# Real
# Cambridge

*For Anglia Ruskin University, with gratitude.*

# Real
# Cambridge

# Grahame Davies

## SERIES EDITOR: PETER FINCH

# SERIES EDITOR'S INTRODUCTION

From the top of Castle Mound, Cambridge does not spread out in front of me in an anonymous sprawl. Instead it is low rise, touchable in that way ancient places often are, and richly green. The grass-covered mound which I've climbed, the motte of King Edward I's stone-walled castle, is about all that remains of the vortex of fortification that was once here – Iron Age Camp, Roman Fort, Norman Castle, Civil War Bastion – all now drained away by time. Even the Shire Hall out there beyond the car park, a seat of government of one sort or another since at least 1067, is rumoured to be moving on.

Below me is the River Cam, one of the reasons the city developed in the first place. At this point its waters could easily be crossed and from here you could readily get to the sea. It became the site of the first Bridge over the Cam, a frontier settlement that was a day's march from the Roman strongholds of Godmanchester and Great Chesterford. And in the fullness of time it also turned out to be a place to be invaded by just about everyone – The Celts, Romans, Anglo-Saxons, Vikings, Danes and Normans. If you want to touch the past then you can do it here.

But I'm in the present, an observer on a first trip, expecting grandeur and finding it. I'm here to check out the mystic forces that still flow in this part of eastern England. To follow the trails of the poets, raconteurs, scientists, engineers, mathematicians, philosophers, and sheer world class geniuses who have clustered. I want to see just what marks this town from the red bricks and glass high rises of other places. Now the whole world is bent on getting itself educated, Cambridge with its stone ancientness has risen to the top.

Oxford might dispute that last claim, being the older place, but given Cambridge's roll call of the great and the good that hardly matters. I've come on a day at the end of term when the town is full of May Balls (perversely held in June) and bursting with young life. There are people everywhere. The river is heaving with punts. These are manoeuvred by young men wielding what look like scaffold poles and loaded with Prosecco drinking couples, boisterous graduates and their extended families. The parents here to see how their offspring have progressed in the world.

Down along St John's and Trinity Streets the colleges cluster. They are set up like walled city states. Independent republics with their own libraries, museums, chapels, gardens, courts, parlours, and lodges. Some, such as Sidney Sussex College, are reluctant to show more than a stone perimeter wall to the outside world. Others, like King's, declare their majesty with architectural thunder and great flashes of green quadrangle that magnificently appear through gatehouses elaborate enough to front a palace. King's serendipitously offers Choral Evensong as I pass. The Christian past still playing in the Christian present, choral polyphony that flies, and a collect chanted in an English made incomprehensible by the echo inside the world's largest fan-vaulted chapel. An elderly Chinese couple for whom this may well be their first Christian experience sit when they should stand and stand when they should sit, the sung psalms rolling through their air around them.

Outside there's a naked bike ride in progress, eighty or more naturists on cycles ringing their bells and beaming. Their Cambridge audience watch, but despite the quantity of in-your-face nudity available, do not seem that concerned. Cycling is a Cambridge mainstay. Bikes cluster in great gaggles at each road junction. Some have wheeled boxes to their fronts carrying packages, groceries, children. These are the Dutch box bikes, a nineties import that Cambridge has made its own. Other cycles go at such speed that I am surprised there are not more two-wheeled disasters. Writer knocked down by handlebar, camera smashed, ribs broken.

As early Cambridge developed it became the destination for refugee scholars running from Oxford. They established the first Cambridge college, Peterhouse, in 1284. Clare, Pembroke, Gonville and Corpus Christi soon followed. The spiritual presence of the place was assured. You can argue, as the ley line hunters have, that the lines of power already crossed here, and well they might have, but it was the clustering of colleges that secured Cambridge's future. But I want to check those earlier powers. Is there anything still in the air?

There's a run of ancient churches that flows through the city's heart. Starting with the Norman Round Church at St Andrew The Great (St Sepulchre's) I follow the alignment passing a total of six further holy spots (St Michael's, Great St Mary's, St Edward, King and Martyr, St Bene't's, St Botolph's, and Little St Mary's) with evidence of there once having been more. This major ley flows on to cross with another connecting with the round barrow on nearby Wormwood Hill. Great ancient power. I am a believer in these things but right now I can't really sense a thing.

Out in the Gog Magog hills at the iron age fort of Wandlebury I have already walked the full ring looking for an earlier history.

Much enigma surrounds this location, a few miles south of the city. In the 1950s archaeologist, explorer and parapsychologist TC Lethbridge claimed to have discovered, in the chalk below the earthen banks, a 3000-year old outline of three giant figures. At the time there was huge dispute and Lethbridge retired into ignominy. There's no sign of the giants today that I could see but that's the joy of mystery. Gog and Magog were ancient goliaths, opponents of the chosen people, according to the Old Testament. They lie in the Cambridge soil their moment still to come.

Back on the corner of Castle Street and Chesterton Lane the Victorian Church of St Giles with St Peter are running a pop-up *Biergarten*. Draft beer in plastic glasses to be consumed while listening to rock music and sitting in the graveyard. The Rev Canon Philipa, who runs the place, offers a welcome to saints and sinners. It's a good line. Opposite is Kettle's Yard, a line of four workers' cottages knocked into one by Jim and Helen Ede in 1957. Ede was the son of a Cardiff solicitor who worked at the Tate Gallery and developed a strong interest in modernism. His dream, fulfilled in Cambridge, was to offer his own living space as a place for art where both artists and enthusiasts would be welcome. The result is unique, neither exclusively home nor quite entirely gallery. Kettle's Yard holds an unrivalled collection of works by Ben Nicholson, David Jones, Christopher Wood, Henri Gaudier-Brzeska, Constantin Brancusi, Barbara Hepworth, Eric Gill and others displayed in a laid-back household setting. Nothing is labelled, objects cover all available surfaces, paintings hang on all walls.

Ede's inventory records that on visiting his father back home, and being reimbursed the £2 train fare, he bought two lustre goblets on the way back to Cardiff station. I find them, still lusting, displayed on the sitting room mantelpiece. Ede's eye collecting perfection.

On Magdalene Street, on the way to the Bridge of Sighs, one of the few city centre convenience stores is closed. 'Due To Eid' explains a hand-written sign, adding, by way of explanation, 'Muslim Christmas'. Unsurprisingly there's a sense of high intellect at work in this town. Casual conversations I eavesdrop are about rhetoric and art history rather than football or drink. Or maybe in addition to football and drink. The World Cup is on screen in every pub I pass and there are plenty of those.

It's hard to turn in the city's centre and not be confronted with some new avenue of scholarly adventure. Museums, libraries and galleries are everywhere. Most colleges have their own and there are thirty-one of those. South of the Zoology Museum and the Sedgwick Museum of Earth Sciences and before you come to the Polar Museum with its statues of a husky sledge dog outside is the magnificent Fitzwilliam. Free to enter and you can photograph anything you like. The world has moved on. The Fitzwilliam teems with armour and vases, ceramic wonders from all corners and at least 1700 paintings including Titian, Turner, Degas and Stanley Spencer. In 2006 a stumbling visitor managed to reduce a Qing vase to a hundred pieces. The repaired ceramic is now back on show more famous than it ever was.

But what I'm really looking for is not the Cambridge of brochure and web site, the one the visiting thousands come to see. The Botanic Gardens and the Mathematical Bridge might be as wonderful as Wren's Library or the facade of Corpus Christi but I prefer to hunt the lesser known. The apple tree at Trinity, a direct descendant of the one in Newton's garden at Woolsthorpe Manor that dropped its fruit on the mathematician's head. The skull of Oliver Cromwell complete with spike hole buried in the gardens of the Lord Protector's old college, Sidney Sussex. Grantchester Meadows, inspiration for Pink Floyd's Roger Waters song of the same name on the album *Ummagumma* from 1969. Not everything in this magic place is of the distant past.

Standing where things might have been or were or where the sense of something still hangs is one of the essences of psychogeography and central to the 'Real' series. Who better as an author to have for the current volume then than arch realist, poet and novelist Grahame Davies. He's got form. His *Real Wrexham* which came out in 2007, went immediately into reprint.

Grahame, who studied at what is now Anglia Ruskin University, makes as much of the people as he does of the places in this splendid new addition to the 'Real' series. *Real Cambridge*, however, does not major on the obvious. In a city where world status seems to have been handed out like smarties Grahame still finds plenty of the new and the oblique and the undiscovered to illuminate. At the back of the Buddhist Centre on Newmarket Road he finds the remains of what was in 1926 "the most progressive theatre in England". He investigates William the Conqueror's approach to Cambridge data protection in the Domesday Book. He checks the Leper Chapel, still extant opposite Abbey Stadium. He walks Fleam Dyke, once the boundary between Saxon invaders and resident Celts. He encapsulates it all with due deference to the city's status and history, its magic, its realism and its fen country thrills.

*Real Cambridge* is as addictive a read as it is stimulating. As a guide it will keep you in the city and environs for months. As a new take on home for local citizens it will illuminate the unexpected and throw new light on the well-known. Best in class? Certainly. Read on.

Peter Finch

# INTRODUCTION

It has something of the theatrical about it – the way this city allows itself to be seen. Driving into Cambridge from the west, you come down Madingley Road, just one more leafy, tree-lined arterial route on the outskirts of town. You take a right into Queen's Road, with its mini roundabout, railings and parking meters.

Then the trees thin out, and there to the left across the river meadows, is the great west end of King's College Chapel, outlined against the endless East Anglian sky. It looks like the front door of heaven. England meets eternity: hard stone against the sky. You will never forget this.

This view isn't revealed with a flourish: there's no bombastic build-up of processional boulevards or triumphal arches like you might find somewhere more assertive, because less assured. Here, the curtain is drawn back without a fanfare. It's a statement, not a speech; a testimony, not a tirade. The English have always known that understatement is the most powerful expression of all. It always leaves you wanting more when the curtain falls. Like the greatest art and the most searching science, Cambridge always asks more questions than it answers.

Like a theatre, too, Cambridge lives on terms with transience. So many of its residents are just passing through this caravanserai for the cognoscenti, this Portland stone portal between adolescence and adulthood. When the show ends, no matter how much they loved it, they can't stay. This city is a first love: the kind that can neither last nor be forgotten.

I was eighteen when it happened to me. Right on schedule. I had travelled from my home in north Wales in my father's Ford Cortina for a college interview. I knew nothing of this part of the country. England, to me, was itself exotic, and the two-dimensional flatness of this fen country was like no landscape I had ever seen: it seemed designed to outline individual features like parts of a stage set; isolated, intentional, giving them a sense of drama and consequence.

We had passed the sign at the city boundary; the traffic had slowed, bikes quietly multiplied, but still, it seemed we were some distance from the city centre, wherever that might be. We took that turn down Queen's Road, and the images of white buildings started flickering behind the trees like a ciné film before snapping suddenly into focus with that perfectly-proportioned wide shot of that astonishing chapel. The shot held for a long moment, until the trees filtered back into the *mise-en-scène* and the frames fragmented again. It lasted seconds. And a lifetime. This is what achievement looks like, it seemed to say. This is how good things can be.

For anyone coming up to college, this view was the gateway to great things. For me, though, it had the allure of the unattainable. I wasn't actually coming here to go to Cambridge University, but to the Cambridgeshire College of Arts and Technology, a college of further education on the other side of town. The meagre currency of my scrappy A Level results wasn't going to buy my way into some ivy-covered academic arcadia. C.C.A.T., 'C-Cat', 'The Tech': these were not names to utter in the same breath as Magdalene ('Maudlin'), Caius ('Keys'), or any of the other nonchalantly coded shibboleths exchanged knowingly by those for whom brains, breeding or brass, or all three, had secured a place at life's Latin-graced High Table. I was, and remain, eternally grateful for the opportunities which my college gave me, not least for taking a chance on me in the first place. But I knew, if I did succeed in graduating, that no-one thereafter was going to be flinging open the gilded doors of privilege at the mere mention of my *alma mater.*

Neither was the campus I was entering going to feature in any tourist guides. No-one's heart was going to miss a beat as they saw the grey concrete slab of C.C.A.T.'s tower block emerge between the unassuming terraced houses of Mill Road. No-one was going to treasure for ever their first glimpse of the utilitarian redbrick of the evocatively-named D Block. No. But although it might not be Cambridge University it was still Cambridge – and there was clearly more to this town than the gown. And by God, I was going to make the most of it.

After all, this East Anglian fenland community is a world city, a place whose name itself denotes not so much a location as a condition; more a state of being than a place to be. This is where Wittgenstein split hairs and where Rutherford split the atom; where Newton sought God through science, where Darwin found that science had taken God's place; where Watson and Crick discovered the DNA that shapes our bodies, and where generations of students push those bodies to their limits. This is where the world went to college: Donne, Marlowe, Cromwell, Byron, Wordsworth, Coleridge, Tennyson, Ted Hughes, Clive James, Stephen Hawking, half of Monty Python and most of Pink

Floyd. But it is also the place that gave us Association Football, the Society for Psychical Research, the Night Climbers, the Cambridge Folk Festival and Katrina and the Waves.

So from the very first, I was acutely conscious of the fact that there are two Cambridges: the one of choice, and the other of necessity; the one where privilege passes noisily through, and the other where the prosaic quietly persists; the one that cannot be ignored, and the one that is scarcely noticed. Like proton and neutron, they have opposing impulses, but occupy the same space; at once independent and interdependent. Neither more authentic than its counterpart; each essential to the other; both of them real.

# CENTRAL

# REALITY CHECKPOINT

Crossing Parker's Piece one foggy night after one too many pints, the young Malcolm Guite suddenly found himself at the junction of two worlds. Out of the mist emerged an ornate Victorian cast-iron lamp standard, decorated with scrolls and sculpted dolphins: scratched on the side were the words: 'Reality Checkpoint.'

Now a poet, academic and Chaplain of Girton College, Malcolm recalls this as an epiphany: "It was surreal. I thought: if this is reality, which side of it would I be? I realised there was this whole divide between the Cambridge bubble and the real Cambridge of Mill Road with its police station and fire station, and all the things you'd find in an English town."

The lamp standard, made by the Glasgow Sun Foundry in the 1860s, marks the centre of the Piece[1], a square twenty-five-acre park on the eastern edge of the city centre, where two diagonal paths make a giant cross. To Historic England, which gave it a Grade II listing in 1996, this is simply 'Lamp Standard. Number 1268376.' To those with a more symbolic turn of mind, this is the very point where town becomes gown; the boundary between the world of mind and the world of matter. Like the lamp-post marking the boundary of Narnia in C.S. Lewis's stories, this is a rusty iron Rubicon.

The term 'Reality Checkpoint' seems to have been conferred clandestinely, as a scratched 1960s graffito. Some attribute it to students from what was then Cambridgeshire College of Arts and Technology – now Anglia Ruskin University – a tribal frontier-marking, a proud declaration that they, at least, were part of the real world. Certainly, by the mid Seventies, the name was well-known enough to feature in the *Varsity Handbook*. Repeatedly painted over, it kept reappearing, like one of those ineradicable handprints in ghost stories, until, in recent years, Cambridge City Council, with admirable good humour, succumbed to the inevitable and fixed the words to its plinth as an official sign – though the unofficial graffito soon reappeared too.

Malcolm Guite first came to Cambridge to read English at Pembroke College, and, like so many, found it hard to leave. After graduation, research and ordination, he combines his pastoral work with poetry, music and academic research, specialising in the poetry of Samuel Taylor Coleridge, T.S. Eliot and C.S. Lewis.[2] Biker, rocker, pipe-smoker and ex-exorcist – though they call it 'diocesan advisor on deliverance ministry' these days – he's been described as: "What would happen if John Donne or George Herbert journeyed to Middle Earth by way of San Francisco, took musical cues from Jerry Garcia and fashion tips from Bilbo Baggins, and rode back on a Harley."

"Cam-bridge. The clue is in the name," he says. "Cambridge should be a place of transition. There's a sense that a checkpoint is not a destination. It's somewhere you have to get in order to get somewhere else. From reality to unreality."

Parker's Piece seems designed to display this dichotomy. On the east side are the long functional grey rectangles of the swimming pool and the YMCA. On the north, the fire station and police headquarters. On the south side are the backs of the shops and offices of Regent Street. So far, so utilitarian. But then on the city side is the imposing outline of the University Arms, Cambridge's first hotel when it was built in the 1830s, and a landmark ever since. The neo-classical architect, John Simpson, has recently redesigned it, retaining the nineteenth-century façade and replacing the blocky 1960s and 1970s extensions with a harmonious ensemble of arches, creamy fluted pillars, and copper-clad turrets, as if to say: this is where the magic begins.

In the shadow of the University Arms is Hobbs' Pavilion, once a crucial piece of cricket infrastructure, now a restaurant, named after the cricketer Sir John Berry 'Jack' Hobbs[3], the greatest batsman of his age, who was born in Cambridge in 1882. On its elegant cupola, a weather vane, shaped like a batsman, is always positioning himself to take advantage of the prevailing wind. These days, most of Cambridge's serious cricketing takes place at Fenners, behind the swimming pool off Gonville Place, a home of first-class cricket since 1848, and one of the country's oldest grounds. But, as I pass Hobbs' Pavilion today, a groundsman is marking out a temporary cricket pitch on Parker's Piece, pacing out its giant white circumference like a magic circle. My path would take me across it, but I hesitate: this space is now sacred. I skirt it carefully, like when, as a superstitious child, I feared to enter a fairy ring.

In fact, Parker's Piece is much more significant in football history than in cricket. It was here, in the early Nineteenth Century, that some of the earliest games of what we now call soccer were played, resulting, in 1848, in the formation of the Cambridge Rules, adopted by the Football Association in 1863.[4] But there's nothing to mark the birthplace of the beautiful game; nowhere for the soccer pilgrim to leave a votive offering of a scarf or shirt. In 2013, the city council planned to erect a statue of a 6ft 7in Subbuteo football referee on a circular display engraved with the rules of the sport. It never got past the planning stage, and was withdrawn after what were described as "commercial issues" and "negative feedback" from the public. Or, in other words, a reality check.

# CITY CENTRE

Once you exit Parker's Piece on the city side, Regent Street funnels you into the city centre past banks, offices, charity shops and restaurants. Park and Ride buses glide past to the bus station at Drummer Street, with their placid cargoes of passengers. Park and Ride users must be the most law-abiding people in the world, mildly submitting to their civic duty, abandoning their vehicles before even sighting their destination, and then queueing obediently to be ferried in. Instances of criminality among Park and Ride users must be close to zero. Outside Sainsbury's, a windblown piece of paper lands at my feet. On one side, in black biro, are the words 'Ned's Pitch. Back in five mins.' On the other side a smiley face and 'Always be happy'. The position of Cambridge's street people seems all the starker by comparison with the city's reputation for affluence and privilege.

That reputation began in the Thirteenth Century. Before she was famous, Cambridge, with a population of about two thousand, was your average medieval town: castle and church, brothel and tavern, stocks and gallows. Simple pleasures. But that all changed in 1209 when the University was founded by a group of scholars fleeing a dispute with townspeople in Oxford. This cuckoo in the nest grew quickly. A Royal Charter was granted in 1231 by King Henry III, and by 1246, there was a Chancellor's Court, exercising legal power over the students and college, who were exempt from civic control. It was a slow-motion civic *coup d'état*. Soon, the University licensed the taverns, controlled the market. set the price of weights and measures and even had rights of entry to private houses, – to police the extra-curricular activities of its members. Houses could be commandeered as student hostels. Townspeople effectively became second-class citizens; when disputes arose, appeals to authority usually resulted in the University students being excused and all others punished.

Small wonder that when, in 1381, the Peasant's Revolt, led by Wat Tyler, reached Cambridge, the rioters exacted long-overdue redress. The University's charters, seals, and other symbols of power were burned in the marketplace, with one woman, 'mad' old Margaret Sterr, throwing the ashes into the air and shouting, with a suspiciously erudite rhetorical flourish: "Thus, thus let the learning of all scholars be confounded."[5] But it was the rebels who were ultimately confounded, as authority quickly reasserted itself, leaving the townspeople with even fewer rights than they had had before. The rivalry continued for centuries, with civic occasions, transport, licensing, law-and-order and public work projects, all becoming flashpoints. Only in 1856, with Parliament increasingly representing the people rather than the powerful, did the University finally, reluctantly, sign away most of its exclusive privileges.

Only rarely is power relinquished willingly, and within the University itself, the barriers to entry came down slowly, and often only after long and sustained pressure. Religious nonconformity was allowed in 1871 – prior to that, students had to be Anglicans. The enforced celibacy of college fellows was abolished in 1882 with the Oxford and Cambridge Act, which allowed dons to marry. And the University's right to send two members to Parliament was abolished only after the Second World War. Women, who had been grudgingly allowed their own colleges from 1869, when Girton was established, were not full members of the University until 1948.[6] As for the other colleges, the first to allow women in was graduate-only Darwin, from its establishment in 1964, followed by Churchill, Clare and King's in 1972. Others followed and in 1988, Magdalene, named after a fallen woman, was the last all-male bastion to fall. Students no longer have to wear caps and gowns outside college; Latin survives only as a linguistic ornament for High Table graces and graduation, and generally the once rigid demarcations between inclusion and exclusion have faded and blurred.

But look a little more closely, and a different picture emerges. For instance, there's the arcane terminology – matriculation, Tripos, Michaelmas – and those pronunciation padlocks Magdalene and Caius, which seem to have been fashioned to keep out all but the chosen few who can be entrusted with the keys. Or the Caius. Think also about the way the colleges present themselves architecturally. James Riley does: he's a Fellow of English Literature at Girton, and co-directs a cross-disciplinary university project called the Alchemical Landscape, which studies:

> "...the artistic representation of the British landscape as an uncanny
> if not haunted space, and the use of comparable 'spectral' language
> to speak about matters of environment, property and value."

An expert in counter-culture, the Beat Poets, Jack Kerouac, and William Burroughs, James is also researching cult road movies, cybernetics, and post-humanism, so is accustomed to questioning the conventional and identifying the counter-cultural.[7]

"The politics of space is arguably more evident in Cambridge than in many other places," he says. "It's difficult to think of anywhere else that has such a high concentration of signs marked 'Private' within close range of its market-square. Any city that develops around a set of older university buildings is inevitably going to have a certain intermingling of spaces with different criteria in terms of use and access. However, in Cambridge it's as if a distinct semiotics of power is at play in the fortress-like appearance of some of the older colleges." Visit the city centre, he says, and look from the crowded street through one of those college doorways: you'll see an open, quiet, palatial space, with public access strictly limited.

Cambridge has a long history of providing a home to people clever enough to criticise it, and yet it survives even the most trenchant attacks. Raymond Williams, the Marxist historian, compared the people he met in Cambridge unfavourably with those of his native Abergavenny: "...nobody fortunate enough to grow up in a good home, in a genuinely well-mannered and sensitive community, could for a moment envy these loud competitive and deprived people."[8] The novelist Piers Paul Read, felt that Cambridge's pretensions "amount to fraud – a confidence trick played on the nation and the world. Its pseudo-aristocratic ideals of idiosyncratic scholarship and convivial Epicureanism, are … another instance of *la trahison des clercs*. Succeeding generations of able, intelligent and idealistic young men are turned into intellectual narcissists as dons, or narrow, complacent careerists"[9]. In Frederic Raphael's 1976 novel *The Glittering Prizes*, a group of gifted college contemporaries, now middle-aged and successful, are accused by an angry younger generation of opposing a flippant facade of superiority against the claims of social justice. "*Cambridge*", says one of the accusers, contemptuously. "They never grow up."[10]

Commerce reflects the priorities shown by the colleges, says James. The shops in central Cambridge are geared mainly towards luxury items. For most household necessities and cheaper groceries, you have to go to Mill Road or further afield. Shopping areas like the Grand Arcade and the Lion Yard, the city-centre mall which, in the 1970s – to the horror of conservationists – replaced the complex of medieval streets and buildings in Petty Cury,[11] have a similar effect. "They're easily accessible and, like the traditional arcades, they invite window shopping, but they're not solely designed as spaces of public assembly and ultimately their use is income-dependent. Quietly, and unconsciously, they seem to say: 'don't come here if you don't have the money.'" Old identities find new expressions, which is perhaps, by now, a kind of tradition in itself.

## THE COLLEGES

Looking at the 'Backs' of the colleges ranged along the banks of the Cam, one might be forgiven for thinking the city was planned as an architectural showpiece. In fact, it grew sporadically, according to the fluctuating political, dynastic, religious, social and financial forces expressed in the University's various institutions. While it may look serene and unchanging today, the complex of buildings developed piecemeal, new uses gradually displacing older ones, as the commercial interests of what had once been an important riverport yielded slowly, and by no means always quietly, to the demands of academia. Over the centuries, plots of land were acquired or, in the case of colleges like Jesus, which were built on former monastic sites, expropriated,[12] and incorporated into the ever-expanding academic estate, which now numbers 31 individual colleges. On these sites, buildings arose in response to periodic injections of resources and ambition from a succession of different patrons: royal, aristocratic, religious or – in the case of Corpus Christi – civic: the college was erected by Cambridge townspeople in a spirited, but ultimately unsuccessful, attempt to beat the University at its own game. Pride, piety, personalities and politics all played their part as the city grew to become, with Oxford, one half of the greatest academic duarchy in the world.

The colleges divide into two main groups, like geological ages, separated by a seismic gap of some two centuries, during which no colleges were founded. The 'old' colleges are those founded in the pre-modern period, between 1284 (Peterhouse) and 1596 (Sidney Sussex), while the 'new' ones were founded between 1800 (Downing) and 1977 (Robinson). The motives behind the later foundations, which are products of the post-Reformation and scientific age, generally reflect the changing priorities of that period, with an emphasis on science, religious tolerance, and the rights of women. Whatever the period of their establishment, each college is now a kind of city-state with its own foundation story, mythology, treasury, pantheon, government, citizens and diaspora. All have been extensively chronicled; each could provide material for a library of books. So a couple of images of the world beyond the college gatehouses in two of the older institutions must serve as holograms.

## PEMBROKE COLLEGE

James Riley was right: there's something symbolic about crossing that boundary of the college gatehouse; leaving the clamour for the cloister. As you pass through the castellated portal, crowds vanish, the pace slows, noise recedes. You're inside. Space to breathe; time to think; an enclosure where, paradoxically, the imagination can be free. It's probably no coincidence that it was two lifelong Oxbridge dons, C.S. Lewis and Lewis Carroll – two men who spent their entire lives crossing and recrossing these thresholds of perception – who produced English literature's two most famous images of magical realms entered through familiar objects: the wardrobe for Narnia, and the looking glass for Wonderland.

In any journey to an alternative reality, the traveller needs a guide. The author and academic Mark Wormald meets me at the gatehouse of Pembroke College to take me through this checkpoint from sunny traffic-filled Trumpington Street and into the shaded courts inside.

Pembroke, founded in 1347 by Marie de Saint Pol, Countess of Pembroke, is the third-oldest of the Cambridge colleges, and has seven hundred students and fellows. Its site includes a fine Wren chapel. Not all architectural interventions here were as welcome, though. In 1875, the Gothic Revival architect Alfred Waterhouse turned his attentions to Pembroke. The aim of the Gothic Revival was, of course, to restore the beauty of the art and architecture of the Middle Ages which it was supposed had been lost through successive centuries of soulless neo-classicism. The Revivalists sighed after stained glass, pined for pointed arches, and hankered for hammer-beam roofs. Which makes it almost incredible that, when Waterhouse wanted to put his Gothicist fantasy into practice at Pembroke, he actually *dynamited* the fourteenth-century medieval hall of the College's foundress, as well as the Master's lodging and an entire range of the Old Court to make way for his neo-Gothic replacement. He was dismissed some years later, and over time, his building, having been found inadequate in several ways, was itself adapted, including, ironically, by having its windows changed back to the original medieval style.

The list of Pembroke's alumni is as illustrious as any in Cambridge. From the world of politics it includes William Pitt the Younger, 'Rab' Butler, and more recently, and most tragically, Jo Cox.[13] In religion, it includes bishops Nicholas Ridley, martyred in 1555, and Lancelot Andrewes, who oversaw the translation of the King James Bible.[14] Among Pembroke's authors are Edmund 'Faerie Queene' Spenser, the Metaphysical poet Richard Crashaw and Thomas Gray, of 'Elegy' fame, who decamped to Pembroke from Peterhouse in a huff after being the victim of a practical joke by fellow students;[15] more recent alumni include the novelists Tom Sharpe and Clive James, whose own memoirs of Cambridge are essential reading. Any one of these, and many others who could have been mentioned, would merit an extensive study. But I have come on the trail of one alumnus in particular; a man who was simultaneously one of the most public and most enigmatic of writers, the late Poet Laureate, Ted Hughes.[16]

Over lunch at High Table, the dining area reserved for fellows and their guests, under the brooding profile picture of Hughes painted by Peter Edwards in 1993, Mark, an authority on Hughes, tells me about the poet's time at the college, where he arrived from Yorkshire on a scholarship in October 1951, following two years of National Service. Pictures of the time show him still wearing his military greatcoat. Transformations and threshold experiences were to play a big part in the poet's life and work, and nowhere more so than in his first years at Pembroke itself.

"History has added quite a lot of myth to his Cambridge," Mark says, "But the key story is that at the end of his second year, he was struggling at 2 a.m. with an essay about Samuel Johnson, which turned out to be more or less his final English literature essay. He fell asleep and dreamed he was back at his desk, looking at this essay, and that the door to his room opened, and a head looked round it."

Here, in Hughes' own words, is what happened next.

The door opened wide and down the short stair and across the room towards me came a figure that was at the same time a skinny man and a fox walking erect on its hind legs. It was a fox, but the size of a wolf. As it approached and came into the light I saw that its body and limbs had just now stepped out of a furnace. Every inch was roasted, smouldering, black-charred, split and bleeding. Its eyes, which were level with mine where I sat, dazzled with the intensity of the pain. It came up until it stood beside me. Then it spread its hand – a human hand as I now saw, but burned and bleeding like the rest of him - flat palm down on the blank space of my page. At the same time it said: 'Stop this - you are destroying us.' Then as it lifted its hand away I saw the blood-print, like a palmist's specimen, with all the lines and creases, in wet, glistening blood on the page.

I immediately woke up. The impression of reality was so total, I got out of bed to look at the papers on my table, quite certain that I would see the blood-print there on the page.[17]

"This is the myth," says Mark. "And probably the reality."

The point, Mark says, was that Hughes saw the study of English in Cambridge at that time as associated with the analytical, critical dismantling of texts, a process he saw as destructive of his own self.

Hughes got the message. He switched for his last year from English Literature to Archaeology and Anthropology, thereby removing the vulnerable, mysterious sensibilities needed for literary creation away from the pernicious, scorching heat of analytical literary criticism.

Hughes told a researcher he had this dream on his second floor room on K Staircase, thereby sparking, in later years, a minor pilgrimage industry where scholars and fans would arrive in the quadrangle and gaze reverently at the rooms which were the scene of Hughes's vision. Except, Mark discovered, they were gazing at the wrong place. Hughes had led them astray. Mark's research showed that the rooms on K Staircase had never been student accommodation; they were the senior tutor's rooms, and no student would have been falling asleep there at two in the morning. And neither do those rooms have the distinctive two steps up into the room and two steps down that Hughes remembers his fox-man having to take. Mark's search of college records revealed that Hughes actually lived in a different set of rooms overlooking the same quadrangle. And those rooms, uniquely, had the steps. Mark completed this literary detective work just as workmen were removing the two steps into the room to make room for a filing cabinet, as Hughes' former sanctuary was being turned into offices. The cabinet is still there today, as are three young members of the college's development office, at their modern desks, with mousemats, coffee cups and holiday postcards. If the fox-man were to visit now, he'd have a heavy cabinet to shift first.

The two steps outside the room are still there though. It seems, Mark says, that while Hughes was ready enough to tell and retell the story of that transformative vision, he nonetheless wanted to conceal its precise location. I wonder if, in that dissembling, there wasn't something of a countryman's instinct not to leave tracks, a poacher's habit of concealing the trail to his most productive covert, a magician's caution not to let too much daylight in upon the mystery. Hughes, it seems, was happy enough to lay false trails. One of the best-known stories about his time in Pembroke has him being confronted at the door of his rooms by the senior tutor who suspected him of concealing a woman visitor there. Hughes is supposed to have answered the door stark naked, and to have flung his arms out and declared, 'Crucify me!"

Mark tells me that, many years later, at Buckingham Palace, Clive James met Hughes who told him that "not a single element" of that story was true. There is somewhat more evidence for the story that in Hughes' third-year rooms, he painted pictures of jaguars on the ceiling above his bed. Why on the ceiling? Because they could best be appreciated by visitors *if they were lying down.*

After graduating, Hughes moved to London, but kept returning to Cambridge to use the University Library, where he immersed himself in a study of occult and erotic literature.[18] During this period, he lived, fox-like, in outbuildings and a succession of temporary lodgings. It was during this period, at a boozy, jazz-filled literary party at the Women's Union in Falcon's Yard[19] on 25 February 1956, that he had the most fateful meeting of his life, and one of the most famous encounters in all literary history – with a young American postgraduate Fulbright scholar at Newnham, a poet called Sylvia Plath. They were instantly attracted, and when they kissed that night, she bit his cheek long and hard, drawing blood. For most men that would be a warning sign; for Hughes it was an invitation. This brilliant, brittle young poet seemed to promise a union with a soul as passionate and as primal as he felt his own to be.

What happened afterwards – the marriage, the fighting, Plath's suicide, the endless subsequent recriminations and explanations by those involved and those far distant in time and sympathies – is too well documented to need recounting, and is still dangerously contentious. That most volatile of literary relationships will remain the topic for endless debate, dispute and division; the two poets like dark twin planets, locked in orbit, their dual gravity pulling in observers as perpetual, captive satellites. Fearing such an attraction, which only emphasises one's own insignificance, I have always kept a safe distance. When I once sat next to Hughes' widow, Carol, at dinner, she told me my poetry should come before anything. I wasn't so sure. That's the right advice for great poets, perhaps, not for minor ones. My work would be no better if I devoted every waking minute to it. I wasn't going to endanger what contentment I had by seeking an achievement I could never attain.

Hughes and Plath's lives and work have long been disputed territories: theatres for the proxy conflicts of later, ever-changing ideologies, alliances and antipathies. In the fog of this war, it can be hard to make out the poems clearly, or to see them free from partisan viewpoints. However, the Cambridge landscape in which the early months of the poets' relationships was enacted can at least be traversed: the pubs overlooking the Cam, the Anchor and the Mill, where Hughes drank, and which Plath sketched; the former rectory of St Botolph's Church where he stayed in the garden shed; Whitstead hall of residence next to the playing fields at Newnham where Plath stayed and against whose windows Hughes threw gravel to get her attention. Walking this ground today is a bit like one of those tours of First World War battlefields in France or Belgium: where, over the decades, destruction has been domesticated and terror tamed.

Mark shows me some more of the materials he has collected on the poet's life. His rooms, overlooking the same quadrangle as Hughes', are decorated with a framed manuscript copy of Hughes' much-anthologised poem 'The Thought Fox'. The cushions on the sofas are in the shape of fishes: Mark has made a special study of the role that fishing played in Hughes's life: as a childhood pastime in Yorkshire, as a shared recreation with members of the Royal Family during his time as Poet Laureate, as a lifelong opportunity for solitude and communion with nature, and as an almost bottomless source of imagery for the submerged powers to which, as poet, he held out his tentative, barbed invitation.

Currently, Mark is working his way through Hughes' dream journals at the British Library, and is gradually bringing back to the light of day the extraordinary symbols which bred and

teemed in the poet's psyche. Those images were frequently those of nature and animals, and these feature prominently in Pembroke's own striking visual tribute to Hughes: the six stained-glass windows by Hans von Stockhausen in the College library's Yamada Room, in which hare, owl, mermaid's purse, moose, ram, and – of course – crow, are depicted, along with quotations from the poetry. One pane shows the pawprint of a fox alongside that of a man: Hughes's own handprint. Unexpectedly, I feel a primal impulse of my own: to put my own hand into that same space on the glass; like you do with a filmstar's concrete handprint on Hollywood Boulevard; like you do with the stones of Jerusalem's Western Wall. Whether your head believes or not, your hand does. I hesitate, though, remembering my long-held caution about closing the circuit with this literary lightning conductor through whom the creative current coursed so strongly, illuminating – and burning. I mean, look what happened to that fox-man ... Then my hand is on the print. It fits perfectly. It could be my own. But for me there is no fire, just the cool touch of the glass.

## QUEENS' COLLEGE

On the flawless green of the Fellows' Garden at Queens' College, a jazz ensemble is playing, the blonde female vocalist barefoot on the cool baize of the grass. Champagne circulates; glasses fill miraculously; strawberries and cream materialise. Here, with the backdrop of the Tudor, half-timbered Long Gallery, all the elements of a perfect English summer's day are present: panama hats, straw boaters, floral dresses, striped blazers, striped lawn. Even the sun, obedient to its RSVP, has shown up punctually. It wouldn't have been so churlish as to do otherwise: if Suzi Digby, Lady Eatwell, invites you to do something, you generally find yourself doing it.

As requested by the invitation, we are all wearing red roses, in one form or another: jewellery, floral dresses, or, in my case, a simple, but, I hope, tasteful buttonhole. This is unusually demonstrative for me. A poppy on Remembrance Day is about as flamboyant as it gets for me usually. Now, I feel positively raffish. In fact, not like myself at all.

That's the thing about Suzi Digby: she has the ability to get people to be more than they think they can be. She's an inspirational choral leader who specialises in getting ordinary people to perform to a standard they had never thought possible, and who coaches professional singers to a level that leaves reviewers struggling for superlatives. Reviewing her staging of Bach's St Matthew Passion with a choir of three hundred children from disadvantaged backgrounds in a former industrial site in London a few years ago, an awestruck *Telegraph* journalist called her "The Mother of all Music".[20] That was only one of a seemingly innumerable series of initiatives she has conceived to take classics across boundaries – some of them obvious, many of them invisible – which separate ordinary people from extraordinary music.

It is a mission which has seen her working with everyone from Yehudi Menuhin to Mick Jagger, founding a collection of choirs and outreach charities, conducting performances across the globe, making recordings, judging competitions, presenting programmes and taking part in television series like *The Naked Choir*. If there's a musical bone in your body, Suzi Digby will find it. Our paths have crossed in the music world, and now I'm working on a project for her new specialist choir, ORA Singers, to reimagine some of the sacred texts and their musical settings used by the late Tudor and early Jacobean composer Orlando Gibbons, one of the greatest figures in English church music. Gibbons' music was described as having "... fine harmony, unaffected simplicity, and unspeakable grandeur'.[21] The reviews for ORA's first two CDs have been equally lavish: "Truly, this is British choral music's new golden age,"[22] "... the ever-reliable English choral tradition is renewed again."[23] And it's not just British critics who are impressed. (In 2018, they won the German music industry's Opus Klassik Award as Best Ensemble of the Year.)

It's a lot to live up to. Before too long, I will need to look at the texts in detail and see what new response might be possible to material which has been hallowed by centuries of performance. But that can wait. Right now there's a party – and an unusually eclectic mix of guests, combining Suzi Digby's musical world with that of her husband, John, Lord Eatwell, the college President, an economist, former senior Labour Party advisor and working peer.

One of the guests – who is working, he tells me, in artificial intelligence – also has architectural interests; he tells me the Long Gallery Hall of Queens' was made in the style of a ship's keel with a long central timber, on which the rest of the building's wooden frame was hung. A rare survival from the Tudor age, it was saved from being refaced in later material by the college's relative poverty during the periods when medieval buildings like Pembroke's were being replaced with newer ones. Poverty, however, is not really an issue now. Queens' is one of the larger colleges, with over five hundred undergraduates and close on four hundred postgrads. It is also one of the older colleges, founded in the late Fifteenth Century, with the involvement of two different queens, (hence the apostrophe *after* the 's'). The first foundress, in 1448, was Henry VI's queen, Margaret of Anjou. Then it was refounded in 1465 by Edward IV's queen, Elizabeth Woodville. There are older colleges in the University, but of all of them, it is probably at Queens', where many early buildings have been preserved, that the visitor gets the greatest sense of continuity with the middle ages.

I find myself talking to a musician who says she is currently trying to memorise a series of works by Chopin. While my knowledge of Chopin's works is, admittedly, pretty rudimentary, I nonetheless sense a chance to shine: I tell her that I recently bought a very useful book on the subject of recollection, and called, appropriately, *You Can Have An Amazing Memory*.[24] "Oh," she says, interested. "Who's it by?" I should have foreseen this before I opened my mouth. "I can't remember," I say. I'm grateful, shortly afterwards, to be able to talk to Nathan Emery and Nicky Clayton, who I find are experts – among other things – in animal behaviour. Nicky has specialised in the study of corvids, members of the crow family, finding that not only can they make tools, but that they're capable of a cognition which can comprehend a past, present and future. I wonder if Ted Hughes – whose rooms were a few hundred yards from here as the corvid flies – knew that? For his part, Nathan is also pursuing pioneering research into animal intelligence, and is the author of a popular science book called *Bird Brain*.[25] In present company, I feel as though that's a description of my own intellectual capacities.

Music, however, I *can* understand, albeit as a layman, and at the level of enjoyment rather than analysis. The party is invited through to Queens' chapel, a late Victorian Gothic masterpiece by George Frederick Bodley. We take our seats, the *habitués* noticeable by the way they seem serenely unaware of the bracing upright posture the wooden pews require you to adopt. The chapel, with its painted ceiling, has, I'm told, superb acoustics. Which is just as well, as the audience could hardly be more discerning. Semi-Toned, a male barbershop group from Exeter University, are introduced by Gareth Malone, the nation's choirmaster. He says that he and Suzi – "who invented choirs"– met while working on *The Naked Choir*. She was coaching Semi-Toned. They won. Today, without the pressure of competition, Semi-Toned have a varied set showcasing their versatility: Dusty Springfield's 'Son of a Preacher Man', some soul classics, even beatboxing. You can see why they won. Afterwards, a student pianist, a newly-graduated triple-starred First, takes his place at the grand piano, beginning with a simple melody and gradually conjuring it into a virtuoso rhapsody. Beneath the embellishments, as though to illustrate how the people's music and professional mastery can live in harmony, you can trace the unspoiled outline of the folk song: 'My Luve is Like a Red Red Rose'.

# THE EAGLE

It sounds rather like the start of a joke: a man walks into a bar, and says: "We've found the secret of life." Except this wasn't a joke, and he really had. The man was molecular biologist Francis Crick, the date was February, 1953, and the pub was The Eagle, in Bene't

Street. Originally The Eagle and Child, this is Cambridge's oldest public house, dating from the early Seventeenth Century. It is owned by Corpus Christi college, and for a while, was the meeting place of the Cambridge Corporation which at the time was largely a drinking club. Today it's leased to the Greene King brewery chain and is a busy city centre hostelry, with guest beers on the bar and little brass numbers on the tables for your food orders. In 1953, this was the regular smoke-filled lunchtime haunt of scientists working in the Cavendish laboratories which were then nearby in Free School Lane. So it was here that Crick, who had been working with his colleague James Watson, announced to the PhD'd punters that they had discovered the double-helix structure of deoxyribonucleic acid, aka DNA, the molecule that carries the genetic instructions for the growth of all living things.

Later that year, Watson and Crick drew up, over lunch at The Eagle, a list of the twenty canonical amino acids which make up DNA. Some nine years later, in 1962, they shared the Nobel Prize for their discovery, together with Maurice Wilkins, formerly of St John's College Cambridge, later of King's College London. This recognition was, however, too late for another scientist who had made a vital contribution to the discovery, Rosalind Franklin, a former Newnham student and later researcher at Cambridge University Physics Laboratory. The work she carried out with Wilkins in London was shown by him to Watson and Crick without Franklin's knowledge, in circumstances which are still controversial. Franklin died of ovarian cancer in 1958. The Nobel Prize Committee does not give awards posthumously. She is, however, commemorated with the other pioneers on the plaque outside the pub. She also has a building and a bust in the garden of Newnham, and, in the Memorial Court of Clare College, a credit on the DNA sculpture donated by James Watson himself.[26]

Franklin was only 37 when she died, but in the back bar of The Eagle, there is a unique memorial to some of the pub's former customers for whom the horizon of life was shorter still. During the Second World War, The Eagle, appropriately enough, became a favourite haunt of British and American fliers. Theirs was a surreal existence: one day, all the comforts of home: beer and bonhomie, girls and glamour; the next day, a fight for survival against the Nazis over occupied Europe. And maybe no next day after that at all. Small wonder that in between ops, they needed to make some kind of lasting mark on the world they might soon be leaving. War poets are few at any time; and in the Second World War they were fewer still, and what these airmen wrote wasn't poetry, and the materials they used – charcoal, candles, lipstick and cigarette lighters – were not the conventional tools of literary creation. But as they burned and scrawled their messages onto the ceiling of the back bar of The Eagle, they nonetheless created what would now be called a participative community artwork; except, unlike the dutiful compilations of artworker-induced adages that bedeck public art projects today, they didn't do it to prove relevance and inclusivity, they did it because they were young, they wanted to be remembered, and they might very soon be dead.[27]

Most of their messages are numbers. At first glance, the ceiling looks as though Watson and Crick had used it for some particularly complicated calculations. But these are actually the squadron codes; numerals that meant everything then – pride, reputation, achievement, honour – and almost nothing now. Swirling through them is a giant silhouette of a naked woman. Among the arcane numerology, it's the personal names and messages that reveal a little more about the youngsters who put them there: men who were mostly only the age of today's undergraduates, and many of whom would never get any older. What do you write, when you're in death's waiting room, and you can, at most, manage to scrawl a few words? Well, your unit number, we know that much. And your name: Frank, Bill, Mac, Jim, Donald, Jimmy, Tony, Frank, Red,

Clark, Chan, E. Ware, Rich, John, Phil, Buck, Beattie, Stiffs, Bob and Tommy. Or a nickname, personal or collective: Kasard's Killers, The Old Standby Kerrane, Bert's Boys, The Pressure Boys, Fighting 98 Boys, Fightin 101, The Darling Squadron, Parachute La La, Sad Sack, U.S. Navy Yanks. A place: Rougham, Yorkshire, Oxford, Inns of Court. Or a message, clear or cryptic: Get Some In, Drunk Again, Joan is here, Tally Ho, The Wild Hare, Merry Xmas, Stars and Stripes, Acheive Your Aim [sic]. Ubique[28], Alis Nocturnis.[29] Oh, and yes, Mother.

## MAY BALL

Along the Backs, the lawns have become a city of marquees, like a travelling fair; there's a full-sized dodgems ride, and swaying inflatable bouncy castles are leaning like drunks against the aloof walls of King's College. Over the sound system, a singer belts out jazz standards. The May Balls, those end-of-term, end-of-an-era, end-of-the world bacchanalias which close the academic year with many a bang, and not a few whimpers, are in full swing. Frederic Raphael called them a place where "the cream of the Cambridge theatre would be able to have a last dance on the doomed vessel of their youth".[30] May Week, another of those terminological *oubliettes* which Cambridge fashions for the unwary, actually takes place in June, and has done since 1882. It's all here: glamour, sophistication, elegance: the smartest people in every sense of the word.

Fast forward to 3 a.m. and there's a queue outside Uncle Frank's kebab van. On the other side of the square, there's an even bigger one at The Trailer of Life, (Established. 1997). The guys have their untied bowties still round their necks, just to show they were *real* bowties, not ready-made ones; the girls wear hotpants, microskirts, ballgowns. Two of them peel away, clutching their doners. "If I can find a place to pee, I'll pee," one of them says, conversationally. At this hour of the morning in Cambridge city centre, being sober feels like a superpower. Everyone else moves as though they're under water. Though water is probably the last thing on their minds. Speech is slow, deliberate, precise – and untintelligible. One young guy in a white tuxedo is trying to explain something to his female companion: "Clearly..." he says, But inspiration fails him.

"Clearly..." he says again. Actually not.

A drunk kicks a taxi. The driver barrels out of the door and bends over to inspect the damage. There isn't any. But he fetches another, larger, taxi driver, and they confront the drunk, who's now being dragged away by his friends and falls over. A slightly more sober friend is remonstrating with the drivers, with the desperate atavistic politeness of the plastered; old courtesies invoked for new offences: "Sir, Sir, I can only humbly apologise..." Two new fares arrive. The driver takes them and drives off.

Music thumps from upper floors. A bearded roadie wheels a speaker back to his car. The white-bearded busker outside the Cool Britannia souvenir shop is playing bluegrass and tapping the percussion with his feet. Street people have set up in doorways. It's nearly closing time for them. A homeless guy I'd seen earlier outside Boots almost knocks me down as he shoots past on a bike, eating a burger with his free hand. Outside the Round Church, two guys have set up a candlelit pitch: with flickering tealights surrounded by inspirational messages on sheets of cardboard. In Cambridge, even the homeless have to raise their game. Coins chink; takings are divided. I search my pocket for change. There isn't any. Most of my payments are now plastic. The millennia-old business model that turned compassion into cash is finally failing. Where does that leave people like these? Or bluegrass buskers for that matter? Not for nothing do they call those cards contactless.

Young women are weaving their way home barefoot, finding their way between the detritus by some sixth sense which has somehow survived the chemical assault on the other five. One of them claps me on the shoulder: "You look very smart," she says appreciatively. "Thank you," I answer. "So do you." A young man in a rumpled dinner jacket reels up to me and stops, pointing at me with both hands: "I want to make love TO YOU!" This is getting to be a good night. I've had more attention in five minutes than I got in three years as an undergrad. Drink-fuelled irony or not, I'll take it. This is already the most successful night of my life. A few minutes' later, a guy distributing nightclub flyers looks at me, and then, of course, looks away again; I'm several decades outside his target demographic. But was there a nanosecond's hesitation before he looked past me? I flatter myself there was. Though it is very dark.

# GOTHIC

The dark is sometimes kinder than the day. At least, that's the thought behind the event I'm attending tonight at St Edward King and Martyr Church in Peas Hill.[31]

'Right. I'd better set up the burning cross,' says Mick.

Suddenly I have second thoughts about this Goth Eucharist. I'd thought it would be all black clothes and monochrome melancholy to the accompaniment of organ music and the occasional tolling bell. Now I'm imagining white hoods, and sweaty backwoods bigotry with a background of chirping cicadas. Since when did Goths carry burning crosses? My hosts, the poet, musician and Anglia Ruskin academic, Mick Gowar, and his wife Ann, an Anglican priest, have noticed my hesitation.

'Not a *vertical* burning cross,' Mick tells me. 'Horizontal. Tea lights. On the floor. In a cross shape. It's more Habitat than Alabama.'

I breathe again. This is The Cure not The Klan.

'Horizontal burning crosses are more inclusive,' Mick says.

Inclusive is the key concept here. Cambridge has scores of churches. One for every flavour of belief, from black-suited Bible-clutching Baptists to incense-swinging vestment-clad Anglo-Catholics, and everything in between. But what about those who might not believe in anything at all? Not to worry: Cambridge has a service for them too. The Goth Eucharist at St Edward's is aimed at those who might suspect that there's nothing above that Cambridge-blue sky but darkness. The service, the first of its kind in the Church of England when it began in 2005, and distinguished by using only secular music such as the work of Bob Dylan, Leonard Cohen, Joni Mitchell, Nick Drake and Nick Cave, and the theatrical trappings of gothdom (participants approached the altar over a carpet of crushed red roses) has attracted national attention, film crews, and comment, including from *The Times* columnist Caitlin Moran, who could see the point:

> ...church services are all about a misunderstood man who got nailed to a cross. They are held in a looming, bell-towered, candle-lit edifice in the middle of a graveyard. Indeed if you go catholic, you get to burn incense and drink blood, as well.

If death and darkness are on your mind, then St Edward's could hardly have stronger credentials. The church is named after the English King mysteriously murdered in 978. Later, during the Reformation in the mid Sixteenth Century, when Cambridge became the cradle for the new ideas of religious freedom which would tear the nation away from Rome, St Edward's was the stage for priests such as Hugh Latimer and Nicholas Ridley to set out their radical views.[32] Both later became bishops and in 1555, under the persecution of 'Bloody' Mary Tudor, were burned at the stake in Oxford. Latimer's Pulpit is still in use at St Edward's every Sunday. Malcolm Guite has a poem on the subject. Mindful of the fires through which Latimer went to meet his God, it ends: "He touched this wood, and kindled love to flame." This is not a place to shy away from harsh realities.

The themes for the first five 'On the Edge' services of the current term are, according to the poster on the iron railings of St Edward's: Despair; Death; Dependency; Depression and Deliverance. No, not the Sam Peckinpah kind, I remind myself (the thought of that burning cross seems to have twanged a banjo string of Deep South imagery) the Jesus Christ kind. The kind represented by that – horizontal – cross of candles laid out on the chancel step in the darkened interior of this medieval vaulted building dedicated for centuries to kings, divine and human, who died a martyr's death.

Even among misfits, the desire to fit in is strong. So I've worn my blackest clothes. A linen jacket bought as a bargain a decade ago and now badly fraying; a waistcoat that rarely sees the light of day, or the night for that matter, and a narrow collarless overcoat which looked like a great idea when I bought it in Zara but looked a lot less great when I got it home and found I couldn't fasten it. But with Goths, I assume, an open, flowing black overcoat is *de rigeur*. And anyway, it's dark. Who's to notice? I'll just blend in.

I've overdressed. The rest of the congregation are in civilian clothes. There's only one other Goth, and he's someone unconnected with the service, whom I've invited myself: Simon Satori Hendley, a member of a rock band, who shares an interest in Cambridge psychogeography. We've arranged to go for a drink afterwards.

The service starts. The minister is Texan. I think I hear that banjo string faintly again. But no. It's just a guitar. Johnny Cash is playing lugubriously in the background. He at least is black-clad, though disembodied. And it's good, actually, the service: readings and symbolic rituals, interspersed with the *ennui*-laden soundtrack of the career melancholic. It's a million miles from the happy-clappy evangelicalism which has captured many sections of English Christianity, but it's pretty darned close to the existential angst and raw grief of the *Psalms* and *Ecclesiastes*, and the despairing cry of the abandoned Christ. For all the artfulness of its velvety externals, this ceremony seems a pretty authentic expression of that darker side of the human condition.

Afterwards, Simon and I have that pint. Simon is a writer, club manager and for nearly twenty years was the frontman of Rome Burns, a four-piece post-punk Gothic outfit, described as the "Politest Band in Goth." He's also the author of *Apathy: A cause not worth fighting for*. It's a history of indifference and lack of passion. The blurb says: "read about great hobbies for the apathetic (sleeping, drinking, watching TV, shrugging, sitting looking at walls), stupid causes, ideal occupations...and much much more." It also generated a gratifyingly non-committal review from John Naylor:

> I bought this book for no particular reason a few years ago. I found this book nothing to get excited about. I could not care one way or the other about it. It will be amusing to some I suppose. I would not recommend it as that would take effort. Enjoy it or don't. It is all the same to me.[33]

We leave the pub to take a round trip up to the Castle Mound, a view Simon says I need to see. On the way, he gives me a Goth's guide to the colleges we pass: Corpus Christi, where the Elizabethan playwright and sometime secret agent Christopher Marlowe studied; King's, where the ghost story writer Montague Rhodes ('M.R.') James lived as undergraduate, don and provost; Trinity, where the man the press denounced as "the wickedest man in the world", the occultist Aleister Crowley[34], studied for four years in the 1890s, leaving without a degree but already with more life experience than most of his contemporaries would ever have.

Simon stops to point out to me the war damage on the back wall of Trinity College's Whewell's Court.[35] where Sidney Street and Jesus Lane meet. There are several pock-marks caused by shrapnel when a German bomber dropped eleven bombs and a host of incendiaries, killing three people, injuring seven and destroying ten buildings. It rather gives the lie to the widely-believed story that there was an agreement between the Allies and the Nazis not to bomb each others' historic University cities: that Oxford and Cambridge, Heidelberg and Göttingen were all saved by mutually-assured non-destruction. The story was current during the war itself, and in his autobiography Stephen Hawking[36] mentions it as the reason his father moved the family out of London. You can see why the story would appeal, providing, as it does, reassurance that even in the greatest darkness, there are points of light – like with the Christmas Truce in the trenches of 1914. Except that the Christmas Truce really happened, with thousands of witnesses, and there's no evidence that the university cities agreement did in fact exist. Cambridge was actually bombed 11 times between 1940 and 1942, with thirty people killed and seventy injured. In fact, the very first civilian deaths from bombing in Britain during that war happened in Cambridge, when four adults and five children – including, by tragic irony, evacuees – were killed on the night of June, 1940.[37]

Of course, compared to other cities on both sides, the university cities did get off lightly. But that this was due to altruism is a difficult case to make: these cities were not vital to the British war effort, and the Germans had certainly showed no respect for heritage when they launched what became known as the Baedecker Raids from 1942 into 1944, deliberately targeting cities – particularly Bath, Canterbury, Norwich, York, and Exeter – of cultural rather than military value. Those raids, named after the

German tourist guidebooks, were a strategic failure, wasting the lives of many highly-trained airmen and losing irreplaceable aircraft in return for hitting targets of negligible military significance. So the fact that Oxford and Cambridge – and their German counterparts – suffered so little may simply have been sheer pragmatism rather than idealism; fear rather than hope. What's more, the destruction wrought on London and its own priceless heritage, and the even greater devastation visited by the Allies on the great cities of Germany like Dresden stands as stark testimony against any naive assumptions of chivalry amid barbarity or light amid darkness. But the myth persists. We want to believe in the light.

Simon and I make our way down Bridge Street, over the river and up Magdalene Street, past terraced houses where, in every window, someone is leaning into a glowing screen. The Castle, now the site of council offices, used to be the county jail. Many hangings took place here. We climb up the nearby Castle Mound, and take in the view over the city. It's certainly dark enough now; the night sky above is starless, just as the bomber crews liked it best in the days when a light in the darkness could mean death. I thought of the themes of the Goth Eucharist: despair; death; deliverance. There can be light that kills and darkness that saves. Nothing is really black or white. Below, the lights of the city stand out like the candles of the burning cross.

## PASSING THROUGH

"The incomparable city", was how the travel writer Arthur Mee described it in 1936: "...there are no English acres to surpass these ... Whenever we come, these colleges are a spectacle unsurpassed in England, but if we come in springtime, we come to an enchanted land".[38] Many writers have called Cambridge home, either just for their student years or for longer as academics and residents. Which means that the city has been the subject of innumerable literary portrayals by many of the most gifted writers in the language. However, as so many of these authors were connected with the University, their perspective is often confined to the college walls; the city's existence limited to the three intense eight-week terms of the academic year. But in the other six months, and in the often-crowded streets outside the college walls, life goes on. If, as is often said, Cambridge is really like a stage set, then it's a theatre that, paradoxically, is much busier when it's closed than when it's open.

Centre stage, of course, is the Chapel of King's College. This is after all, one of the great buildings of the world. The vision initially of Henry VI, it was erected between 1446 and 1515, and finished under Henry VIII, after the dynastic convulsions of the Wars of the Roses. A straight-backed rectangle of English Perpendicular Gothic in Yorkshire stone, it manages that English feat of being both restrained and expressive at the same time, maintaining an impeturbable exterior while reserving its emotion for the sensitive stained glass and the expansive decorative fan-vaulting inside.[39] It is the sheer white cliff on which the wave of tourists breaks.

On King's Parade, the street is wall-to-wall visitors. A bride and groom go past, followed by their photographer. A hen party in blue and white striped matelot shirts, with sailor hats and sashes. A guy sweeps past in a floor-length rainbow cloak and a jester's hat, carrying a clipboard with the logo of the Cambridge Folk Festival. On the pavement outside King's a woman sits in cross-legged meditation, while nearby colleagues hand out *Falun Gong* literature. Many of the female Chinese visitors seem to have a 1920s thing going on: cloche hats, Louise Brooks-style straight fringes and bobs, and *eau-de-nil* drop-waist flapper dresses. Perhaps the 1920s theme is appropriate: one of the particular attractions of Cambridge for tourists from China is that, in the 1920s, it inspired one of the most famous Chinese poems of the Twentieth Century, making it a destination for literary pilgrims ever since.

Xu Zhimo, born in 1897, was a visiting scholar in King's from 1921 to 1922. Revisiting in 1928, he wrote what is now his most famous poem: 'Farewell to Cambridge', seven stanzas of delicate valediction, which end:

> Softly I am leaving,
> Just as softly as I came;
> I softly wave goodbye
> To the clouds in the western sky.[40]

The first and last lines of the poem are carved, in Chinese characters, on a memorial of white Beijing marble, erected in 2008 on the Backs behind King's. Here, thousands of Chinese visitors come each year to see the place which inspired a literary classic. In the UK, a poem on the curriculum guarantees the lucky poet an audience of hundreds, perhaps even thousands, of students. But this poem is on the national curriculum *in China*, and generations of children have had to learn it by heart. In a country of nearly 1.4 billion people, that makes for a readership in the hundreds of millions.

You don't have to be Chinese to appreciate Xu's vision. Only mortal. 'Cambridge' and 'farewell' are really inseparable. For most who come here, the clock is ticking from the moment they arrive. The apparent timelessness of the sight of the college buildings along the river only sharpens the knowledge that this cannot last. And the more you appreciate the beauty, the greater you know the pain of departing will be.[41]

> Quietly I am leaving,
> Just as quietly as I came;
> Gently waving my sleeve,
> I am not taking away a single cloud.

It was in the clouds, only three years after he wrote that poem, that Xu himself took leave of life, aged only 34. His plane crashed in Shandong Province after heavy cloud obscured the mountains through which it was passing. China lost one of its most original voices, a moderniser, an experimenter who introduced Western forms to Chinese tradition, and a vital bridge between East and West. But his work in bringing the cultures together goes on, visitor by visitor, snapshot by snapshot, on the banks of the Cam. Some corner of an English field that is for ever China.

I sit on the wall of King's College to watch the crowds. Groups of language students stream past, in their obediently colour-coded gear, marshalled by guides using umbrellas, flags and selfie sticks to navigate through the crowds. Punt touts hail prospective punters with an all-purpose, non-gender-specific "Hi Guys!" One elderly man, dressed as though to show that he is emphatically *not* a tourist, in raspberry cords, flat cap and tweed jacket, strides through the throng with his head aloft as though pretending these hundreds of his fellow human beings did not exist. In one hand is a walking stick more suited to a hike across the Cumbrian moors; in the other a lead on which he pulls a poodle. He pauses as the dog drops two small but venomous-looking deposits on the pavement, then walks on, studiedly oblivious. I decide to do the more than decent thing and clear them away, and am searching my pockets for a tissue, when a hastening tour guide accounts for one of them. In a moment or two, amid squeals of disgust, a language school party has picked up more than just new vocabulary and has accounted for the other. With a sense of relief mixed with guilt, I stop searching. At least the thought was there. Sitting nearby are two homeless guys. They don't stop talking. Both of them at the same time. Occasionally, I find myself tuning in to them. They have vehement views on everything under the sun. It makes for an exhausting listen. They've no shortage of opinions. But then, I reflect, they've got little else.

You could teach a course on British history just by walking along this street. In one direction is Corpus Christi, founded by the town guilds in 1352, but soon to become much more gown than town. In the Sixteenth Century, Archbishop Matthew Parker bequeathed to Corpus' library some of the greatest treasures of any collection, including the oldest manuscript of the *Anglo Saxon Chronicle* and the sixth-century *Gospels* of St Augustine, on which the Archbishops of Canterbury take their oath of office. The novelists John Cowper Powys and Edward Upward studied here, as did Christopher Marlowe, the original Cambridge spy. His portrait hangs in the college hall.

Towards the Market Square, past 1 Trinity Street, which has been a bookshop – Britain's oldest – since 1581,[42] is Gonville and Caius. This was established in 1348, as the fourth oldest college, and it gained the second part of its name two centuries later when a successful alumnus, Dr John Keyes (he preferred the Latin form

'Caius'), became Master and gave his *alma mater* a heavily symbolic makeover: entry through the Gate of Humility, then the Gate of Virtue, and finally the Gate of Honour. Whether Keyes himself practised those qualities is, however, debatable: he was famously cantankerous and wasn't strong on equal opportunities, refusing applications from the "deaf, dumb, deformed, lame, confirmed invalids or Welshmen." He may have been the model for Dr Caius in Shakespeare's *Merry Wives of Windsor*, and was certainly a very distinguished physician, though some of the remedies he tried in order to prolong his life – such as breast milk from nursing mothers – might be regarded as fringe therapies today. Nonetheless, Caius – the college, that is – enjoys an impressive medical and scientific reputation. It was the college of Watson and Crick, and numbered Stephen Hawking among its Fellows. The noticeboard outside its porter's lodge used to carry a picture of him holding a teddy bear in the college colours, and the slogan 'Smarter than your average bear.'[43]

Next door is Trinity, which, with six hundred undergraduates, is the largest Oxbridge institution, and which counts thirty two Nobel prizewinners among its members, half the total for Cambridge as a whole. Its alumni include Ludwig Wittgenstein, Vladimir Nabokov, Bertrand Russell and Sir Isaac Newton, whose statue by Louis-François Roubiliac, stands in the college chapel, against a backdrop of the names of members, including the poet Rupert Brooke, killed in the First World War.[44]

Trinity's centrepiece, the Great Court, is the place where, on matriculation day, undergraduates traditionally attempt to race around the 383-yard perimeter in the 43 seconds it takes the clock to strike twelve. The Great Court Run was immortalised in the 1981 film *Chariots of Fire* in which, in 1919, the Jewish sprinter Harold Abrahams, played by Ben Cross, defies scepticism and prejudice to become the first to achieve the feat. In reality, Abrahams never even attempted the run: the first, and so far only, person to complete the full circuit – running on the outer perimeter flagstones rather than the shorter route on the inner circuit of cobbles, which is now permitted – was David Lord Burghley in 1927. Olympians Steve Cram and Sebastian Coe both attempted it in 1988, and narrowly failed.

Opposite the ornate frontage of Trinity gatehouse[45] is Heffers bookshop, established in 1876, and the largest in the city. Entering here for the first time as an undergraduate, I can recall looking around at that cavernous space, where the stepped terraces of shelves rose and dropped away on all sides like the galleries of a slate quarry. Contemplating the tens of thousands of volumes, I told myself that this, if anything, should cure me of the foolish ambition of being a writer. What difference could one more book make? Assured of my own insignificance, I felt relief at being absolved of the need to seek recognition, however minor. It didn't last.

Cambridge Market Square has occupied the same place since Anglo Saxon times.[46] In 1553, it was the scene of a dynastic and religious turning point. As he lay dying, the fifteen-year-old King Edward VI, who had continued the Protestant reforms of his father Henry VIII, had been persuaded by his chief minister, the Duke of Northumberland, to settle the Crown on his Protestant cousin – the Duke's daughter in law – the sixteen-year-old Lady Jane Grey, thereby safeguarding the Reformation, and bypassing Edward's half-sister, Mary Tudor, who had a stronger claim to the throne but who was Catholic. When Jane was proclaimed Queen, Mary fled to Framlingham Castle in Suffolk, with Northumberland and a large force in pursuit. But public opinion swiftly changed. London proclaimed Mary Queen, Northumberland's forces deserted him, and he, hoping to save himself, also belatedly proclaimed Mary Queen, in Cambridge market place: It didn't work. He was arrested in Cambridge the next day and executed shortly afterwards, as was his unfortunate daughter-in-law, the Nine Days' Queen.

Today, among the takeaways and souvenir stalls, a group of evangelical students in pale blue – Cambridge blue – teeshirts have set up an open-air 'prayer station', with a vertical banner advertising their services. One of them approaches me: "Hello. Is there anything you would like me to pray for?" I want to oblige. I think hard. There's always world peace and an end to hunger, of course, but that's all a bit Miss World. And there are always, sadly, the sorrows and sicknesses of friends. It's just that, put on the spot like this, not a single example of human suffering comes immediately to mind. Not one. "No, I think I'm OK, thanks," I find myself saying, in the upbeat tone you use in a restaurant when the staff ask if you need anything else. The student smiles and moves on, leaving me feeling rather chagrined at my own failure to rise to the occasion. Offered a direct line to the throne of grace, a personal introduction to the deity from someone who clearly knows Him well, and given a complete blank sheet for my petition, the best I could come up with was a cheery "No, I think I'm OK, thanks."

But, on reflection, that statement may have been simple, but it was still true. And after all, gratitude itself can be a form of prayer. Do I need anything else? Really? No. Thank you. This is fine. I don't need anything more than this. As expressions of the existential condition go, it might not be Newton, or Wittgenstein or Hawking, but it feels fitting enough on this spring day in this East Anglian market square, under that endless Cambridge blue sky.

## Notes

1. Named after a former tenant, college cook Edward Parker.
2. University of North Carolina website.
3. 1882-1963.
4. Martin Garrett, *Cambridge. A cultural and literary history*, (Massachusetts, 2004), 10. See also, Richard Tames, *An Armchair Traveller's Guide to Cambridge*, (London, 2013), 254.
5. C.R. Benstead, *Portrait of Cambridge*, (London, 1968), 63.
6. Girton was followed by Newnham (1872), Hughes Hall (1885), Murray Edwards, formerly New Hall, (1954) and Lucy Cavendish (1965).
7. https://www.english.cam.ac.uk/people/James.Riley/
8. Ed. Ronald Hayman, *My Cambridge*, (London, 1977), 59.
9. *Ibid.*, 203.
10. p.240.
11. Probably derived from 'small cookeries': i.e. street food.
12. Benstead commented: "seldom were the proceeds of robbery better expended." *Op.cit.,* 48.
13. Tragically murdered by an extremist in 2016.
14. Jesus Green saw Cambridge's only Protestant martyrdom, when John Hullier was burned at the stake on Maundy Thursday 1556 under Bloody Mary's persecution. David Barrowclough, *Bloody British History; Cambridge* (Stroud, 2015), 27.

15. Morbidly afraid of fire, he kept a rope ladder in his room. Lured out by a false alarm, he climbed down into a carefully-placed water tub. Benstead, *op. cit.,* 40. *Cambridgeshire,* (London, 1939), 46.
16. 1930-1998.
17. *Winter Pollen: Occasional Prose,* (London, 1994), 8-9.
18. Many still bear his annotations.
19. Off Petty Cury, later demolished.
20. *Daily Telegraph* November, 2011 http://www.telegraph.co.uk/culture/music/classical music/8913501/Suzi-Digby-is-the-mother-of-all-music.html
21. Sir John Hawkins, in his *General History of Music* in 1776, quoted in F.A. Keynes, *By-ways of Cambridge History* (Cambridge, 1947), 78. Gibbons, (1583-1625), was a scholar and later student at King's, his family having moved to Cambridge from Oxford when he was a few months' old.
22. Claudia Pritchard, *Independent on Sunday,* February, 2016.
23. Sir Nicholas Kenyon Guardian, April, 2016. https://www.theguardian.com/music/2016/apr/17/ora-upheld-by-stillness-vol-1-byrd-review
24. Dominic O'Brien, eight times winner of the World Memory Championships. Published London, 2011.
25. (Brighton, 2016). https://featheredape.com/
26. Watson's college, Clare, commemorates his achievement with a double helix symbol at Memorial Court. Tames, *op. cit.,* 81. Crick's former house in Portugal Place, behind St Clement's Church, has a golden helix above the door. Tames, 242.
27. The graffiti had been obscured by later layers of tobacco smoke, but a regular, James Chainey, rediscovered and restored it. Malcolm 'Ozzie' Osborn, 'A Famous Ceiling', *http://www.398th.org*
28. Latin: 'Everywhere', motto of The Royal Artillery and The Royal Engineers.
29. Latin: 'On the wings of the night', motto of 58 Squadron, RAF Bomber Command.
30. *op. cit.,* 90.
31. Peas Hill, Market Hill and St Andrew's Hill are not hills; at one time the name simply meant an open space. Tames, 17. In *Cambridge Street-Names. Their Origins and Associations.* (Cambridge, 2000), 12. Ronald Gray and Derek Stubbings suggest the area, a former fish market, was named for the Latin pisces.
32. On October, 1555. Followed five months later by Archbishop Cranmer, another Cambridge man. Arthur Mee cites the Reformers as evidence of Cambridge's genius for innovation: "...as Oxford was the home of lost causes Cambridge was the nursery of the new", *Cambridgeshire, op. cit.,* 13.
33. On the Goodreads website.
34. 1875-1947.
35. This stone-faced Victorian residential court was long the home of the poet A.E. Housman (1859-1936). For a period, the philosopher Ludwig Wittgenstein lived on the floor above. Housman denied him use of his private toilet. Martin Garrett, *op. cit.,* 174.
36. In his book *Black Holes and Baby Universes and other essays,* (London, 1993). 1.
37. The houses destroyed included ten of the twenty bought in Vicarage Terrace by the early social housing pioneer Dr Henry Sidgwick. F.A. Keynes By-ways of Cambridge History, (Cambridge, 1947).
38. Arthur Mee, *op. cit.* 28
39. Cromwell's soldiers used it as a drill hall. Henry James described it as "the most beautiful chapel in England". Ruskin described it as a " piece of architectural juggling ... a table upside down with its four legs in the air".
40. Translation from ed. Peter Pagnamenta *The University of Cambridge: an 800th Anniversary Portrait,* (London, 2008), 29.

41. Cambridge produces 'instant nostalgia' according to John Vaizey, later Lord Vaizey, the economist. "The Phrase 'It won't last, you only have eight more – seven more – six more – terms' was repeated to me every day", Hayman, *op. cit.,* 117.
42. Tames *op. cit.,* 264.
43. The catchphrase of the TV cartoon character Yogi Bear.
44. See this book's West section. On the other side is Ferenc Békássy, a member killed fighting for the Central Powers. Of the 14000 current and former members of the university who took part in World War One, over 2000 were killed and 3000 wounded, C.R. Benstead, Portrait of Cambridge, (London, 1968).
45. Where since time immemorial the statue of Henry VIII has the sceptre in his hand replaced with a chair leg.
46. Tames *op. cit.,* 17. Its layout has changed, though. At one time, much of it was tenements.

# NORTH

# CHESTERTON

"Go home! Go HOME!"

The woman behind the counter in the convenience store is shouting at the older Eastern European guy who is standing, bewildered, by the door. I have just come out to buy some groceries and here I am on the ugly frontline of communal tensions.

The woman is pointing at the door. She's not someone you'd want to mess with.

"Go! Home!"

A middle-aged female customer is watching all this, motionless, saying nothing. But that's always the way. For the triumph of evil, all that's necessary is for good people to do nothing. That's what they say. I'm going to have to step in. I just hope there's CCTV. The papers love this sort of thing.

The shopkeeper whirls round to me now. She points at me.

"You speak Italian?"

"Er, no. Why?"

"Him," she says, pointing back at the older guy, who, meanwhile, has picked up a bunch of flowers and is offering them to her, still smiling apologetically. "He can not speak English. And he is *drunk!*"

She says "drunk" with the same tone of outrage as though she were saying "mass murderer". Actually, the shopkeeper has a marked Eastern European accent herself. What exactly is going on here? But she's in full flow now.

"I keep tell him. You are *drunk!* You must go *home!* He been in four times. Always more drunk. He has a fat wallet. All fifties. Somebody watching him – he will be robberied. Or murder. He has to go home." She turns to him again. "Go! Home!"

A younger guy has now walked in. Well-dressed. Professional-looking. The shopkeeper turns to him.

"You speak Italian?"

"No. Why?"

"Him," she indicates the older guy. "He is *drunk!*"

The younger guy turns to him, and speaks a few words. The drunk's face lights up.

"Romanian", the young guy tells the woman, matter-of-factly. Speaking to the drunk in his own language, he guides him quietly out of the shop – but not before the older guy has first paid for the flowers – a peace offering in the interests of domestic harmony, no doubt. He wobbles away on his bike.

Inside, all is quiet again. The lady customer who has been watching all this speaks for the first time. She's English.

"I *told* 'im 'casa'," she says.

There has always been something a little different about Chesterton. Safely distant on the north bank of the Cam, the village retained some independence from the college-dominated centre of the city, and, rather like the South Bank in London in Shakespearean times, became a place where those weary of rectitude could relax. It infuriated the College authorities. In 1592, having forbidden students to attend performances by travelling players in Chesterton, they issued a warrant authorising constables to prevent any such performance. It was ignored, and the playbills appeared on the College's own gates. So the University complained to the Privy Council about Chesterton, "which town hath and doth continually annoy our University". But in a rare occasion of officialdom siding with town rather than gown, for once, no action was taken.[1]

Perhaps something of that same spirit of independence was at work some four hundred and twenty years later, when, in April 2017, a protest against powerful interests in Chesterton came to international attention. In response to the demand for attractive riverside homes, a developer had built a new collection of houses in Water Street, priced at well over a million pounds. There was already local concern over house prices, and the apparently unaffordable cost of these latest additions proved the last straw for one disaffected party. Overnight, a huge graffiti slogan appeared across the weatherboarded gable-ends of two of the properties. Normally this would have merited a few paragraphs in the *Cambridge Evening News*; it would hardly have generated worldwide media interest. But the graffitist had pulled off a publicity masterstroke. The message was *in Latin*.[2] 'Only in Cambridge!', the gloating headlines read. 'Vandal with classical education sprays Latin on houses;' 'Educated vandal,'; 'Here's how they do graffiti in Cambridge' and so on. A pleasing image of a better class of vandal, a satisfying suggestion of continuing civility in a seemingly disenchanted world and, let's face it, an ingrained deference to high culture, all combined to promote a collective suspension of judgement at wilful damage to property and disrespect for the rule of law.

Except there was a catch. While the use of Latin was undoubtedly a brilliant publicity coup, the vandal probably didn't know the language at all. The graffito *'Loci Populum! Locus in Domos'* is not actually coherent Latin, and a quick check with Google Translate showed that the protestor had simply typed 'Local Homes for Local People' into the automatic translator, producing a garbled result. Still, the point was made. *Opus bonum*, as they say in Google Translate.

Chesterton has also been the scene of another long-running dispute over accommodation. Along the banks of the Cam here, there are some 100 houseboats, or 'liveaboards' as the residents of these converted narrowboats call them. Some are gleamingly-restored museum-pieces, others are the floating equivalent of a battered VW camper. But they're all homes, and people have lived along this shore for many years. Many local house-dwellers regard the 'boaters' as an essential part of their area's character, and as a welcome human presence along an otherwise lonely stretch of the river. The boaters guard their chosen lifestyle jealously. But not everyone shares this view, and the council which has the necessary but unenviable task of balancing the city's books as well as balancing the competing claims of house-dwellers, river dwellers and river users, has been engaged in a long wrangle with the river-dwellers over mooring fees and health and safety. The boat dwellers fear eviction from their current low-cost city-centre accommodation being replaced by a gleaming – and expensive – new marina.

But, by necessity, the boaters are a resourceful bunch. And none more so than one of their main spokesmen, Bill Jenks. As a former army officer and marketing director of a multinational company, he's used to conflict and strategic change. And he's a survivor, who came to Cambridge by a more roundabout route than most. "I caught salmonella eating a snack in an up-market Dutch whorehouse," he says, frankly. "Could have been worse I suppose." That episode forced him to cancel his existing career plans, and, in search of an alternative path, brought him to study at the old Cambridgeshire College of Arts and Technology. Later, a chance conversation in the Green Dragon pub led him to buy Mizpah, an old-school pitch-pine, oak and mahogany river cruiser. Over 20 years he then got to know the collection of eclectic characters who make their home on the banks of the Cam. Later, when the council's new licensing policy for houseboats seemed to put his friends' lifestyle under threat, he joined the Camboaters campaign group.

They see themselves rather like the indigenous people of the river. They actually *live* on the Cam, while the rowers and – on the upper stretches – the punters, are just passing through. Rowing has expanded hugely, Bill says, fuelled not so much by the long-established University usage, but by the growth of the city itself, whose rowing clubs primarily use the river after work. "There are nearly nine hundred hulls on the river," he says. "It gets absolutely chocka. It's like Heathrow airport trying to use the river now." The sense of being forced out by gentrification fuelled a feeling of resentment, he says.

Speaking to Bill's fellow boaters at the Fort St George pub on the riverbank one evening, it's clear they're keen not to be seen as part of an identikit counter-culture. Yes, they're marginal, one of them says, a community within a community, strong-willed, free-spirited, with a big independent streak, but most of them have strong networks in the wider city, either through work or personal associations. The river community includes an archivist, a neurosurgeon, a tree surgeon, a builder, some teachers, engineers, carpenters, lawyers, PhD students, adventurers, retired folk, people with young families, and – yes – lots of musicians, "But we all have a practical bent," he says. There's something about the reality of life on the river, with the cold and the wind, the flood. There's great freedom, and friendship. And you can move."

But only when you want to. Being moved on against your will is a very different matter. And all that river-borne resourcefulness will be at work in making sure that they stay right where they are. On the table in front of Bill, I spot a copy of the writings of Marcus Aurelius. This is only circumstantial evidence of course, but all the same... "Were you responsible for the graffiti on those houses?" I ask him. "No," he says. "If I had been, it would have been proper Latin."

## ARBURY

I meet James Murray-White at his house in Carisbrooke Road. It's easy to find, he tells me: white handrails on the front path, next to a vegetable patch. A front-garden veg patch, like a front-garden sofa, is usually a sign of an independent spirit. I'm not wrong. Trained in drama, James steered into journalism, mainly with an activist, environmental bent. As reporter and film-maker, he's travelled widely: five years in Ireland, enough to pick up some Irish; five in Israel, ditto Hebrew. Now, he's back in Cambridge, the city where he was brought up from the age of two, and he's making films with artists and activists, causes and campaigners, always looking for the edge where art meets science, where creativity meets conservation.

We walk out through the somnolent suburban streets to find the latest quiet conflict zone which has attracted his lens: the northern margin of the city where developers have bought up a huge tract of land for a new housing development to be called Darwin Green. On our way to the chainlink fence which marks the boundary, we pass a fine little late nineteenth-century, or possibly early twentieth-century house with an attractive pillared portico and a decorated lantern. It's boarded up and overgrown. Next to it, James points out an old, glass-roofed laundry. I assume they'll preserve the house as part of the new development. Sadly not, he says. It'll be demolished. We push through a collapsed wire fence into the old paddock next door. The old piggery, James says, with the orchard trees that once provided windfalls. This is going to be built on too. Round the corner, we strike out for the building site itself, along a service road leading to an encampment of grumbling generators and JCBs, stationary on this Saturday afternoon. We're aiming for the strip of ancient woodland on the far side of the building plot, which is due to be preserved when the field turns into houses and hardstandings.

Halfway through, we encounter a single huge Alsatian tethered to a fence and barking furiously. If he's a guard dog, then his short lead limits his effectiveness drastically. We'll be able to pass by easily. Even while barking, he's wagging his tail madly. Is he trying to be friendly? Has he been abandoned? Perhaps we should check. He's in the middle of nowhere here, after all. Maybe he has some I.D. on his collar. "Do you mind dogs?" I ask James. "Not at all," he says. Nor do I. When I was a small child, our village lived in fear of a huge savage shaggy Alsatian called Sultan who guarded his disabled master Hugh Parry, the draper, with ferocious passion. He guarded not only Hugh's person, but, for good measure, the entire road on which his house stood. If Sultan was on guard, which he usually was, no-one could pass by. No-one, that is, except me. I was a weedy, bespectacled child, who looked like a frailer version of the Milky Bar Kid. This lack of physical presence, a painful liability in a tough industrial village in the 1970s, was a major asset when it came to Sultan. Sensing no danger, he would let me pass without so much as a growl, and would even let me pat him affectionately as I did so. It gave me a minor celebrity I badly needed. Ever afterwards I've been convinced I have a special rapport with even the fiercest canines. They're all just Sultans to me. This one would be no different.

I strode over to him confidently, speaking brisk, fearless words of reassurance. For his part, he worked himself into an ecstasy of aggression, writhing and gnashing like Hitler at a Nazi rally, his barks scarcely distinguishable individually, more an unbroken torrent of uncontrollable fury. By now, he should have been letting me pat him, should be looking up at me with chastened eyes, guilty for his misplaced suspicion, grateful for my magnanimity. Instead, his red eyes were blazing with unmitigated hatred. For the first time, I felt fear. Was that foam in the corner of his mouth? It was. My nerve broke. "I think he really *is* a guard dog," I said. My bravado evaporated. Fifty years of confidence destroyed in seconds. I will never be invincible again.

We walked round him. A minute or so later, a little van marked 'Security' drew up behind us and stopped next to the dog, which had dialled its rage down from rabid murderous frenzy to mere snarling malevolence. I looked back at the guard, and made a walking gesture with my fingers to indicate our intention. He gestured back with a double thumbs-up. We made our way along the edge of the field of churned-up heavy clay, keeping to the edge until we got to the brook which marked the boundary of the ancient wood. It was only about five feet wide, but looked deep after the recent winter rains, and steep-banked. Eventually, we found a way over: a narrow metal girder, some four inches across. It was like that scene in *Indiana Jones and the Last Crusade*, where Indy crosses to the Grail sanctuary.

Having passed this first threshold, we're inside: a wilderness of briars and butane cans, impenetrable undergrowth and sudden clearings. Bent double, we push our way through to the centre of the wood, where we find a large tent surrounded by plastic chairs. We approach carefully, If someone has set up home here, they're probably not expecting visitors. James tells me of the tent-dwelling migrants who live on Stourbridge Common, just behind the Leper Chapel. Maybe this is something similar. But as we get closer, we see it's deserted, and in fact was probably never anyone's home. There's no sign of domestic habitation. A coolbox lies on its side, and the ground is strewn with bottle tops. Some kind of shebeen for boozing and drug-taking. Shortly afterwards, we find another, smaller tent. This one, though deserted now, clearly was someone's home at some point. Beyond, is a blanket of snowdrops. "I think there may be a fox here," James says He's right. The smell is unmistakeable.

It's time to go back. But we can't find the bridge. Time and again, we push our way through the briars and overhanging branches to find the brook bridgeless, impassable. We're marooned. We might have need of that tent yet. Eventually, we find a fallen tree which might serve as a way across. James crosses it, steadying himself with one of the overhanging branches: a dangerous move in the depths of winter, when the sap is at its lowest and even quite sturdy-looking branches can snap. As he is halfway across, I remind him, helpfully I hope, of that scene in *King Kong* where the adventurers try to cross the chasm by means of a fallen tree, only for Kong to shake them off to what their leader Carl Denham later called "horrible deaths". Thankfully, no such fate awaits James. Or me either, as he pulls me safely across. We retrace our steps, passing the guard dog, who looks at me now with an air of quiet triumph.

Further on, we reach the far northern outskirts of the city, where the A14 forms a barrier of traffic noise. We walk through the Orchard Park development of flats, new houses, a Premier Inn and Travelodge. We don't pass another living soul. There isn't even any traffic. It's like the place has been hit by a neutron bomb. As we're passing the business park, where James points out one of the units whose windows are coated with photovoltaic energy-generating cells, a jogger stops to greet him. "Chan!", says James. Soon, they are deep into a discussion of Cambridge art politics: the pressure on studio space, the way property prices are driving artists out of the town centre. Chan Ny works in a studio at Christ's College, but it looks as though he and his fellow artists will have to leave due to the site being redeveloped. It's a common story in this fast-growing city. Chan needs to be fast-moving too. He jogs on.

We're now at the Cambridge Guided Busway, the longest such track in the world, stretching sixteen miles from St Ives in the north to Trumpington in the south along a disused railway line. It's comprised of guiderails between which buses can drive, kept on track by small horizontal kerb wheels fitted to the vehicle. The buses can operate on normal roads as well, and, because they have the busway to themselves, they can run to time like trains. Before its opening in 2011, the project was beset by doubts and cost overruns, but once it opened in 2011, it's proved popular; millions of journeys have been taken on it.

The busway passes the Moulton Park Industrial Estate in King's Hedges. One of the units here houses Daily Bread, a Christian-based workers' co-operative wholefood shop, which opened in 1992, and which now employs 22 people, with a particular emphasis on providing opportunities for those with mental health or physical issues. The company's rigorous 'People Before Profit' principles make the Sermon on the Mount look a bit undemanding by comparison. I need to buy a few necessities, so we go in. As I'm browsing the organic, artisan, gluten-free, low-salt, high-welfare, hypo-allergenic, fairly-traded wares, I gradually notice a more subtle difference from normal shops. It's not just the goods. It's the pace. People here *move* differently. In the queue for the checkout, it isn't the usual hurried grab, bang, scan and swipe, with the items stashed like swag into a plastic bag which will later poison some unfortunate marine creature. Here, the movements are measured, economical, graceful as tai chi: each item is lifted reverently and then laid down thoughtfully, to be packed into the cloth bags that everyone – *everyone* – has brought with them. The young man on the checkout is solicitous; he might be a young doctor inquiring about my health rather than a cashier scanning a couple of groceries. All the customers look ethical. Already, I find my own natural impatience subdued by the serenity around me, and I have slowed to the considerate pace of my fellow shoppers. The dimly burning wick of my conscience begins to glow a little more brightly, and I decide to buy some of the fairly-traded chocolate on sale at the checkout, just to give them some custom. I drift outside, effortless, virtuous, calm.

It's getting late, the light is fading, and I remember it's been a long while since lunch, and it's still quite a while until dinner, and we have an hour or more's walk until then. I remember the chocolate I've just bought. It should be enough to bridge the gap. I fetch it out of my satchel and try a square. It tastes faintly soapy. It cost twice as much as a normal bar – how can it taste worse? I try another square. The same. It goes in the nearest bin – but in the bit marked 'Recycling'. It's what it would have wanted.

On the carpark outside the Ship pub in Northfields Avenue a family with a white pitbull are buying kebabs from a van. Opposite is the squat brick pillbox of North Arbury Chapel, windowless at ground level, lit by skylights only. A sign at the door says 'You are so precious to God'. The only other sign, on the featureless wall next to the car park says: 'No ball games'. We cross the Nun's Way

playing fields, and into Campkin Road, where I lived during my
second year at college. The house has changed. It's in a sight better
shape than it was in my time. I look up at what had been my
bedroom when I was nineteen. Only one thing is visible: a large jar
with a home-made sign: 'Beer Fund'. Actually, maybe it hasn't
changed so much after all. From the Arbury community centre
comes the sound of clapping, cymbals, drums and chanting; an
Indian cultural evening. On the wall outside, a sticker: 'Migration is
not a Crime'. Three young teenage girls, aged thirteen or fourteen
maybe, pass us on the way to see some boys they have met on social
media. They catch the first sight of them, leaning on their bikes in
the middle of the footpath, and turn on their heels; "Omigod!" says
one of them, "Why are they, like, *four* years old?!"

We walk on to the Arbury Court shopping centre, a small
courtyard of shops and flats, where a wall has been decorated with
a mural by the French graffiti artist El Seed, whose swirling shapes,
based on Arabic calligraphy, are interwoven with words by the
Cambridge poet Veronica Forrest Thomson. Two Deliveroo cyclists
cut through the snarled traffic. They are both as thin as bicycle
chains. In the grey cubes of their delivery boxes, thousands of
calories are being ferried to waiting waistlines.

I'm approached by a well-dressed, middle-aged Englishman,
carrying a plastic bag, full, apparently, of papers. He has a
confidential air. "Do you know about Princeton, New Jersey?" he

says. "A little," I answer, cautiously. "Have you heard about the Philadelphia Experiment?" he asks. I have, unfortunately. Enough to know that it's a favourite among conspiracy theorists who believe that during World War Two the US Navy tried to make a warship invisible, with disastrous consequences for the crew. My interrogator is now looking at me with an air of deep significance. "It's all true," he says, and stares at me again, waiting for the import of his words to sink in. Right now, I'm wishing I could become invisible myself. There's no point in arguing. "I know," I say, and then, slightly *sotto voce*, and with what I hope looks like sincere frustration: "But they'll never believe it!" He seems satisfied. As I edge away, he reaches into his plastic bag, takes out a bottle of red wine and takes a long draught.

Residents of Arbury are understandably wary of the generalisations that are often applied to their district by outsiders. As a former resident myself, I sympathise. According to the Index of Multiple Deprivation, this isn't actually Cambridge's poorest area: that distinction belongs to Abbey, and then to King's Hedges, but Arbury is not far behind. These things have to be seen in perspective. We're not talking the South Bronx here, but there is no mistaking the fact that, but less than 10 minutes' cycle ride from King's College Chapel, you can be in a very different Cambridge, a very different England.

Outside the Carlton Arms in Arbury Road, James is stopped and embraced by a young French guy, a friend of his, who launches into a story of his domestic challenges. Like with Chan, earlier, but now in a mixture of English and Franglais, James is patient, thoughtful and insightful. After some fifteen minutes, after much Gallic embracing, the friend moves on: the clock is ticking on his problems at home. "So, you just dispense counselling on the street?" I ask James. "Oh, not really," he says. "I just know him because he's the partner of my friend Annie." As he speaks, Annie cycles past, stops, and we reprise the earlier scene, before she cycles off again.

At the junction of shop-lined Chesterton Road and Hawthorn Way, is a little bridgehead of hipsterdom on the north bank of the Cam. Straight-spined women in Birkenstocks, with yoga mats slung over their pulled-back shoulders glide into the Satyam Yoga Wellbeing Centre. Next door, Stir – 'Local, Social, CB4' – is doing a brisk trade in single-origin Guatemalan roast coffee. Bikes with wicker baskets are stacked outside, leaning together as though for company: wicker baskets become rarer as you head further north into Arbury, where people cycle to save money, not the planet. Further along the road, on a tiny triangle of municipal planting, at the junction with Mitcham's Corner, stands a small stone water trough with a memorial to one of the city's most unlikely friendships. The inscription reads:

1934
In memory of Tony, a dog who gave him friendship and happiness during his Cambridge years. This trough is erected by His Royal Highness Prince Chula of Siam.

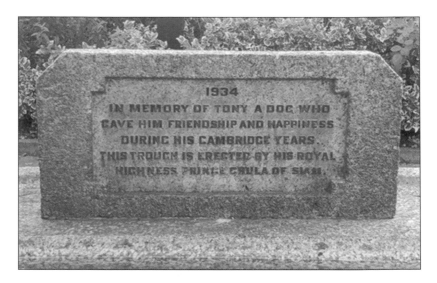

Chula Chakrabongse was the son of Prince Chakrabongse Bhuvanath and his Ukrainian wife, Ekaterina Desnitska, and a grandson of King Chulalongkorn, the ruler whose modernising programme managed to ensure that Siam was one of only three countries in the world (Japan and Abyssinia were the others) to escape European control at the height of imperial expansion. To meet the would-be colonisers on equal terms, he ensured his family had a European education, so Prince Chula spent his undergraduate years at Trinity, picking up English manners, including, of course, a love of dogs. After he left, he gave money for the trough in memory of Tony who had been his constant companion. Prince Chula later married an Englishwoman and moved to Cornwall where he died in 1963 aged 55 – but not before erecting two more memorials in that county to his canine friends.

There's time for a pint, so James and I go into the Waterman Arms. The Scotland v England rugby game is on the television. I order a pint of Adnams Ghost Ship for myself, and Mosaic for James, and we find a table.

In the background, among the England fans around the screen, the beers are going down. So too, sadly for them, are England, who are unexpectedly trailing the Scots by some margin. A lone Scot at the bar growls encouragement at the screen. At our table, James and I discuss roots, belonging, place and people. He says that when he retires, he's thinking of going back to Ireland, to the Gaeltacht, learning Irish properly and really making a contribution. He wants to grow some roots. Maybe it's the Ghost Ship, but I'm moved to straightforward disagreement. "You've *got* roots," I say. "They're right here in Cambridge, where people embrace you in the street, where you know the names of the passers-by. You're one of the most rooted people I've ever met."

Cambridge is changing more quickly than just about any city in England. It needs its roots and its remembrancers too, and James, it seems to me, was born to do that. Far be it from me to discourage someone who wants to learn a Celtic language, of course. Thank God for those who do. But Celts don't have a monopoly on roots, or the need for them. It's that English diffidence again: worried at their power, wary of their past, they leave it to the Celts to stand proxy for patriotism, like their pets stand proxy for their affections. It's commendable restraint. But unnecessary. We all know where love of our own begins and dislike of the other starts. You don't have to say all love is dangerous in order to avoid hatred, any more than you have to make out that all drink is evil in order to avoid becoming a drunk. James nods, thoughtfully. In the background, the TV commentary is shouting of a Scottish victory: 25-13. Scottish voices are raised in raucous, unabashed triumph. The English fans keep their disappointment to themselves, holding their feelings close, like their beer.

# THE KINDERSLEY WORKSHOP

It seems to be the fate of many poets that their friends are separated from them by time, sometimes by centuries. When the struggling author could have used the companionship, the commissions, even a few coins, where were they then? Not born yet. That's where. Long after the poet has gone to the grave – too often hastened on the way by poverty, sickness, lost love, despair, or just by the cold indifference of the world – then, and only then, do they have admirers in abundance.

This struck me on one of my occasional visits to Bunhill Fields, just off City Road in Spitalfields in London. This crowded cemetery, originally 'Bone Hill', is the last resting place for around 120,000 people. From the Seventeenth Century onwards, it was particularly associated with religious dissenters, who included some of the greatest names in English literature. Daniel Defoe is buried here, his grave marked with a tall obelisk, its surfaces covered in admiring inscriptions. John Bunyan is a few yards away, his tomb marked with relief sculptures of scenes from *The Pilgrim's Progress*, and topped with a recumbent statue of the author. Both these impressive memorials are the work of later admirers of these feted bestsellers. A few yards away is a simple unadorned gravestone with the inscription: 'Near by lie the remains of the poet painter William Blake 1757-1827 and of his wife Catherine Sophia 1762-1831'.[3]

For a natural anti-authoritarian like Blake, who never saw a convention he couldn't question, or a power he couldn't challenge, it seemed fitting that the grave should be so austere and undecorated, without even a quotation. His words, after all, are lapidary enough; their mysticism as profound as any saint's, their radicalism as dangerous as any revolutionary's. It seemed enough that the bare stone should only ever carry the occasional transient tribute: a faded sweet william, or a few coins left for the street people to later take away, a gift from one outsider to another.

On this particular August day, though, I arrived to spend my customary few minutes in this little green patch of tranquillity among the tower blocks, to find that the poet-painter's belated fan club had turned out in force; the Blake Society was holding its annual gathering on the anniversary of his death. Picnic rugs were spread out on the grass; glasses chinked, salads and dips were shared. So was poetry. A white-bearded man in a waistcoat and a hat with sweet williams entwined round the brim strides into the middle of one of the groups. He clutches a sheet of foolscap paper: "Listen to this, everyone! Listen to this! I've got a poem! This is *amazing*!" He's right. It is. He declaims to the cemetery at large, and at length, concluding – eventually – with a denunciation of: "The hateful! Hateful! *HATEFUL! HATEFUL! HATEFUL!!!* steam-driven Satan-mills, that boosted productivity…" There is polite applause. "William would have liked it," one man says at length. "William *does!"* says an excited lady with a flower garland round her neck, correcting to the present tense: "William does!" Next to her, a beautiful young woman dressed entirely in orange sits cross-legged, staring straight ahead, her face a serene impassive mask beneath her long dark centre-parted hair. By her side is a foot-high stack of well-used black Moleskine notebooks. On the other is a little silver bell, which she lifts and tinkles occasionally as though to summon unseen servants. Her neighbour offers her some salad from a Tupperware. The young woman closes her eyes and inclines her head sideways almost imperceptibly. That's a no. Then she reaches out to lift and ring her bell. One of the cemetery maintenance staff trundles past with a wheelbarrow. The flower garland lady, recumbent on her tartan rug, champagne glass in hand, hails him proprietorially: "Don't cut down the buddleia!" As I left, I thought that, on the whole, Blake had had rather a lucky escape.

Years later, though, standing in front of Blake's replacement gravestone in Lida Lopes Cardozo Kindersley's stonecutting workshop in Victoria Road, West Chesterton, I'm ready to revise that view. Blake's twenty-first-century friends have done him proud. The Society has commissioned a superb piece, with a quotation from his poem 'Jerusalem';[4] "I give you the end of a golden string, Only wind it into a ball: It will lead you in at Heavens gate, Built in Jerusalems wall". I'm worried about the missing apostrophes. Won't people think they're a mistake? Won't pedants go on pilgrimage there for the rest of time, just so they can point out the errors? But the Society's right: that's how Blake wrote it, in his own manuscript, which he printed and published himself. The society is being true to his vision and his way of doing things, not making him conform to later sensibilities. That's true friendship for you.

In commissioning the piece to replace the original gravestone in August 2018, the Society knew exactly where to go. The Kindersley workshop, in a converted Victorian school, sets the standard for letter-cutting in the English-speaking world. It was founded by David Kindersley,[5] who had been apprenticed to the father of English letter-cutting, the sculptor Eric Gill, before becoming a highly sought-after artist in his own right, one of the major figures in twentieth-century art. After leaving Gill in 1936, Kindersley made Cambridge his base, starting his first workshop in 1945 in Barton, just west of Grantchester, then moving in 1967 to Chesterton Tower, a mid-fourteenth-century building near Chapel Street, before finally settling, in 1977, in the former school in Victoria Road. Here, he continued working on a flood of commissions for memorial sculpture and inscriptions of all kinds from both sides of the Atlantic, with a seemingly endless number of major projects including the war memorial in Trinity College's ante-chapel, the carvings at Madingley American Cemetery, plaques and memorials in Westminster Abbey and Canterbury Cathedral, and the spectacular gates at the British Library in London, which he designed with his third wife and former protégée, the Dutch-born artist Lida Lopes Cardozo Kindersley, whom he married in 1986, and with whom he had three sons. David Kindersley died in 1995 and is buried in the churchyard of St Luke's Church, only a few yards from where he worked for the last decades of his life.

In the high-ceilinged, light-filled calm of the workshop, Lida continues the tradition, with her team of craftspeople and apprentices. The commissions are still flowing in steadily, so much so that the business produces a booklet – a little work of art in itself – to explain in detail to the prospective client how the process works: everything from the choice of material, the type of letterforms, the spacing, interlinear spacing, the finish, and the fixing. A headstone can cost anything from three and six thousand pounds. The practice keeps a record of its commissions so detailed and so orderly it would put the Cambridge University Library to shame.

The artistic approach is rooted in the Arts and Craft tradition of personal vision which formed Eric Gill and then David Kindersley himself: "Through our love for letters – for the alphabet, for writing and lettering – we aim for perfection in the transmission of meaning," the booklet says. "It is our reason for being." Clients are invited in to meet the artists, as a relationship is essential to a satisfactory outcome. If someone is about to spend thousands of pounds on setting some words in stone for all time, you can bet that some pretty profound feelings are involved.

"By the time people come to us they know they want lettering done by hand," says Lida. "They want something human, something understood, something to reflect the humanity of our being. We try to reflect the beauty of the person, and the beauty which we human beings can give the world."

So widows and widowers come, with their albums and their memories. Children who have lost their parents come. Parents who have lost a child. Sometimes their words come with a difficulty that makes the painstaking task of carving seem easy by comparison. Lida recalls one grieving father who could not even speak his dead son's name. Only when she used his name when describing the proposed inscription could the father eventually, for the first time, let his tears flow. "If you work with letters, you are in the middle of life and death," she says.

The work is carried out in silence. There's no background music, just the sound of hammer and chisel. It's an industrious, concentrated, intentional silence, verging on the reverential: the kind that is better than speech. And it's contented. Hammer-strokes can heal. There's something therapeutic about the attention, the absorption, the materiality of this work. It was a similar impulse that led Lida and her childhood friend, the Dutch ceramicist Els Bottema, to carry out an art project which has become a modern legend: the Shingle Street Shell Line.

It didn't begin as an art project, though; simply as a way for two old friends, both recuperating from cancer, to spend their time at a remote row of cottages on a deserted Suffolk beach. They started collecting white whelk shells – just the whitest ones, and just whelks – and laying them end to end in a fragile gleaming line towards the sea three hundred yards away. Visit after visit, working together side by side in silence for hours, and in all weathers, they crafted this fragile lifeline all the way to the water's edge. Made from 20,000 discarded homes of tiny creatures, it can now be seen from space on Google Earth, and has become a symbol of persistence, of survival. Their book, *The Shingle Street Shell Line*, tells the story in poetry as bare and frail as the delicate white line across the shore:

> nothing new was brought to the beach
> the shells were there, thrown from the sea.
> beautifully white and tempting shapes
> we had to pick them up, the best
> the least battered ones
> they are all a little broken
> we are all a little broken

Working with such ephemeral, natural, found material in a fluid and unstable landscape seems the very opposite of the order and permanence of Lida's daily work. It is, however, perhaps a necessary counterpoint: a reminder of the fundamental wildness of the material of existence on which we try to carve our meanings. The morning light which floods the former schoolroom catches the lettering on one of the completed plaques, Cato's advice to the orators: *Rem Tene Verba Sequenter*, "Grasp the subject: the words will follow". The artists, who have been enjoying their coffee break around the big central table, are back at work. The only sound is the arrhythmic percussion of steel on stone as love is transferred into letters, blow by blow.

## FRONTIER

"You're going to *Arbury*?" a friend had said to me with mock horror. "You'd better be careful. I've heard they only read Proust *in translation*."

Certainly, Arbury's gritty reputation may be overstated, but its position as the city's overlooked, forgotten northern province is not. Lacking a historic centre, devoid of a focal point, and efficiently drained of its population each day by arterial roads, it is one of those places designed not to retain people, but to expel them: to facilitate their departure to places of employment elsewhere. Much of Milton, King's Hedges and Arbury is a network of closes and courts and cul-de-sacs threaded by a few tree-lined thoroughfares. Front gardens have been turned into hardstandings for vans with business logos; plastic picnic furniture awaits summer days; posses of wheelie bins, roughly painted with house numbers, loiter on the patchy grass verges.

Although the area was developed mainly during the Twentieth Century, its roots, and its name, are among the oldest in the city. In their study of Cambridge street names, Ronald Gray and Derek Stubbings say that Arbury Road is the only street-name in the city that has connections with prehistoric times. In thirteenth-century documents, it is spelled Herburg and Ertburg, meaning earthwork – a reference to Arbury Camp, at the north end of the road, a low circular Iron Age bank and ditch about 100 metres across, believed to have been an animal enclosure."[6] Later, it was used by the Romans, and excavations in the 1970s found a fourth-century house with painted walls, a tessellated floor, a tiny bath, burial sites and a mausoleum.[7] Building work in the 1950s unearthed the skeleton of a Romano-British woman in a lead-lined stone coffin; she was accompanied in her resting place by a mouse and a shrew, whose bones are also on display, with hers, in Clarke Hall in the Archaeological Museum in Downing Street, where they inspired a poem by Sylvia Plath called 'All the dead dears', which begins:

> Rigged poker-stiff on her back
> With a granite grin
> This antique museum-cased lady
> Lies, companioned by the gimcrack
> Relics of a mouse and a shrew
> That battened for a day on her ankle-bone.

The remains of the Arbury earthwork itself, long ploughed over and built upon, lie within the new Orchard Park development; their presence marked by the road names; 'Ring Fort Road', 'Iceni Way', 'Chariot Way' and 'Chieftain Way', next to the Premier Inn and the Travelodge. Although now tamed, this was, until quite recently, the city's edgy borderland. Here in the early summer of 1970, a husband and wife, driving up Arbury Road at dusk, encountered what they believed was the legendary East Anglian hell-hound, Black Shuck. As large as a wolf, it bounded over the bonnet of their car – even then in 1970 a vintage model – and vanished into the nearby allotments, leaving behind it a deadly sense of cold. The witness, Mrs Celia B. Dale, told the story a few years later to the historian and folklorist Ivan Bunn; she blamed Shuck for the ill luck which seemed to curse the family ever after the appearance.[8]

The sense of north Cambridge being somehow on or beyond a boundary has inspired the work of the artist Ian Rawlinson, who was born and brought up in the area, and who, like myself, is a former student at the Cambridgeshire College of Arts and Technology. I first encountered Ian's evocative sketches, etchings, collages and prints of Arbury in an exhibition entitled *Frontier* at the appropriately-named Edge Café on Mill Road. In his hands, images of pylons, maisonette-block staircases, or a housing estate pub became haunting, atmospheric reflections on the spirit of place. These were parts of Cambridge which were undiscovered, or, even worse, which were ignored by other artists. Art, like wealth, is drawn gravitationally to existing centres of power and influence; the already-successful exercising a magnetism on the aspirational; the already-celebrated demanding yet more fame. Against such centripetal forces, it takes determination to take a centrifugal path. But that's what Ian has done, in his resolve to apply to the marginal the same thoughtful attention as the centre, he pushes against the flow of expectations as though against a strong east wind.

There's certainly a strong east wind blowing when we meet at Cambridge North station, one rainy September Saturday. The station is very much on the pioneering fringe of Cambridge: opened in 2017 on the Fen Line in anticipation of this area's expected growth as a residential district for commuters to the city centre and to London. Build it and they'll come. Currently, its no-nonsense metal-clad structures stand in the middle of an empty windswept tract, surrounded by a car park which seems to have enough disabled spaces to cater for the whole British paralympic squad. Around the deserted bays, nervous learners in driving-school hatchbacks practise cautious three-point turns. On the other side of the tracks – literally – is Fen Road, the biggest of

Cambridge's two main Traveller sites, where, in a corridor of land between railway and river, hundreds of Traveller families occupy their long-accustomed space of adjacent apartness, a paradoxical island of rooted stability as, on its daily mass migrations, the settled world streams past.

We go to the Science Park, the first of its kind in the U.K. established in 1970 on farmland owned by Trinity College and left derelict after its use as a military base during the Second World War. In its day a visionary conception, now much-copied, the Science Park is a sprawling 173-acre campus which is home for ninety biomedical, technology and research businesses whose names range from the familiar – Philips, Toshiba – to ones whose alien amalgams of consonants sound like characters in *Game of Thrones*: Xaar; Vix; Roku; Sigma-Aldrich; Jagex. However, what we have come to see is very much old tech, and relates to a conflict far more real than any in Westeros. During the last war, this site was a United States army camp where fighting vehicles were prepared for the D-Day landings. Some veterans of that campaign are still with us – just – but much of the physical evidence of that conflict has gone.

Unless you know where to look. And Ian does. One of his pictures in the *Frontier* exhibition shows an angular grey shape, with one single watchful dark square aperture. The whole blocky assemblage is overlain with thin lines of what look like branches.

A World War Two pillbox. It's hidden now in the overlooked unkempt scrub next to the drainage ditch behind the car park of Cambridge Consultants ("we help clients identify, create and launch breakthrough products and services that disrupt their markets"). To get to it, we have to push our way through a determined defensive screen of brambles, which twist and catch at you in that uncanny almost sentient way they have. The grey concrete fortification is almost enveloped by them: a few barbed tendrils have even snaked through the windows into the black interior. Luckily, I'm wearing a thornproof coat, and Ian hands me a broken fence slat which becomes an improvised machete. In a few minutes, and at the cost of a few scratches, I've cut my way through. I had hoped to get inside, but the whole structure is so heavily wrapped in thorns that it would have taken hours. I content myself with looking through the gun port to where, had the day ever come, some young GI would have been ready to hold the line for his country, and ours. It's hard to imagine. No, almost impossible. Those days seem as distant as the Iron Age when our ancestors, in the face of who knows what threat, put up the ramparts of Arbury Camp.

We make our way through the rest of Arbury and King's Hedges, past Ian's old primary school. All that remains of the buildings of his day is the sloped hardstanding of the bike shed. Past the house

where, thanks to a friend's record collection, he discovered punk rock; past the former Jenny Wren pub, wrecked and graffiti'd; past what had been a row of independent shops, now a single Tesco; past the subject of another of Ian's pictures, the Snowcat pub,[9] now a *Sikh gurdwara* with orange flags fluttering from cloth-wrapped poles. Finally, we pass the fenced-off overgrown piece of waste land between Hawkins Road and Downhams Lane where the carcasses

of anthrax-infected horses were buried after germ-warfare experiments in the Second World War. The site was concreted over, and sealed with a membrane, and in 2003 was declared anthrax-free by the council and opened up for development – though one mysterious undeveloped corner remains.[10]

In King's Hedges Road, four young teenagers sweep round the corner; three boys riding mountain bikes, and a girl pushing a yellow Ofo bike, which is designed to be immobilised and unlocked only after electronic payment; she's pushing it with its only moveable wheel. A blond boy of perhaps fourteen, clearly the leader, is wearing a full black mask over his nose and mouth, highwayman style. He takes the Ofo off the girl and leans it against the hedge, then jumps into the bushes and emerges with a rock the size of a housebrick. He thumps the Ofo's sealed unit smartly. The bike beeps in protest and releases the wheel. "Wot a dodgy geezer!" says the girl, admiringly, and they all ride off.

As the suburbs spread across the fields in this part of Cambridge, there were some attempts by planners to vary the monotony. Ramsden Square, despite its name, is actually a concentric circle of houses, with an orbital road on the outside and a circular park in the middle. In Nun's Way, we walk through a housing scheme designed, ingeniously – but optimistically, given the East Anglian climate – along the lines of a Mediterranean courtyard, with a gateway leading into an enclosed space onto which all the houses' front doors open. Great for the *bambini*: all one big happy *famiglia* in the dappled shade of the olive trees. Today, in the autumn rain, all the doors are shut.

European–style architecture may not have blossomed here, but the European community certainly has. Ever since the U.K. opened its doors in 2004 to residents of eight new member states of the E.U., – the Czech Republic, Estonia, Hungary, Latvia, Lithuania, Poland, Slovakia and Slovenia[11] – Cambridge, like many towns and cities across the country, has become the home to sizeable numbers of people from Eastern Europe, helping fill the demand for labour in one of the country's fastest-growing cities. For many of the new arrivals, this was terra incognita; but for one group, at least – the Poles – there were long-established compatriots ready to welcome them.

At the end of the Second World War, more than 160,000 Poles, mainly service personnel and refugees, were exiled in Britain when their home country passed from Nazi into Communist control.

Across the country, they formed their own communities, drawing together the threads of family, language and Catholicism, to try to keep whole the fraying garment of identity, against the cold winds of assimilation. In Cambridge, in 1976, the Poles bought 231 Chesterton Road, a fine red brick town house on the corner of Chesterton Hall Road,[12] to be their community centre. Thirty years later, after Poland joined the EU, the centre's fortunes were revivified, and Klub Polonia opened, a Polish restaurant, offering long-time expats and new arrivals alike a taste of home.

Poland was one of the first foreign countries I ever experienced. Shortly after the Berlin Wall came down in 1989, I took part in one of the many volunteer relief convoys which took medical supplies from the West to what had been the Iron Curtain countries. We passed through Checkpoint Charlie, which was still in operation, drove through the strangely unkempt countryside of East Germany, and over the border into Poland. It was springtime, and, as far as the eye could see across that level hedgeless landscape, the fields were filled with wildflowers. I was young, the year was young, and so was Poland's freedom; its future as limitless as those endless unfenced fields. Days like that do not come often, and you do not forget them.

My affection for Poland was sealed years later, when, lecturing at the Catholic University in Lublin, I was gratified to see the large hall packed with an attentive audience numbering in the hundreds.

Which is hundreds more than I'm used to. Only after I had finished my talk, and had done my best to answer the thoughtful, respectful questions, did I find that the audience had come under the mistaken impression that I was *Sir Norman* Davies, the distinguished Polish-speaking historian, and author of *God's Playground*, a magisterial history of the country. Nonetheless, the audience had stayed and could not have been warmer. That kind of generosity buys a lot of loyalty.

So, as Ian and I call into Klub Polonia for lunch, I feel on fairly familiar ground. But not familiar enough for me to find my way to the dining room at first attempt. Two young men have come into the building ahead of us, and have walked purposefully, from the old-fashioned wood-panelled lobby up the stairs. I follow them, only to find them genuflecting and crossing themselves before the altar of a Catholic chapel in the main first-floor room. Back downstairs, in the entrance hall, which is decorated with posters for choirs, festivals and church services, and where a table serves as an improvised bookstall, I try another of the doors, this time with success. Inside the dining room, we're greeted by a young woman in a light-blue blouse embroidered with flowers. We take a table in the window overlooking the road. Around us, the other customers are mainly young people with children, and conversation is predominantly, but not exclusively, in Polish. The menu is, of course, traditional home cooking, with plenty of goulash, mashed potatoes and sauerkraut. The whole room has the feel of a village tavern in the old country. The shelves behind the bar seem to have a vodka for every day of the week. On the wall, in pride of place, hangs a picture of a Spitfire fighter, a symbol of the conflict which first brought Poles in large numbers to Britain, and of the contribution they made to the freedom of their adopted land. The British connection with Poland is by now an old one, but if the brisk trade and young clientele of Klub Polonia is anything to judge by, it's good for a couple of generations yet.

# ST ANDREW'S CHURCH

Diversity is sometimes assumed to be a product of the mobile society of the late twentieth and early twenty-first centuries. In fact, of course, it has much deeper roots than that. Races, languages, classes and creeds would have coexisted, with varying degrees of amity or enmity, at least from the time the Romans set up their 'castrum', the camp which gave Chesterton its English name.[13] Over the centuries, cultures and colonists clashed and competed: pagan Anglo-Saxons displacing Christian Romano-Britons; pagan Danes conquering the by-now-Christian Saxons, only to be Christianised and Saxonised in their turn. Then came the Normans, establishing over an English-speaking nation a ruling class which remained French-speaking for more than three centuries. And through it all, until the time of the first Elizabeth, Latin remained the language of the Church, of diplomacy, and, of course, of the University.

Hidden away in the centre of a modern housing development in Chapel Street, Chesterton, is a building which is a legacy of the complex geopolitics of the middle ages. Chesterton Tower,[14] a squat two-storey building with corner towers, which now stands opposite a row of domestic garages, was built in the Fourteenth Century to house the priest of the local St Andrew's Parish Church. Two centuries earlier, the parish had been given by a grateful Henry III of England to the Papal legate, Cardinal Guala Bicchieri,[15] who, in the dying days of the reign of King John, had been sent by the Pope to keep order in an England which was threatening to tear itself apart in a power struggle between high-handed monarch and rebellious barons. Over three tumultuous years, this tough-minded Italian fixer stood in for the Archbishop of Canterbury, knocked heads together, brokered deals and acted as the official protector of the new young king until, with peace restored, he returned to Italy. The parish of Chesterton which Henry had given him, he gifted in its turn to his home abbey of Vercelli, who ran it for the next three hundred years until links with Rome were finally severed during the time of Elizabeth I.

St Andrew's Church dates from some thirty years after Bicchieri's return to Italy. Its tall spire is one of the city's most prominent landmarks. Inside, the church is light and spacious; the sudden quiet accentuates the birdsong from outside and the ticking of the huge clock in the tower. Above the crossing, some recently-uncovered medieval wall paintings show surprised-looking souls rising naked from their boxy tombs on Resurrection Day. But the story isn't over for them: some, looking with relief towards the angels, are being spirited away to heaven; others, faces covered with their hands, are being snatched away by horned, beaked devils. The disturbing medieval vision leaks into the building's immaculate present, where posters for Alpha courses and the Mission Praise hymnbooks mark it as belonging to the evangelical tradition. High up, a nineteenth-century stained glass window shows a golden-haired Christ blessing a child while being watched by admiring disciples. This church, as so often, is a palimpsest, each successive generation adding its own overlay of dogma, decoration, or both.

On the outside wall of the church is a plaque commemorating the death in 1797, of Anna Maria Vassa, aged four, 'daughter of Gustavus Vassa, the African'. Vassa, whose real name was Olaudah Equiano[16], was kidnapped as a child from what is now Nigeria and lived for many years as a slave before buying his freedom and travelling to England where he published a bestselling memoir of his time in captivity and became one of the most prominent figures in the abolitionist movement, working alongside William Wilberforce and Thomas Clarkson, both of whom were themselves former students of St John's, Cambridge. The three are commemorated in a Collect prayer of the Church of England for 30 July. Equiano married an Englishwoman, Susannah Cullen, and the family and their two daughters lived in her home village of Soham, just east of Cambridge. Susannah died aged 34 in 1796, and Equiano a year later aged 52, followed by Anna Maria a few months later.[17] The sonnet on her memorial draws the visitor's attention to the resting place of "a child of colour haply not thine own," who now "is gone and dwells in that abode, / Where some of every clime shall joy in God."

Some, not all. The evangelical Protestantism of Equiano, Wilberforce, Clarkson and their circle was colour-blind when it came to admission to heaven. Religion, not race, was the key. Whatever captivity Equiano may have endured, he, like so many in those days when faith fused with social activism to move mountains of injustice, believed that the truest freedom awaited beyond this life. The same belief is chiselled in the words of hope on the surrounding gravestones: 'passed away', 'sleeping peacefully', 'Underneath are the everlasting arms.' In the lichen on one of the graves I see what looks like the face of Jesus. But it's a simulacrum; when I take a step towards it, it vanishes.

## FEN DITTON

This little village on the east bank of the Cam, on the northern fringe of Cambridge, has, according to the 2011 census, a population of 760. This particular May Saturday, though, that number must have more than doubled. It looks like there are at least that many in the beer garden of the Plough. I have come here, along with what looks like a substantial chunk of the local population, to watch the annual May Bumps. This rowing race has existed since 1887, as a development of the earlier Lent Bumps, which began in the early Nineteenth Century. The race, held over a four-day period involves something like 150 college crews, with over 1,300 individual rowers, in a series of intense chases along a stretch of the River Cam east of the city centre. Because the river, unlike the Thames, where the more famous Oxford and Cambridge Boat Race takes place, is too narrow to allow boats to race side by side, they race in line, with the boats behind trying to overtake or physically touch the boat in front in order to force it to pull over and make way. Over the days, by a process of calculations so complicated it would have made Stephen Hawking's head swim, boats can climb up the rankings until the overall winner in each category is declared. Each boat's position is then recorded ready for the following year, where the competition resumes from where it left off. Spectators can buy a guide which shows the skeletal diagrams of the scoring system in bewildering detail. It looks like a combination of the periodic table and the double-helix diagram for DNA.

The good news is that you don't need to understand it to enjoy it. After all, from any of the individual vantage points along the riverbank, your only view of the race is when the crews swing into view and vanish again with a rattle of oars, a snap of splashed water and a torrent of shouted instructions. It's a spectacle, and Fen Ditton is making the most of its ideal position in a bend of the river. There's bunting in the streets, and tea and cakes on sale in the church. In the wooden-tabled pub garden, it's panama hats, sunglasses, cycle helmets, gazebos, marquees, plaid picnic blankets, blazers. A Norwegian girl is telling her friend how the YR weather website is better than any other. Everything in Norway is better than anywhere else. The Pet Shop Boys' 'I Love You, You Pay My Rent' belts out from the bandstand speakers. In between tracks, the commentator discusses a disputed bump. At the riverbank, a portly young man, dressed as though for a country show in tweed jacket, check waistcoat, flat cap and cords, and looking rather like Ratty from *The Wind in the Willows*, stands supping his beer thoughtfully.

On the opposite bank, cyclists race past to the accompaniment of applause and whoops, following returning boats whose crews' heads are decorated with greenery – the sign of a successful bump. The male cox of one boat, bearing no greenery, is singing the coloratura passage from the Queen of the Night's 'Die Hölle Rache' aria from *The Magic Flute*. A group of male supporters of Lady Margaret Hall's crew stroll past in orange mankinis, rather too slowly. A women's crew are sporting shirts whose slogan, 'Dangerous and incompetent,' can only be an insult-turned-badge-of-honour. One of the coaches is telling a friend his crew had given all they could: "They left it all out on the water..." Long accustomed to bellowing over the distance between riverbank and boat, his normal speaking voice has settled many decibels higher than necessary on the volume dial.

The DJ's soundtrack has shifted to hits of the 1920s: a scratchy version of 'You're the cream in my coffee' with the muted brass and high-pitched constricted vocals of the period. The garden is getting pretty crowded now. A table occupied by a group of Americans has amassed a dozen empty coke bottles. I decide to check out the scene from the other bank. There's a little motor boat whose owner is charging £2 for a river crossing. I pay my two coins like one of Charon's passengers, step aboard, and with the faintest whiff of diesel and the merest growl of the outboard, am ferried across in all of seven seconds. Pound-per-inch, that must be the most expensive commute in the world. But, even if only for a few moments, it has at least got me out on the river, and today, that's most definitely the place to be.

## Notes

1. Eds. Glynne Wickham, Herbert Berry, William Ingram, *English Professional Theatre, 1530-1660*, (Cambridge, 2000), 115.
2. Latin was widely used in the University until Elizabethan times, when the visiting Queen Elizabeth I's desire to hear a play in English was met with puzzlement.
3. Originally erected in 1927 over Blake's grave and some seventy yards from his wife's later burial, it was moved some twenty yards in 1965 to be closer to the other authors. The stone is now placed on Blake's actual resting place.
4. Not the poem famously set to music by Sir Hubert Parry – that was an extract from the preface to Blake's poem 'Milton'.
5. 1915-1995.
6. Gray and Stubbings, *op. cit.*, 1.
7. Tames, *op. cit.*, 16.
8. https://www.hiddenea.com/shuckland/cambridge.htm   Letter from Mrs. Celia B. Dale to Ivan Bunn, February 1976.
9. Opened in 1959, renamed The Grove in 2001, and a gurdwara since 2011.
10. 'Assurance on anthrax burial land', BBC website 14.10.2003 http://news.bbc.co.uk/1/hi/england/cambridgeshire/3189662.stm
11. Joined, two years later, by Bulgarians and Romanians.
12. F.R. Leavis lived at 6 Chesterton Hall Crescent during his early years in Cambridge..

13. Tames, *op. cit.*, 16.
14. Later, it was for a while the studio of the letter-cutter David Kindersley.
15. c. 1150–1227.
16. 1745-1797.
17. The surviving daughter, Joanna, inherited her father's estate, and later married a Congregationalist. She died in 1857.

# EAST

# ANGLIA RUSKIN UNIVERSITY

Visitors arriving at Cambridge railway station are greeted by a large sign on the platform, proclaiming, cheekily: 'Welcome to Cambridge – Home of Anglia Ruskin University.' It always makes me smile. Underdogs have to make the most of their opportunities.

I came here in 1982, when it was called the Cambridgeshire College of Arts and Technology. I was responding to a newspaper advert offering a straight English Literature degree. I had messed up my A Levels: too much time wandering the hills and trying to write poetry; not enough time spent revising. No university would take me. Strings were pulled. They broke. I had made no insurance applications to other institutions. C.C.A.T. was my last hope.

John Tyler interviewed me in an office in a now-vanished terrace on Bradmore Street, just off East Road. The course had already reached its allotted 40 places, and they were now only interviewing for reserves. I'd take that chance. Many of the college's students came from the East of England, and this tongue-tied Welsh-speaker from north Wales was a rarity. Did I know the work of R.S.Thomas, he asked me. Know it? I'd met him (thank God for Wrexham Library's outreach programme). We spoke about Thomas; his politics, his poetry. Shortly afterwards a letter arrived offering me a place. I took the chance C.C.A.T. gave me, throwing myself into everything it offered, and I've never forgotten the debt.

C.C.A.T. may have struggled for profile compared to Cambridge University, but we had a secret weapon: Pink Floyd. We used to tell people the band was formed at C.C.A.T. It wasn't strictly true. It was formed in London largely from people who knew one another from Cambridge, two of whom, Syd Barrett, the first frontman, and David Gilmour, the guitarist and vocalist, had attended C.C.A.T. But even that made it way cooler than anything the University could possibly offer.

Roger Keith 'Syd' Barrett was born in 'Jesmond', Number 60 Glisson Road, a three-storey, double-bay-fronted semi in a quiet residential street near Cambridge country cricket ground. When he was three, the family moved a mile away to 183 Hills Road, a brick-built two-storey semi, opposite the entrance to Homerton College. Another founder member, the bassist and later lyricist and vocalist, Roger Waters, three years Barrett's senior, was growing up just around the corner in Number 42 in a street whose name foreshadowed his later career; Rock Road.

The band was at the heart of the psychedelic underground scene in late-sixties London, and went on through decade after decade of invention and reinvention to become the soundtrack to a generation. But it went on without its charismatic central founder, Syd Barrett, who, having done enough drugs for that whole generation, dropped out and returned to his mother's house in Cambridge to live as another kind of legend – a burned-out monosyllabic recluse. He became the object of endless curiosity for fans who would spot him – or imagine they had – making his daily trip to the newsagents for cigarettes, or shopping at Sainsbury's with his sister Rosemary, who looked after him in his later years, by which time he'd moved to a semi in St Margaret's Square, a few minutes from his childhood home, and, appropriately enough, a cul-de-sac. He lived there from 1981 until his death from pancreatic cancer in 2006.[1]

In June 2017, Rosemary unveiled a blue plaque to her brother in the middle of the Anglia campus on the redbrick wall of the Cambridge School of Art. This is actually the oldest institution in Anglia Ruskin. Founded in 1878 as the Cambridge School of Art, in 1960 it became the Cambridgeshire College of Arts and Technology – providing the model for the lightly-fictionalised 'Fenland College of Arts and Technology' in the 'Wilt' novels of Tom Sharpe which, based on his own experience at the college, feature the hapless lecturer Henry Wilt. Next it became, successively, Anglia Higher Education College, Anglia Polytechnic University, and finally, in 2005, Anglia Ruskin University. The connection with Ruskin is actually pretty tenuous, he delivered the School of Art's opening address, but that was it. Still, like Pink Floyd, he was a big name. And like I said, underdogs have to take their chances when they can.

## MILL ROAD

Mill Road is the part of Cambridge where clever meets cool. It has always had a reputation for independence. Originally an area of working-class housing, built during the late nineteenth-century railway boom, the area was fertile ground for socialism. Romsey Town, just further east over the bridge, was known as Red Romsey. Though now steadily gentrifying, the area's progressive credentials are still strong: radical bookshops, vegetarian cafés, Socialist Worker posters declaring 'Kick out the Tories', others, more conciliatory, advertising the Wholesome Fair, Daily Bread Co-Op; People Before Profit. Letterboxes carry stickers 'Save the Trees. No junk mail please' The window of one of the terraced houses is decorated with stickers supporting everything from cycling to veganism to windpower. On the windowsill is a single book: *On Palestine*.

Windpower actually has a long history in this area. Mill Road is named for the windmill which once stood at the corner of Covent Garden,[2] on the site of what are now numbers 56 and 56A.[3] In 1843 it was demolished and replaced with housing as the railway brought huge population growth: in 1801, there were only 252 residents in Mill Road. By 1831, 6651; by 1861, 11848, and by 1891, 25091.[4]

In the Urban Larder café in Romsey Town, I meet the Irish artist Jim Butler, who's been recording the subtly-changing streetscape for over 10 years since he took up a job in the Art School. He's fascinated by the contrast between the historic colleges, with their planned appearance and well-documented changes, and an area like Romsey Town, where sometimes more far-reaching transformations happen with less comment. For example, there's the seemingly endless proliferation of cafés like this one, showing how, on a rising tide of lattes, the area has been borne up from working-class to middle-class, and, at least among its younger residents, has acquired a character owing more to Europe than East Anglia.

Densely-populated, active and fast-changing urban spaces like this have something of the montage about them, Jim says. His deft black-and-white line drawings of the buildings, roads and street furniture, sketched using a stick picked up at the Cambridge Folk Festival, are partially overlaid by asymmetric patches of colour which, on closer inspection, turn out to be details from ephemera: bus tickets; cloakroom receipts; envelopes. He collects these 'scraps', as he calls them, according to their colour and keeps them in separate bags, ready to be incorporated into his work, bringing their embedded histories and his own autobiography.

"Photography gives you all the information you need," he says: "But also all the information you don't. Drawing slows you down, and you can notice things. I'm noticing blocks of colour and bringing them out, but by using these scraps it can never be mistaken for reality." Barcodes become balconies; tickets become traffic signs; the fine, pink, rectangular pattern of a Lufthansa boarding pass becomes a stretch of terraced brickwork, highlighted as though by a patch of sun.

Later that day, in one of the street's many other cafés, Relevant, I meet Allan Brigham, who has himself watched Cambridge change over the decades, and from a more street-level perspective than most. As a road sweeper, he helped make the city presentable each day, rather like, he says, a theatre stage hand. His passion for local history made him a Blue Badge guide and earned him an honorary Master's from the University. This, combined with his day job, brought him celebrity: presenting history snippets on Anglia television, complete with orange overalls, barrow and brush. When he raised some mild objections to this stereotyping, the no-nonsense TV executive was having none of it. "He said all TV historians have a gimmick, and there are brighter people out there than you. But none of them have got a broom and a barrow," Allan says: "So I had to come along, sweeping, and then stop and do my piece about the history of prostitution or whatever." Now retired from the day job, he can concentrate on his work as Chairman of the Friends of the Museum of Cambridge, and his business, Town Not Gown Tours, specialising in the places other tours overlook.

Places such as the David Parr House, at 186 Gwydir Street, the unassuming terraced home of David Parr,[5] a working-class Victorian artist-painter who worked for the F.R. Leach decorative arts company and who brought back to his own modest house his passion for Arts-and-Crafts-style stained glass, Gothic Revival

mouldings and William Morris-inspired hand-painted wallpaper. This extraordinary legacy was preserved unchanged by his grand-daughter, Elsie, until, after her time, the property passed to a local trust which, helped by Lottery money, turned it into a time-capsule museum Allan describes as "Mill Road's cultural gem," What was once just accommodation has added even more cachet to what is now a seriously hip neighbourhood.

Allan tells me that the cellar in Relevant is a great vinyl store. I go to check it out. I've never been that knowledgeable about popular music. As the youngest child, I grew up with whatever my elders played: mainly old 78s and middle-of-the-road stuff. I seem to remember Simon and Garfunkel was about as cutting-edge as it got. My own record-buying was largely comedy novelty records. Although, now I come to think of it, there was an early foreshadowing of melancholy in my making a special effort, aged eleven, to order James Taylor's mournful *Wandering*, and the Carpenters' bittersweet *Yesterday Once More*. Otherwise, apart from a dutiful interest in heavy metal in the late 1970s, which, for a friendless geeky teenage misfit like myself, was obligatory for even minimal social acceptance, I don't recall really keeping up with the music scene. I didn't even understand cool, let alone know how to be it.

But entering this reverent, library-like space today, I realise my memory has been selective. I must have listened to much more music than I've chosen to remember. There's one familiar album cover after another. Forgotten faces reappear with shocking familiarity. It's like attending a school reunion after forty years, except no-one has changed. There's a re-release of Jeff Wayne's *Musical Version of War of the Worlds*, with its cover of the ironclad 'Thunder Child' taking on a Martian fighting machine. How many times had I played that album? I knew every line of Richard Burton's tobacco-roughened narration. At £25, the price for this slice of nostalgia is too high. But there are plenty of others: Queen; Crosby, Stills, Nash and Young; Bryan Ferry; Gerry Rafferty. All for £3. I take *Roxy Music's Greatest Hits*. A minute or so later, I'm out on Mill Road, passing the hipster cafés and the vegan cycling collective workshops, with a big square of vinyl under my arm. Look at me, geeky teenage self. Look at me now.

## CAMBRIDGE BUDDHIST CENTRE

The Cambridge Buddhist Centre on Newmarket Road is run by the Triratna order. The name means 'Three Jewels', those being: the Buddha himself; Dharma, his teachings; and Sangha, his followers. But I'm here in search of one of the hidden architectural jewels of Cambridge: the former Festival Theatre.

I came across it in *With My Own Wings*, the 1994 autobiography of Raymond Lister,[6] an ironworker, blacksmith, author and artist perhaps best known as the expert witness in the 1976 trial of the art forger Tom Keating. Lister himself was something of a treasure of Cambridge's past: a survivor from an earlier city not just of academics and scientists, but of working people: engineers, blacksmiths and printers; a Cambridge of illiteracy and barefoot children living in poverty.[7] He was born in Soham House, 113 Newmarket Rd,[8] to an extraordinary family of artisans, engineers and craftspeople. His grandfather was a Sunday School teacher and chapel deacon, of whom Lister said: " … his craftsmanship became an aspect of his religion; it was a way of life as real to him as the Tao is to a Taoist".[9]

Lister, a polymath, straddled the worlds of industry and art.[10] He joined the Festival Theatre on Newmarket Road, which had opened in 1926 as "the most progressive theatre in England".[11] This enterprise, which continued until 1939 – and which, despite the name, was unconnected with any festival – was based in the early nineteenth-century former Theatre Royal. Although no longer a working theatre, it has survived as part of the Cambridge Buddhist Centre, and Taradasa Dharmachari, one of the members, has agreed to show me around.

Entering through the tastefully-restored Art Deco sunburst-design main doors, I am greeted at reception by a smiling white-bearded gent who looks seventy-five going on twenty-five: clearly a beneficiary of whatever enlightenment is on offer here. Taradasa will be with me shortly. Inside the sunlit lobby, the day's activities are just starting. A group of women, one of them barefoot, glide past serenely on their way upstairs, carrying cups of some milkless infusion. That's one of the things that would put me off Buddhism: the prospect of a lifetime of herbal beverages. I'm not saying the devotees aren't looking well on it – they're positively glowing – but at what cost? No caffeine. And no alcohol either, I'll bet. And no lots of other things too. Suddenly I feel wretchedly superficial. Already, the place is getting to me.

Taradasa arrives: a thoughtful-looking bearded Englishman of around my own age. He offers to show me around the centre, which is spaced across several floors in a converted Georgian town house. We go upstairs, pausing to let infusion-bearing women drift past with silent smiles. There are rooms for meditation, for yoga, for counselling. In the shrine room, where kneeling cushions are piled in corners, the decoration behind the statue of Buddha is made of tin cans, their ends flattened into wheels and sunbursts, their bodies rolled out flat, embossed with Buddhist texts, burnished, and snipped into delicate curling metal fringes. It all glows like white gold; the prosaic, utilitarian vessels transformed into means of grace, their interiors, once dark and soiled, now shining. Outward humility, inner radiance. There's a faint fragrance of incense. And considering that we overlook Newmarket Road, one of the city's busiest thoroughfares, there's an uncanny silence too. I look through the window as an articulated lorry outside glides past soundlessly. How is this possible? The place is getting to me. Inner stillness grows silently; the outward world with all its empty distractions fades away. Taradasa notices my absorption. "Secondary glazing," he says.

Tour over, we're back in the lobby, where Taradasa opens a door to reveal the building's real inner secret. Stepping through from the cool, minimalist reception area, you're in the foyer of the former

Festival Theatre, facing the curving outer wall of the auditorium. Opening the wooden door in that curve reveals one of Cambridge's most extraordinary spaces: a tall, deep, three-balconied theatre dating from 1814.

Today, the only audience is half a dozen or so statues of Buddha, watching in silence a non-existent play. A metaphor for the spiritual life. The frayed leather upholstery on the handrails is original; so are the wooden floorboards; so is the frame of cast-iron pillars. The front panels of the balconies still carry biblical texts from the time when this was a mission hall, though these are now covered for safekeeping. One reads: "where sin abounded, grace did much more abound,"[12] a reference, surely, to the fact that the building had been converted from a theatre into an evangelical mission. And rather a catty reference too, when you come to think of it.

We have the place to ourselves, so Taradasa takes me into all the secret passages. Under the stage, among the machinery, a pantomime donkey stands next to a shelf full of Buddhas. Tibetan prayer flags are strung between the rusty metal jacks holding up the stage; a festival in the underworld. An abandoned carpenter's workshop stands waiting, its patient tools unused. Backstage are pictures of luminaries who appeared there: Robert Donat, George Bernard Shaw, Dame Flora Robson. Some claim Dickens performed here. He certainly performed in Cambridge, but the location is uncertain, and the Buddhists are too honest to let supposition become certainty. On the empty stage, a giant gold dharma wheel leans against the wall. We open the curtain, looking out on that spectacular three-tier auditorium. The Buddhas look down, regarding every move with the same ineffable smile.

The theatre was built in 1814 as one of a circuit for a touring company called the Norwich Players. In 1878, it became a mission hall, and then, after a brief period as a boys' club, became the Festival Theatre under the direction of Terence Gray[13], a millionaire vineyard owner and racehorse owner brought up on his family's estate in the Gog Magog Hills. Gray's experimental staging techniques attracted the greatest talents of his day, including Yeats and Dame Ninette de Valois, who was Gray's cousin. The theatre project, though influential – indeed controversial – was short-lived. After seven years Gray moved on to other interests, eventually re-emerging as Wei Wu Wei, a Taoist and Buddhist philosopher, and author of many serious volumes of non-dual spirituality.[14] He's almost forgotten now. Though, for someone who spent so long preaching the illusion of individuality, perhaps that's not too bad an outcome. The theatre was forgotten too, a neglected storage space for many years until – fittingly enough, given Gray's own leanings – the Buddhists gave it yet another lease of life. Another reincarnation; another chance; another turn of the great wheel of dharma.

We're back in the lobby again, sitting on the sofas. Taradasa has made me a cup of coffee. Real coffee. Well, real instant coffee. With real caffeine. I think he had noticed my hesitation as we approached the refreshment bar. He has been generous with his time, so I ask him a little about himself. It probably won't mean that much to someone devoted to overcoming the restrictions of personal identity, but still, it's only polite.

Originally an East Ender, he worked for a classical music charity before a mid-life crisis moved him to try meditation, and then to make it his whole lifestyle. He has been living until recently at Abbey House, reputedly the most haunted house in Cambridge. Now, he lives with a community of other male followers. He doesn't use the term 'monk', but, unmarried, without children, and devoted to his religion, that's pretty much what he is. He doesn't try to convert or convince. But I'm impressed, and I think it only fair that I should reciprocate with some spiritual autobiography. I try to keep it short.

Nominal Christian upbringing; teenage atheism, then, at eighteen, a spontaneous experience of unitive consciousness, sparking a lifelong search which took me to evangelical Anglicanism and, some years later, out the other side, scarred by its conservatism and literalism, but still needing to believe. A brief recuperation with Anglo Catholicism before settling for liberal middle-of-the-road Anglicanism while simultaneously pursuing deepening interests in other practices: Judaism, Sufism, shamanism, and Jungianism. I'd like to say I've lived my life in the light of my threshold experience. But it would be truer to say I've lived in the shadow cast by that light. But even that shadow was brighter than what would otherwise have passed for illumination. Taradasa nods; he understands. I put the coffee cup down, and thank him for his time. He accompanies me quietly to the door with the sunburst pattern. As it opens, the roar of the street begins again.

## EAST ROAD

The district, in the angle of Newmarket Road, East Road and Parkside, used to be known, due to its distinctive shape, as 'The Kite'. Until well into the Twentieth Century it was an area of workers' housing: a city-centre enclave of poverty. The answer seemed to solve two problems at once: remove the poverty and provide the city with much-needed extra retail space. The area was earmarked for redevelopment. The plans were opposed: residents and radicals, conservationists and celebrities[15] lined up to resist it.[16] Petitions were signed; funds were raised. But of course, this rearguard action failed. In the 1980s, the bulldozers moved in and the glass conservatory roof of the Grafton Centre mall appeared above streets which had once been family homes and artisan businesses. For conservationists, the fight to save The Kite has mythic, elegaic status, a Cambridge Culloden.

Thirty years on, the Grafton Centre is already showing its age. In today's showery weather, its glass roof is leaking, and customers carrying their bags from Debenhams and Boots have to weave around the buckets placed to catch the drips.

A little later, the rain has cleared, and I decide to head across to Mill Road. Emerging into the sunlight from the subway underneath the junction of East Road and Elizabeth Way, I find myself surrounded by naked people. It's the middle of the afternoon. And it's not even particularly warm. Almost all are men. As the traffic streams past, they swig from waterbottles and tinker with their bicycles with the conscious nonchalance of the publicly unclothed. Lacking pockets, their restricted repertoire for casual fidgeting is – along with everything else – painfully exposed. A hand, or even both, on the hip seems the default setting – a pretty assertive stance at the best of times, but positively defiant when stark naked in a town centre on a Saturday afternoon. Their leader wears a hi-vis and a sign proclaiming, somewhat unnecessarily, that this is the Cambridge Naked Bike Ride. It's part of a worldwide network of events intended to "challenge dependency on fossil fuels, highlight the vulnerability of cyclists and celebrate body freedom," though cycling must surely be one of the least suitable activities to undertake when naked.[17] Eventually, tinkering over, they set off towards Parker's Piece at scarcely more than walking pace while cars and clothed cyclists streak past.

On the opposite side of the road, hidden behind the trees on the corner of the junction between Newmarket Road and Elizabeth Way, is the Abbey House which Taradasa mentioned. This is one of the few remnants of what was once one of the most important monasteries in the area. Barnwell Priory, founded around 1092 by the Augustinian Canons, was suppressed during the Dissolution in the 1530s. By the early Nineteenth Century virtually nothing remained apart from some masonry used in the wall and garden of Abbey House (built in the 1670s on the site of the priory itself), and, just round the corner in Beche Road, the Cellarer's Checker, the monastery's former trading post, an unimposing square block. The only other surviving building is the early thirteenth-century St Andrew The Less Church on Newmarket Road. The Priory was never actually an Abbey, though the informal upgrade has been adopted by the whole area. There is little other sign of those centuries of sacrifice and service on the part of the monks. I wonder what they would have made of the naked bike ride.

The cyclists have now passed the main entrance of Anglia Ruskin University. Here, on the corner of Broad Street, is a cycle stand, whose unusual configuration (the supports are a wide distance apart, as they once accommodated an instruction board) reveals this as one of the few traces of one of Cambridge's less successful experiments: The Green Bicycle Scheme. For what is possibly the cleverest city in the world, this was a pretty dumb idea.

In 1993, the council decided to solve a range of problems at a stroke: get more people cycling; let offenders make a positive contribution, and make use of the many abandoned bikes impounded by the police. Its inspiration was the legend that Amsterdam had operated – possibly even *still* operated – a scheme where white-painted bicycles were left around free for anyone to use, and to leave at the end of their journey for the next public-spirited citizen. If this two-wheeled utopia worked in Amsterdam, then why not in Cambridge? In reality, though, it had *never* worked in Amsterdam. The initiative had been the brainchild of an Anarchist group, the Provos, who in 1967 really did paint fifty bikes white and leave them around like a virus in the body of the capitalist system, ready to multiply and cause its host body's demise. However, the antibodies of officialdom were prompt: the scheme broke a city law which banned leaving bikes unlocked, and they were all confiscated. But a legend was born. That year, the band Tomorrow recorded a song 'My White Bicycle'. In 1984, the actor Nigel Planer recorded a cover version in the persona of his character Neil the Hippy from the television series *The Young Ones*:

My white bicycle. My white bicycle

Policeman shouts but I don't see him
They're one thing I don't believe in
Find some judge, but it's not leavin'.

My white bicycle. My white bicycle

Nine years later, Cambridge City Council tried to make Neil the Hippy's vision a reality. Three hundred impounded bikes were renovated and painted green by offenders serving community service orders, and then left around the city for a grateful populace to share. They lasted a day. When the rubber met the road, when altruism met realism, the world was just not ready for such a grand gesture. The bikes vanished into private ownership overnight.

Bike-sharing schemes these days use electro-magnetic locks, commercial sponsorship, smart technology and micro-payments to match high ideals with human nature. Perhaps the free-sharing scheme should be viewed as a control experiment, one of the necessary failures that lead, gradually, to success. And there's still something immensely endearing in the fact that Cambridge should have thought that the scheme *could* work.

> The rain comes down but I don't care.
> The wind is blowing in my hair.
> Seagulls flying in the air.
> My white bicycle. My white bicycle.

# MUSEUM OF TECHNOLOGY

"The seer does not like to dwell upon what he saw enter the room," those were the words that did it for me. I was nine years old and had picked up a book from the mobile library that visited my tiny village school. It was a collection of ghost stories called *Nightfrights*. And it lived up to its name.

In 'The Haunted Doll's House', a man watches ghastly events unfold in the lighted windows of the miniature house in his bedroom. I wasn't quite sure what a 'seer' was, but that didn't matter: I got the idea: something, some *thing*, was entering the bedroom where the unsuspecting children slept. I now know that the author was M.R. James, who specialised in suggesting horror rather than showing it. The compilers of *Nightfrights*, however, were taking no risks that their young audience might miss the point: James' carefully oblique description was accompanied by a line drawing of the creature entering the tiny room. It was ... no, I can't describe it. To this day, I still can't sleep with the bedroom door open.

Montague Rhodes James was born in 1862, the son of an Anglican clergyman, and brought up in the rectory of Great Livermere in Suffolk. As an undergraduate at King's in 1882, he was an outstanding antiquarian and medievalist. He stayed as a don, became Director of the Fitzwilliam Museum, and finally Provost of King's. He left in 1918 to become Provost of Eton until his death in 1936. During his 36 years in Cambridge, he accomplished the herculean task of cataloguing the vast numbers of medieval manuscripts in the University's libraries. The ghost stories he would read aloud to select groups of friends were a by-product. Often taking antiquarian concerns as their material and their setting, and often located in the eerie, haunting emptinesses of East Anglia, the tales are masterpieces of the genre.

Countless readers have admired James. Many writers have imitated him. Few, however, have taken their admiration to the same lengths as Robert Lloyd Parry, who has actually *become* M.R.James. With the aid of a tweed suit, slicked-back hair, some round spectacles and a pipe, this unassuming former art historian transforms into the master of terror: performing James's tales in persona around East Anglia and beyond.

For Robert, it was a different James story which started his lifelong interest. 'Canon Alberic's Scrap-Book', written in 1894. I shan't spoil it for you. Suffice it to say that if, like me, you are an arachnophobe, this *tour de force* carries a major health warning. Here, the speaker is looking into the eyes of the appalling creature haunting the decaying cathedral of Saint-Bertrand-de-Comminges:

> There was intelligence of a kind in them – intelligence beyond that
> of a beast, below that of a man.

The more you think about that image, the more unsettling it becomes.

"It's one of those stories people read when they are young," says Robert. "I was probably twelve or thirteen. I was a fan of Sherlock Holmes, Dungeons and Dragons and H.P. Lovecraft, and my dad gave me a copy of James' stories..."

Many years later, while working on an exhibition of medieval manuscripts at the Fitzwilliam, he had a 'flashback', realising that images in the stories he'd read as a child seemed to have their originals among the materials so familiar to James. After all, 'Canon Alberic's Scrap-Book' is based on the character encountering a particularly lurid image in a medieval volume. Showing me around the Fitzwilliam, Robert explains the connections. "Certain images in M.R. James come from the psyche," he says. "He was able to articulate these latent fears – like the teeth and hair under the pillow in 'Casting the Runes'. I believe he must have got that idea from an image of St Mary of Egypt[18] by the Master of the Lubeck Bible, or a similar image to that." Sure enough, inside the glass case, there's St Mary on the illuminated manuscript, and, apart from her breasts, she's entirely covered in hair.

Even more disturbing is the large seventeenth-century picture 'L'Umana Fragilita', by Salvator Rosa. A mother holds a baby, who in turn holds a scroll on which are written, in Latin: 'Birth is pain, life is short, death a necessity.' Shadows and sinister figures crowd around. Towering above the mother and child is a huge leering, skeletal, winged Death. That's bad enough, but then Robert drew my attention to the creature's ribcage, eight ribs of which stand out starkly. Just eight. And it becomes instantly clear: it looks for all the world like a giant spider suspended upside down above the mother and child. Hidden in plain view. Innocuous at first sight. Horrifying at second. Which is the essence of James' art.

Robert recalls visiting the Church at Great Livermere, in Suffolk, in whose rectory James lived from 1865 until 1909, and being amazed at the size of some of the spiders he saw there. "I would not be surprised if he moved a hymn book and disturbed one of these big spiders," he said. I make a mental note to take Great Livermere off my list of places to visit.

Increasingly fascinated with James' work, Robert began giving readings in persona in James' old rooms, the Founder's Library, and then expanded his repertoire to include other great Victorian and Edwardian writers like H.G. Wells, Sir Arthur Conan Doyle and E.F. Benson, perfoming them in suitably evocative locations, including, in Cambridge, the Whipple Museum of the History of Science, and, of course, the Leper Chapel on Newmarket Road.

Tonight, however, the location is the Cambridge Museum of Technology,[19] an imposing former pumping station on the south bank of the Cam, opposite Chesterton. And Robert's material is gentler fare: Kenneth Grahame's *The Wind in the Willows*. The setting, among the monumental machinery of the Victorian steam age, could hardly be more fitting for the story of Mr Toad's escapades with his newfangled motor cars. There's a smell of engine oil and wood polish. The eclectic audience – accessorised with everything from lip studs, heavy tattoos and Converse All Stars, to tweeds and black Labradors – are attentive.

In the distance, the thumping music from Midsummer Fair can be heard faintly. A police siren wails. Outside the window, sycamores, and – yes – willows, are swaying slightly in a damp south-west breeze. Robert has moved on to the chapter 'The Piper at the Gates of Dawn'.

In Robert's reading, the central characters, Mole and Ratty, searching for a friend's lost child, find themselves encountering, unnamed, but unmistakable, the great god Pan.

"Rat!" he found breath to whisper, shaking. "Are you afraid?"

"Afraid?" murmured the Rat, his eyes shining with unutterable love. "Afraid! Of *Him*? O, never, never! And yet—and yet—O, Mole, I am afraid!"

Then the two animals, crouching to the earth, bowed their heads and did worship.

I find myself wondering if – apart from in explicitly devotional works – there is, anywhere else in English literature, such a heartfelt, unembarrassed approach to the divine. For all its familiar world of tweeds, pipesmoke and country houses, there is something not terribly *English* about it: the unguarded sincerity, and, in particular, the lack of defensive, self-conscious irony. I wonder if Grahame only managed to achieve this because of his masterstroke of making his characters *animals*: the creatures who, in English society, so often stand proxy for emotions and impulses which an unusually uptight human society finds too difficult to express. As the reading concludes, I notice the black Labrador, which has lain patiently on the floor throughout; it is looking steadily at the face of its mistress, with something of the expression with which Ratty gazed at the great god Pan.

# THE CAMBRIDGE MUSEUM OF COMPUTING HISTORY

The Cambridge Museum of Computing History is squeezed into a dogleg of industrial estate land between Coldhams Lane and the railway line, along with the offices of the Cam Cabs minicab firm, the Cambridge Snooker and Pool Centre, – its burglar alarm wailing unheeded – and the Belfast Beds warehouse. A couple of units away is the City of Zion Church ('Bringing Purpose Into Your Life'), in its improvised compound of single-storey buildings, marquees and portacabins, and, nearby, the Unite Christian Church ('Truth, Love, Faith'). Spiked railings, interlaced with brambles; flattened cans of Red Bull in the gutters. Why do people who consume energy drinks not have the energy to put them in a bin? Like all such estates, this is somewhere you're expected to drive to, not walk.

The Museum occupies a two-storey unit. I pay the entrance fee, and find myself in a lobby with a few tables, some bits of electronic kit in glass cases, and, around the wall, a floor-to ceiling display of circuits of blinking lights like something out of a low-budget seventies sci-fi series. I've planned to spend roughly an hour here. But suddenly I'm wondering how I can spin it out that long. Although I was an early adopter of internet technology in the first part of the nineties, and worked full-time in what was then called 'new media' for the best part of a decade, it was only ever a tool for me. I was never a techie. Still, I want to get my money's worth, so I take what I hope looks like a studious interest in the banks of flashing lights: the James Newman megaprocessor; input and instruction decoding; Special Purpose Registers; Arithmetic and Logic Chart; ARM Processor ... Actually, I'm not even going to pretend I can understand all this. I'm going to struggle to spend much more than half an hour here.

I go through into the next room, The 80s classroom. That's more my generation: beige Amstrads and dot matrix printouts, a world of innocence before the world wide web was even a twinkle in Tim Berners-Lee's eye. These machines are survivors from that era, witnesses to a bygone age, their testimony more valuable with every passing year, like those last World War One Tommies used to be. Everything here is hands-on. It's worth a go. It might stretch out a few minutes more for me.

Half an hour later, I am immersed in the archive of the Domesday Project, one of those well-meaning, slightly bossy BBC initiatives which seeks to engage an entire nation in some improving activity. In this case, from 1984-1986, the Beeb had corralled schoolchildren into commemorating the 900th anniversary of the Domesday Book by recording information about their local communities and storing it on what passed for the compact discs of the day – which were almost the size of old 33 rpm LPs.

This 1980s data itself now seems to belong to a vanished world. To access it, I have to manipulate a mouse the size of a housebrick, with a trackball that looks like it was borrowed from the Cambridge Snooker and Pool Centre. But it's certainly absorbing. Once you get the hang of the system's rudimentary, pixillated on-screen navigation, you can summon all kinds of information from the distant 1980s, from the year of Bowie's 'Absolute Beginners', Bon Jovi's 'Livin' on a Prayer,' Madonna's 'Papa Don't Preach,' and Whitney Houston's 'Greatest Love of All;' the year of *Top Gun*, *Crocodile Dundee* and *Platoon*. What did those digital Domesday chroniclers say about those far-off days in Mrs Thatcher's Britain? The entry for Cambridge has the following information on 'Technology'.

> Some of the associated buildings are architecturally modern and even futuristic and catch the eye as one passes the city on the new motorway or bypass.

Yes, one could say that. One certainly could. The entry continues:

> No other English University and no similarly small area has engendered such a concentration of modern developments. Certainly, Oxford has but a tenth of such businesses.

"But a tenth"... He might as well have said "tithe". Ancient rivalries had transferred effortlessly to what was the newest technology of the day.

It wasn't new for very long. The discs were quickly superseded, and soon oxidisation – 'data rot' – threatened to make the data unreadable. That never happened with the original Domesday Book. The Museum has saved the 1986 information for posterity on more durable formats.

As I emerge from the 1980s, I become aware of the background chatter in the room. It's some kind of gaming club: guys in their late teens or early twenties deep into some kind of freewheeling gaming seminar to the accompaniment of tyre screeches, gunfire, explosions and the eerie, bleeping fairground music that seems to be what computers choose to listen to when left to themselves. Super Mario leaps and dives, joysticks and cables rattle. "Die!" urges one of the gamers: "Die!"

I'd almost forgotten. In the next room, among worthy exhibitions about computer pioneers like Charles Babbage, Ada Lovelace, Alan Turing, Steve Jobs and Bill Gates, there's a collection of vintage arcade games. This is what digital technology was invented for – killing aliens. Please let there be *Space Invaders*. And *Missile Command*. And perhaps, if the computer gods are kind, even *Uniwars*, which I spent hours, and hundreds of ten pence pieces, playing in the fish and chip shop back home. I would be awesome at *Uniwars*. Even after all these years.

There's no *Missile Command*[20] or *Uniwars*, But there's a good substitute for the latter, *Xevious*, a vertically scrolling shooter dating from 1983, with joystick and fire buttons. And best of all, it's all in the entry fee. Unlimited lives, and the luxury of starting over, time and time again, as your hand-eye co-ordination improves. Almost Buddhist really. But with more shooting. Whatever; it's heaven for gamers. My spaceship shimmers into being at the base of the screen. At the top, a fleet of alien vessels edge downwards. Missiles start falling like the first drops of rain before a storm. I hit the red Fire button. Die. Die!

Awesome is not the word to describe my performance, but, game by game, my initials gradually inch, pixel by pixel, up the leader board. Another half hour passes. Elapsed time on this visit is now two hours. I've earned back my entry fee twice over in gameplay. I decide to give the rest of the exhibition the once-over. There's Binatone ping pong; the Ur-computer game; the gaming equivalent of Stephenson's Rocket. There's *Pac Man*. There's *Space Invaders*, still maddeningly addictive. There's the Apple i-Mac, 'now considered a design classic', and, to be fair, still looking pretty funky. And that blocky, slow-scrolling but reliable TV information service Teletext.

After three hours I have to drag myself away. When I come out, I have the choice of walking the long way round the industrial estate's perimeter road, or taking what planners call a 'desire trail' between the brambles, up the steep bank and on to the bridge through a trodden-down gap in the chainlink fence. I take it. For the last three hours I've been a teenager again, and I'm going to make the most of it.

## THE ABBEY STADIUM

I grew up in a football-mad family. Saturday afternoons on the terraces; travelling to away games in a rattling Ford Cortina with scarves trailing from the windows; the clanking turnstiles; the crackling tannoy announcements; the tang of tobacco smoke in the winter air; the greasy hamburger from a mobile stall as you made your way home, elated or deflated depending on the result. And all the paraphernalia: the rosettes, programmes, sticker books, press cuttings, badges. I loved it. It gave you everything a religion could give: high days, histories and holidays; pilgrimages and pageantry; victims and villains; hope and hatred; shrines and saints; belonging and belief.[21] And I believed in it all; heart and soul I believed in it.

And then I stopped. When I moved away at eighteen, all that fervour stayed behind like once-loved children's toys; like the books you once read until they fell apart, but which now you'll never read again. This passion was not portable. Removed from its native environment, it withered away. And like so many who have been raised religious but whose faith faltered at the boundary between adolescence and adulthood, the fever, now broken, left me inoculated. At college, in a half-hearted attempt to graft my sporting past to my student present, I attended two Cambridge United games, against Sheffield Wednesday and Leeds United in 1983. But it didn't take. Not even seeing Les Cartwright, a former hero of my home-town club Wrexham, in the Cambridge line-up, could make any difference. Whenever Wrexham won, the tinny tannoy at the Racecourse Ground used to play the opening bars of Pilot's 1974 hit single 'Magic' across the emptying terraces: "Oh, oh oh, it's magic, you kn-o-ow. Never believe it's not so." But the magic had gone.

I realised how far it had gone when I called in Asda one Saturday afternoon to pick up some photographs I had left for developing. As I handed over the slip with the details, the attendant, a man of about my own age, leant towards me with a solicitous air: "How are they doing?" he asked me. I must have looked blank. How were *what* doing? Did he mean the photographs? Surely he was in a better position to judge than I was. He must have seen my puzzlement. "England," he said. "How are they doing?" I twigged. A World Cup qualifier that day. It had scarcely registered with me. I could hardly tell him that I didn't know or care – I had to rise to the occasion. Inspiration came. "I'm sorry," I said, "I haven't heard." I thought this was pretty clever: suggesting that I would have *liked* to have heard, but had simply been prevented from finding out by cruel circumstance (a broken car radio, perhaps? Or a lost mobile phone?). He seemed satisfied, and leant in closer. "Last I heard, they were losing two-nil." This raised the stakes. This called for solidarity, comradeship. I searched for the right phrase. Nothing. I searched again. Nothing. He was looking at me expectantly. "Oh dear," I managed: "Let's hope they ... catch up ... soon..." Even as I said it, I felt the crushing weight of failure. I was only glad the men of my childhood, my duffle-coat-clad father and uncles, my scarf-draped elder brother, were not there to hear it. They would have died of shame.

Some days later, I shared this humiliation with a friend who's a genuine football fan. I told him I needed some stock phrases. Easy, he said. All you need to say is: "They've got a mountain to climb now." Of course. Brilliant. Why hadn't I thought of that? Even better, he said, just shrug and say; "Same every year!" Of course.

So it was with a keen sense of my own limitations that I found myself waiting outside Cambridge United's fans' caravan on Newmarket Road on a Saturday afternoon to meet the person who was going to introduce me to the world behind the amber-painted walls of the Abbey Stadium.

Michael Hrebeniak is not your typical football fan. Or your typical Cambridge don, come to that. He's a lecturer in English and Director of Studies in English at Wolfson College, and a Lecturer in English at Magdalene. Before that, he lectured in Metropolitan Studies at NYU (London), and, at the Royal Academy of Music, he held the glorious title of Lecturer in Humanities and Jazz. He's a saxophonist and jazz journalist, when he's not writing obituaries for the *Guardian*, producing Channel 4 documentaries or making psychogeographical films.

But today, it's football. Conscious how academia can sever you from everyday realities, Michael has made the effort to reconnect with the game he grew up with. Not for nothing is a football stadium known as a "ground". In fact, if my own home town had a symbolic heart, that's where it would be. The ground of my being. Michael grew up supporting Watford, and when he moved to Cambridge, he started attending Cambridge United games, using the principle for deciding sporting allegiance described by the comedian Frank Skinner – simply draw a line on a map from your house to the nearest football club. Easy. The fact that Cambridge play in the same colours as Watford meant he didn't even need any chromatic re-coding, Michael says. In his case, the grafting worked. He's a regular. His son Louis works as a goalkeeping coach for the club, and Michael is struggling heroically to introduce his younger son Ambrose to the game too.

The Abbey stadium's filling up. The portacabin is out of programmes. On the way to the terraces, we pass through old-fashioned turnstiles so cramped that they feel like something in the biblical parable of the narrow gate that leads to life. It's certainly narrow. I'm not sure quite what life it leads to though. The metal stile clanks open. "Welcome to the Nineteen Fifties" says Michael. He's right; the ground should have a preservation order. With the spindly legs of its floodlights towering above the neighbouring streets, this ground is not, like so many others these days, a generic corporate concrete bowl on an out-of-town retail park surrounded by TK Maxx and McDonalds. This is the kind of football ground I remember: a turnstiled, terraced time-machine.

Just the other side of the turnstiles, another portable building is serving teas, coffees and beers. It looks very small for the number of people in the ground, and I wonder if I shouldn't order the interval drinks now. Then I realise that this question should *never* have occurred to me. There was a time when I knew how football culture worked, when I could have reeled off the names of all 92 league clubs; their nicknames, the names of their grounds, and the colours of their strips. Not any more. Once again, I'm reminded that it's a very long while since I've been to a match.

On the terraces, the roof is supported by rusty pillars, and the camera gantry is reached by what looks like a flimsy loft ladder. There are nearly six thousand fans in the ground, over five hundred of them from Wycombe. They're in the next section of the terraces and are keeping up a steady racket, led by someone with a drum thumping out a heady, mesmerising shamanic beat.

Michael tells me Cambridge United used to have cheerleaders, although he was scathing about the fact that they wore skimpy

costumes, with the name of a skip hire company emblazoned on their cut-off bra tops. Commodification, he says. It was the gimmick of Mick George, the club's main sponsor. He does skips, hardcore, plant hire. That explains the costumed Bob the Builder mascot character on the touchline. In his spare time, Mick George breeds alpacas.

Cambridge fans have the reputation of being easy-going. That 1950s thing again. The Amber Army is, of course, a good 90% male. Many have travelled in from the surrounding villages. These are the kind of men, Michael says, that the dons don't know or think about, and the tourists don't notice. "The University might as well be on the Moon for all it cares about this side of the city" he says. There are not too many dons here today, I'm pretty sure of that.

I'm willing Cambridge to win while trying to resist the emotional pull of partisanship. I don't want to care that much. I can forego the elation in order to avoid the dejection. Sports fans always seem to live on an emotional rollercoaster of despair, anger or frustration. Seldom do they have a spring in their step because of success. Even more seldom do you find them philosophical at failure, generously conceding that their player really *did* deserve to be sent off, that their disallowed goal *was* offside. That isn't the point. We're not talking reason here; we're talking allegiance, loyalty, hope, fear. Fans always remind me of gamblers, except the currency isn't hard cash, but emotion. Almost always, disappointment is the only return.

Only rarely, very rarely, does the punter leave with hopes fulfilled and pockets full. Like in the Kenny Rogers song, you have to know when to walk away. I've done that, and I'm not going back. Still, come *on*, Cambridge.

The U's are struggling though. Wycombe's striker, Adebayo Akinfenwa, is a giant: five-eleven and sixteen stone. He's nicknamed The Beast. I've never seen a football player with such a physique. He could be a rugby prop, and a hefty one at that. Apparently, he's the strongest player in the Football League and can bench-press 200kg, twice his own bodyweight. He even has his own range of clothes for big men, called Beast Mode On. His ball skills are impressive, and he seems simply impossible to knock off the ball. It's causing some frustration for the home fans. "You fat bastard," one of them shouts as he comes within earshot. Homophobia and racism are supposed to have been kicked out of football, but not body-shaming. Not yet.

One section of the South Stand is covered with a large gay pride flag. It's the only section entirely empty. From the nearby sections come the squeaks and squeals of boyish voices in the family enclosure. A stray clearance sends a ball over the stand. That wouldn't happen in a modern stadium. You'd need a howitzer to clear those skyscraping roofs. "That's another £65 gone" says Michael. These things count when margins are tight. This is not a wealthy club, even though the land belongs to Grosvenor Estates, Britain's biggest private landlord. In one corner, next to the former broadcasting room which looks like an abandoned World War Two radio hut, part of the terrace, built on landfill, has subsided.

It's goalless at half time. As the players file back inside, a yellow Mick George mini-skip is wheeled out, together with a supply of footballs. It's time for Skip Challenge, where a member of the public tries to kick a ball into a yellow mini-skip. It's more entertaining than the game. Mick George skips are the cheapest in the area, Michael tells me. By far. He's used them gladly several times.

The deadlock is broken just after half time, by Wycombe. Just inside the penalty area Ebere Eze picks up a pass from Akinfenwa, finds himself in space and curls the ball round the defender and into the top right-hand corner, leaving the keeper flat-footed. It's a good move. So good that ten minutes later, he does exactly the same thing again. Two nil. On the touchline, Bob the Builder puts his big foam head in his big foam hands in despair.

Wycombe Wanderers are apparently renowned for gamesmanship. I can see why. When tackled, their players fling themselves to the floor and writhe like cut snakes as they try to wring a penalty from the ref. When a decision goes against them, they protest as though incredulous at the wickedness of the world, and throw the ball away, far enough to annoy, not enough to get a yellow card. At set pieces, opposing players are hassled and crowded. I feel the faint stirrings of tribal hatred. They always cheat. The ref always ignores it. Same every year. I mustn't allow myself to care. Nonetheless, it's starting to get to me.

With eight minutes to go, Cambridge convert a penalty. Hope sparks briefly. Watches are glanced at. There's time for an equaliser. Then Wycombe score again. Despair empties the terraces like sand from a broken hourglass. Four minutes are added for stoppages. It seems more like a threat than an opportunity.

The final whistle goes. There's that familar feeling: money and time expended, and nothing gained but disappointment. "Are you still sure you want your son to experience this?" I ask Michael. I realise I've used the kind of tone in which people used to ask their friends not to send their sons down the coalmines. "Certainly," he says. "It's my moral responsibility as a father. Ruinous, desultory. What better preparation for life?"

## STOURBRIDGE COMMON

After the game, we make our way through the streets towards Stourbridge Common, past the temporarily crowded pubs. Stourbridge Common, a riverside nature reserve and pasture between Newmarket Road and the river, is named for the Stour brook, a tributary of the Cam. When I lived in Chesterton, I used to walk or cycle across the common on my way to town. More recently it's where I walk if I have a writing project: its emptiness somehow invites the words to come. But I knew almost nothing about the area's history. With its grazing cattle, and its 'scrapes' – the little hollows which fill with water but which dry up in warm weather – I had assumed it was one of those little bucolic enclaves which chance or enlightened policy has managed to preserve close to the centre of the city. But I was wrong. This emptiness is not old, but new. For centuries, for almost a month every year, this Common was the commercial heart of England.

Stourbridge fair dates back at least as far as 1199, when King John gave permission to the Leper Hospital – the chapel of which still stands opposite the Abbey Stadium – to hold an annual fund-raising fair. Fairs were the equivalent of a government franchise today: limited, sought-after, and, if you could get a licence, extremely lucrative. Because of its location, at a point where the Cam, still navigable by sea barges, crossed the Newmarket road, Stourbridge became England's largest fair, with a month of trade and festivity from late August every year. Following the 1381 Peasants' Revolt, the fair was handed over to the town.

Its scale was legendary: entire streets of stands were devoted to single products; its 'duddery', selling cloth and garments, set the going rate for such products in the entire country. The fair had playhouses, pubs, courts and pulpits, all erected temporarily; all dismantled after it was over. In the Seventeenth Century, John Bunyan[22], a travelling tinker before he became a Puritan leader, found in Stourbridge the inspiration for his Vanity Fair, which he depicted in *The Pilgrim's Progress*, seeing it as a symbol of how, in a fallen world, everything has its price: "houses, lands, trades, places, honours, preferments, titles, countries, kingdoms; lusts, pleasures, and delights of all sorts". In 1724, the fair was visited by Daniel Defoe [23], who marvelled at its size.

That was at the fair's greatest extent. As industrial towns grew, and as the canal and railway network expanded, trade moved to the new urban centres. The last fair was held in 1933, when Florence Keynes,[24] Cambridge's first female councillor and the mother of the economist John Maynard Keynes, officiated as mayor at its last rites: a proclamation witnessed only by two women with babies in their arms and a youth with an ice-cream barrow. Today, there's nothing to show that this was once the scene of commerce and revelry so immense as to give the English language a byword for ostentation and excess.

Almost nothing. For the practised eye, there are still some clues, and Michael Hrebeniak has such an eye. Attracted to the overlooked, intrigued by the ignored, he has for years conducted an intense psychogeographic and historical study of the area, which included producing a 2019 full-length poem-film *Stirbitch: An Imaginary*[25] showing the hidden layers of history underneath the concrete of the apparently workaday district next to Newmarket Road.[26] He's always been drawn to the fringes, where marginalia reveal more than the text. Perhaps it's because this district has always been the place where the city has located things it would rather forget: the lepers; the fair; the sewage works; the football stadium, and the retail park, that trans-national trading post where transience is designed in.

Michael's study summed up the Newmarket Road retail park well: "an agitational terrain, eliminating the desire to linger, enshrining the ecosystem of automobile and ensuring that crowds will not be allowed to form, but rather, move directly between car and retail shed. Its banal spatial legibility concretizes an ideology of superficial transparency, reorganizing the subject's vision into a split field where gazes are no longer designed to meet."[27]

For Michael , the recognition of the rejected, the recovery of the repressed, the retrieval of the past, is an act of social conscience, defying all the forces, natural and human, that would sweep away all traces of the lives of the overlooked, just as the fair was erased each year once its usefulness was over. He points out how the names of the quiet streets of terraces leading to the Common – Mercer's Row, Garlic Row, Oyster Row – show where the market used to be, recalling when these were rows of stands not houses. As Bunyan said: "… there are the several rows and streets, under their proper names, where such and such wares are vended." The market's pattern is still 'encoded' Michael says, in the streetscape which has supplanted it.[28]

Not just that, but there are also more tangible reminders. He takes me over to the children's playground near the path, deserted now on this rainy evening. "There's almost nothing left today to show where the fair took place. Except this". He points at the base of the trees. In the circle of earth at the base of the trunk are little shards and shapes of pearly white.

"Oyster shells" he says. "Hundreds and thousands of them were eaten here. They were plentiful; a poor man's meal. And the shells were discarded."[29] Now, the soil is giving them back, pushed to the surface by the tree roots. I pick one up: craggy on one side, silky on the other. I decide to keep it. A talisman. A pilgrim's scallop shell, John Bunyan would be proud of me.

We make our way across the Common to Chesterton, joining the straggle of defeated Cambridge United supporters trailing homewards in the pouring rain. At the footbridge, the river is deep and wide. "I love this view", Michael says, looking downriver towards Fen Ditton. He points out that one of the very few pictures ever taken of the fair, showing a gipsy horse gathering, was taken from this spot. On the opposite side of the bridge is the Green Dragon Inn, a pub since the 1730s, and once the location of a ferry plying across the river.[30] This was my local when I was a final-year student. It's changed, of course, but not radically. There's exposed brickwork and bistro tables, but it's still very much a local. This evening, it's providing solace to some of the defeated Amber Army, grumbling about defensive errors and surrendering the midfield. As I'm waiting at the bar to be served, one of the regulars turns his red-veined face towards me. "Bloody shambles, wasn't it?" he says. I think for a moment, but only a moment. "Aye," I say, with an air of weary resignation: "Same every year."

## STOW CUM QUY

My daughter's sister-in-law Halie and her boyfriend Isaac are visiting from Texas, and I've taken them out in the car for the day. On the roundabout at the end of Newmarket Road, I see a sign for a steam fair. I've always wanted to go to a steam fair. Well, not really. Only for about thirty seconds since I saw the sign. But 'always' has to start somewhere. The yellow event signs guide us to Stow cum Quy – known locally simply as 'Quy' – population 544, a village about four miles east of the city. How to explain a steam fair to American visitors? Like a State Fair, I say, but smaller. A lot smaller. And with traction engines. Traction engines? Don't worry, I say; you'll get the idea. It'll be a real slice of traditional England.

It is. Right down to the downpour which begins the moment we get out of the car, and which continues, almost unbroken, for the rest of our visit. We take shelter in the beer tent where the singer Johnny Dee, in his yellow Teddy Boy jacket with black collar and cuffs, and his red ruffled shirt, is just beginning his set. The shout-outs first: "Anyone here from outside Cambridge?" "Ely!" says one guy. That's about fifteen miles; not bad. "March!" says another, upping the ante; it's a good thirty miles away or more. "Suffolk!" says a woman, with a hint of triumph. We could beat that, but were not going to risk drawing unnecessary attention. Let Suffolk be as exotic as it gets. "Come on, Stow cum Quy!" says Johnny, rather in the way Bruce Springsteen might shout "Come on, Glas-ton-berry", and Johnny's off into Curtis Lee's 'Under the Moon of Love', followed by 'Shake Rattle and Roll,'" to the accompaniment of a backing track and the drumming of the rain on the canvas.

After a while, there's a brief break in the cloud, and we venture out, as do most of Johnny's crowd. For the rest of the day, as dictated by the rain, his audience ebbs and flows like the tide. Outside, there's a classic car exhibition. The owners are mostly sitting inside their vehicles, sheltering from the drizzle, with

sandwiches and thermos flasks. Interesting how it's the most prestigious cars that tend to get preserved: the Triumph Stags, the E-Type Jags, the Jaguar Mark 2s. Back in the day, these were the big beasts of the automotive jungle: mythical creatures, rarely glimpsed. Now, they're all that survives. The rest of us rattled round in clapped-out Allegros, Hillman Imps, Morris Marinas and Austin Maxis, which have vanished from existence. If future historians ever tried to understand our motoring past from the vehicles we've preserved, they'd think we all only ever drove sports cars. History favours the victors.

From the beer tent, we can still hear Johnny Dee: 'You're Sixteen', 'Daydream Believer', 'Summer Holiday', and finally, a version of Black Sabbath's 'Paranoid'. That's versatility for you. Now the traction engines are lumbering into a procession, crawling round the show ring while a commentator calls out their finer points over the tannoy. There are steam wagons, steam rollers, steam tractors, ploughing engines, road locomotives. The shire horses of the vehicular world: obsolete; magnificent. Halie and Isaac are the perfect guests: fazed by nothing; appreciative of everything, the craft tent; the gypsy fortune-teller; the country-wear store; the vintage medal collection. But all the same, especially with the bad weather, I'm going to struggle to spin this visit out much longer. I decide to give one of the sideshows a go. There's a shooting gallery, with little tin targets, the shape of human outlines, waiting resignedly for the air-rifle marksman with the skill to take them down.

He's right here. As kids, my brother and I had an arsenal of air weapons. We practised obsessively. I hate to think what we would have been like if we'd grown up in a country with access to real weapons. But airgun or real gun, you never lose a skill like that. These tin men are as good as scrap metal. I ask Isaac if he wants a go. He has a look at the toy-sized air rifle in my hands and politely declines. He's Texan: I somehow imagine he's seen more, and bigger, guns than this. No matter. I'll show him I also know a thing or two. The row of tin men are six feet away. Maybe eight at extreme range. I put the rifle to my shoulder and take aim. As I do so, I suddenly realise I face a terrible choice: I can focus either on the sights or on the target; not both. In the thirty years or so since I last picked up an airgun, my eyesight has deteriorated so much that I can't aim properly. I decide to focus on the sight and I line it up on what has now just become a ghostly outline of the target. Perhaps it's better this way. I've seen *Enemy at the Gates*, the film about the sniper duel in Stalingrad. I know it's better not to look too closely at your hit. I squeeze the trigger. The tin man clatters down. So, in turn, do the other three. It's still there, the old skill. After all these years, I've still got it.

"Anything from the bottom shelf," says the stall lady. The hunter's spoils. There's selection of cuddly toys: plush puppies;

bears with imploring glassy eyes; kittens with expressions of mute adoration. I'd hoped my marksmanship would have produced something a bit more ... macho. But then I spot it. A killer whale. An orca. The terror of the deep. She hands it over. True, it's a bit soft and fluffy for the most feared predator in the ocean, but somehow I sense what he's saying to me: we are kindred spirits, you and I. Killer and killer. I conceal the label which says 'Cuddle Pals' and I take him with me as we make our way out of the showground. Privately, I worry about what I've learned regarding my eyesight. I mustn't let that clean sheet fool me. That was my one last case. I got lucky. My days of military usefulness are clearly over. If my country ever calls, I'll be of no help. Unless, of course, we're ever invaded by six-inch-high, stationary tin men. In that case, I'm your man.

## BOTTISHAM

A few miles further east again lies the village of Bottisham. My wife, Sally, and I have come to visit my friend Will Beharrell, who lives with his wife Lucy and their three young children in a wing of a former manor house. A polymath – medical doctor, charity worker, academic philosopher – I met him through his work as trustee of a charity striving to preserve traditional crafts in Afghanistan (he speaks Pashto). We're going to discuss his latest project over dinner, and his neighbours, husband and wife Arthur Gibson and Niamh O'Mahony, are to join us.

And a jolly evening it is too. Niamh was a BBC Russian World Service producer and writer, and is now an academic researcher and editor when she is not working as a film extra, or what they call these days a 'supporting artiste'. She's just been working on the Harry Potter spin-off, *Fantastic Beasts*, which means I must have seen her. But the work is being threatened by automation, she says: the actors' motions have been captured and digitised so that it can be done virtually in future.

After dinner, I find myself talking to Arthur, a benign-looking, mild-mannered gent in, perhaps, his late sixties, with a halo of curly grey hair around his high domed forehead. He must be, I've decided, a local historian, the kind of person for whom I have the greatest respect. My own father was just such a man: the founder-chairman of the local history society in our home village, about which he knew a great deal and which he firmly believed was the centre of the universe. It turns out Arthur knows a great deal too, but not just about Bottisham, or Cambridge, but about the rest of the universe as well. He mentions his current university work, editing recently-discovered papers of Ludwig Wittgenstein. Thank goodness, I'd just read a book about Wittgenstein and am able to ask about his famous dispute with Bertrand Russell: which was, I seem to remember, something to do with sets, and – apparently – quite a fundamental business. Arthur answers, easily, fluently, with no hint of condescension; I feel his attention lighting up my understanding like a torch briefly flashing around a darkened lumber room. Now we're talking about particle physics. How can I be talking about particle physics? I don't know anything *about* particle physics. But this is an after-dinner conversation, not a public debate; there aren't any rules. Anything is fair game.

So anyway, I tell him, I wrote this poem which used the imagery of attraction and repulsion in particle physics to describe a touching moment of exchange I once witnessed between a homeless man and a child. Arthur liked that. He looked away for a brief moment, and, to my astonishment, he wiped away a tear. We were on to metaphysics now. He'd written a research book on the subject. Niamh thought it was too obscure. I'd like to read it, I said. I was enjoying this. Yanis Varoufakis, the former Greek finance minister, with whom Arthur had been corresponding since they met in Cambridge (we're on to economics now), had sent him the book on the table there. He and Yanis brainstorm. That was when Arthur was also advising a government facility on Big Data policy and a senior Nato centre on the security situations in various countries. I could feel connections forming between previously separated areas of knowledge; my brain racing as I tried to follow Arthur's multiple trains of thought. I couldn't keep up, of course, except in the way a novice rider keeps up with a runaway horse: not in charge; not knowing where it's going. But boy, what a ride.

I'm beginning to think I might have misread this whole local historian thing, so I excuse myself on a pretext and, in the next room, on my mobile phone, I quickly Google 'Arthur Gibson,[31] Cambridge'. Immediately, the results come back: "The Cleverest Man in Britain, Professor Arthur Gibson;" "preternaturally gifted to a Mozartian degree,"[32] "Good Will Hunting parallels, but don's life is stranger than fiction,"[33] the latter a reference to the Matt Damon character in the film *Good Will Hunting* – a janitor found to be a mathematical genius. Gibson is cleverer than that, the article says. A whole lot cleverer.

He was brought up in poverty in a Bradford slum with a vicious, violent alcoholic father for whom, from the age of about five, he was forced to calculate bookies' odds, and who, if he made any mistakes, burned him with cigarettes for the amusement of his drunken friends. His father punished him if he brought a book into the house. He left school at fourteen with no qualifications and ended up doing casual labour, his academic potential unrecognised despite his astounding gifts, his immense, encyclopaedic, self-directed library learning, and his photographic memory. Only through the care and vision of some patient academics, who spotted his talent and went the extra mile to help him overcome the crippling emotional difficulties caused by his upbringing, was he able to enter academia.

But what an entrance. His first IQ test gave him a score of over 210. Einstein's was 160. He's not just the cleverest man in the country; he's the third cleverest in the world. He consumed the most complex subjects seemingly with no more effort than a boy scout collecting badges: philosophy; literature; ancient Near Eastern languages; jurisprudence of international law; mathematics; semantic logic; cosmology; poetry, and seemingly endless combinations of the same. When experts find their expertise is exhausted, they call him; when statesmen are stumped, they call him; when scientists are stymied, they call him. He advises governments on everything from quantum computing to terrorism. I'm reminded of how Sherlock Holmes describes his even cleverer elder brother Mycroft in Arthur Conan Doyle's short story, The Adventure of the Bruce-Partington Plans:

> He has the tidiest and most orderly brain, with the greatest capacity for storing facts, of any man living ... The conclusions of every department are passed to him, and he is the central exchange, the clearinghouse, which makes out the balance. All other men are specialists, but his specialism is omniscience. We will suppose that a minister needs information as to a point which involves the Navy, India, Canada and the bimetallic question; he could get his separate advices from various departments upon each, but only Mycroft can focus them all, and say offhand how each factor would affect the other. They began by using him as a short-cut, a convenience; now he has made himself an essential. In that great brain of his everything is pigeon-holed and can be handed out in an instant.

I re-enter the dinner party a wiser man. My I.Q. is no higher, but I've certainly learned something. He had mentioned none of this background. Cleverness was not important, he said: depth and originality are. The conversation is continuing; Arthur and Niamh are an endearing double act.

"What I'm trying to get at here is..."

"Arthur, what do you *mean*..?"

"A slight digression, but, I hope, a worthwhile one..."

"Where is this going, Arthur...?"

"Am I embarrassing you, my dear?"

"Yes, a bit."

"Is it just selfconsciousness? It will pass. Now, should I make just two points ...?"

Genius here defers to wisdom. Niamh has adopted a scissor gesture with her fingers to indicate the need for him to edit a part of the current discourse. I see Sally note this with interest and show me with a warning glance that I can expect these scissors to form part of her own equipment in future.

I'm grateful I didn't know Arthur's reputation before we met. Overawed, I would never have experienced that electrifying conversation. Thank goodness for that English modesty, that meant that I first met the man, not the Mozart.

After a later meeting, I read Arthur's book, *God and the Universe*. It's a substantial 377-page Routledge hardback with full academic apparatus, and when I pick it up, I'm surprised by its physical weight: it seems to be made out of some super-dense material, like the centre of a neutron star. The back cover carries a quote from Professor Sir Frank Kermode[34], which says that the author: "...combines a temperament as cheerful as an open coal fire with a mind like a pressure cooker." He's right. The book is an overview of a huge range of disciplines – cosmology, philosophy, history, art, music, particle physics – all woven into a thesis which manages to be serious and playful at the same time, as the subject titles show:

"Can a name be transcendent?"; "Has the universe strung us along?"; "How much space has the universe for dimensions?"; "Are some pulsars spin-doctored?"

Arthur believes in God, even if not in the traditional anthropomorphic sense. Niamh, to whom the volume is dedicated, doesn't, not in any sense. Arthur describes her in the Preface as an "Irish Catholic atheist", and credits her for challenging him and enabling him to refine the book's ideas. Having seen that process of challenge at first-hand gives me greater confidence in *God and the Universe*: if the arguments have survived those finger-scissors, they must be pretty sound.

It's a stimulating work, and challenging. Sometimes, at a passage I find particularly difficult, I stop, try to work it out, fail and lose the thread. But if I keep on reading, maintaining a forward momentum despite not understanding everything, if I keep surfing across the depths, I find I discern an outline of his vision: holistic, panoramic, integrative. I'm glad I have my recollection of my conversations with Arthur, which have shown me how to follow the thesis, albeit at a great distance, like watching an aerial display. Has it convinced me there's a God? No. I'm not clever enough to understand the arguments. But it's convinced me that Arthur Gibson believes there's a God, and, if reason and faith mean anything at all, that will have to be good enough for me.

## Notes

1. At home, after treatment in Addenbrooke's Hospital, where his physician father, Max, had worked for many years as the University Morbid Anatomist and Histologist, and where a Barrett Room was named in his memory.
2. Ronald Gray and Derek Stubbings, *Cambridge Street-Names. Their Origins and Associations.* (Cambridge, 2000), 13.
3. It dated from at least 1777: Allan Brigham, Gordon Clark and Peter Filby, *Mill Road Windmill, Cambridge*, (2013), 4, 8. The critic F.R. Leavis (1895-1878) was born above 68 Mill Road, at the time, his father's piano shop; now a sandwich bar.
4. Gray and Stubbings, *op. cit.*, 61.
5. 1854/5-1927.
6. 1919–2001.
7. *Ibid.*, 35.
8. Now demolished. The family later moved to 66 Abbey Rd.
9. *With My Own Wings, the Memoirs of Raymond Lister*, (Cambridge, 1994), 6.
10. *Ibid.*, 104.
11. *Ibid.*, 77.
12. Romans, 5: 20.
13. 1895 –1986.
14. Wei Wu Wei, *Why Lazarus Laughed: The Essential Doctrine Zen-Advaita-Tantra*, (London, 1960).

15. Including Clive James, Michael Palin, Terry Jones and Gruff Rhys Jones.

16. Malcolm Guite, another campaigner, described it as being like the eighteenth-century Enclosures.

17. A legal grey area. The Crown Prosecution Service's guidelines recommend against prosecution "where there is no intention to cause alarm or distress," and no sexual context.

18. c. 344–c. 421 Patron saint of penitents.

19. Built 1894, closed 1960, and being developed as an industrial heritage centre.

20. There's a great online version: http://my.ign.com/atari/missile-command

21. See Iwan Russell Jones: https://www.regentaudio.com/collections/iwan-russell-jones/products/great-sporting-liturgies-fields-of-praise

22. 1628-1688.

23. 1660-1731.

24. 1861-1958. In 1932, at 70, she became Mayor of Cambridge. She chaired the committee responsible for the building of the new Guildhall, completed 1939.

25. A provocative, and genuine, variant of the usual spelling: https://vimeo.com/michaelhrebeniak

26. Michael Hrebeniak, "'Where Is the Dust That Has Not Been Alive?'": Screening the Vanished Polis in Stirbitch, an Imaginary," in Eds. François Penz and Richard Koeck; Cinematic Urban Geographies, (New York, 2017), 155-173.

27. Ibid., 158.

28. Some names recall still earlier times: Saxon Street and Godesdone Road both commemorate the supposed location of the hut of the Saxon hermit Godesone ('God's Son'), near a pre-Christian holy well. His wooden oratory was dedicated to St Andrew: the dedicatee of the church on Newmarket Road.

29. Martin Garrett, op. cit., 223.

30. Once, also the location of a cockpit. Barrowclough, 57.

31. https://boisdalelife.com/2016/09/08/the-cleverest-man-in-britain-professor-arthur-gibson/

32. Ibid.,

33. https://www.timeshighereducation.com/news/hunting-parallels-but-dons-life-is-stranger-than-fiction/419411.article

34. Emeritus King Edward VII Professor of English Literature at Cambridge.

# SOUTH

# RAILWAY STATION AND CB1

The train from London is approaching Cambridge station. In the seat opposite me, a young woman – Spanish, possibly, by her accent – has been talking on her mobile for a while: "No Daniel, not this weekend. I'm sorry, OK?" She has the air of someone who has said this a lot recently, and is prepared to keep on saying it. "No, not this weekend. I need just some time for my own. I'm sorry, Daniel." She doesn't sound sorry. Between her brief responses, Daniel seems to be talking a lot. A lot. As he does so, she carries on reading her book: *El camino de la autodependencia*. Daniel had better make other plans for the weekend. The tannoy announces that we're stopping; "I got to go, Daniel. OK?"

It always mystifies first-time visitors why Cambridge railway station is so far from the city centre – a full mile and a half from the Market Square. The answer dates to when the railway first came, in 1845. The University Vice Chancellor saw it as a mortal threat to the city's purity, particularly as, on the Sabbath, it would carry passengers who "having no regard for Sunday themselves, would inflict their presence on the University on that day of rest." The battle of religion and railway ended in an uneasy truce, with the station built, but at a daunting distance from the colleges, and with the railway company banned on pain of a hefty fine from carrying any university students.

It carries plenty today though. Not just students, but tourists and commuters to and from London King's Cross, which, on a good day and by express train, is only 45 minutes away. And thanks to extensive recent developments, the station area itself is not quite as run-down as it once was. Although neither is it what the city hoped it would be when it conceived ambitious plans for its regeneration. The CB1 development has been one of Cambridge's more controversial projects. An unloved area would be developed into a mixed-use business and residential district. Starchitect Sir Richard Rogers would provide the design. Students, young families and business people would make their homes there alongside a new heritage centre and public square. An urban idyll.

Except it didn't turn out that way. During a decade of disappointment for the city planners, the Rogers scheme failed to catch the public imagination and was dropped when the 2008 financial crisis crashed the company promoting it. The firm which emerged from the ashes pushed through a development which the architecture critic Oliver Wainwright described as a "generic clone-town scene more like a suburban retail park than an illustrious seat of learning."[1]

It's fair to say CB1 is not an architectural gem. But it's all relative. Compared to many a provincial residential and retail complex, CB1 is fine. Compared with one of the most harmonious and exquisite ensembles of historic buildings in the world, though, it's a different matter. At street level, it's a complex of glass and beige concrete canyons, only relieved by the occasional generic frontages of chain coffee shops and restaurants. Any sense of place seems to have been carefully designed out. The only sign you're in one of the world's great university cities is a hoarding around one of the yet-to-be-occupied lots, composed, shrewdly, of images of the spines of books. Someone's done their homework: every volume has a Cambridge connection: Douglas Adams; Charles Darwin; Stephen Fry; Hugh Laurie; Andrew Marr; John Milton; Siegfried Sassoon; David Attenborough. Craftily distributed among this distinguished company are other contributions to the canon: page-turners like Modern Workplace Environments; Open Space Public Art; Prime Business Location; Mixed-Use Development; Shops and Restaurants; 30 Minutes to Stansted, and that bestseller, New 3000-space Car park.

Of course, it's still early days. Communities aren't built overnight. There is plenty of potential here. In one corner of the site,

Cambridge Junction, a multi-purpose art theatre built in 1990 on what had, until 1976, been the city's cattle market,[2] shows how it could be done. For nearly three decades, this charity and social enterprise, and self-styled "edgy urban venue that is proudly more town than gown", has provided the city with the kind of carefully-curated diet of contemporary culture not consistently available elsewhere. In this blocky barn-like structure of uncompromising concrete, steel and wood cladding, the likes of Blur, The Manic Street Preachers and Coldplay performed, as well as experimental artists of every description. In its foyer – all exposed construction techniques, exposed brickwork, and flyers for films with exposed camerawork – you can sit on the battered club-style sofas, drinking the local Moonshine brewery's craft beer and check out the brochure promoting the B movie festival and the Punjabi DJ's spoken word and electronic string fusion set.

Outside, in the apartment complex, some of the flats have tiny balconies crowded with a whole garden's worth of kids' toys, garden chairs, bicycles, and even, in one case, a Space Hopper, which, at three floors up, must count as an extreme sport. It's already apparent that, for the summer, the student accommodation here has become an enclave for hundreds of young teenage Chinese language students. I'm stopped by a middle-aged Chinese lady with a pull-along suitcase, a clipboard and a lost look. "Are you local?" she asks. Well, these things are relative. I'm probably more local than she is, so I try my best to help. She's trying to find the accommodation allocated to her as a tutor on one of the language courses. Her English is excellent. The directions she's been given are not. We're puzzling over them with the help of Google Maps when three young women, genuine locals with vapes and Red Bull cans in hand, stop and help. They're as mystified by the directions as anyone, and the tutor sets off hopefully in the best-guess direction we can offer.

It's seven in the evening, and scores of Chinese students are streaming from their temporary apartment lodgings to the ground-floor feeding stations to be given their nightly noodle boxes. Some of them eat while sitting in the laundry room, watching the machines go round while texting home. Many carry Cool Britannia and Union Jack shopping bags. Their clothes bear the logos of enterprises like the Cambridge Accelerator Course and a variety of aspirational slogans which make up in enthusiasm what they lack in idiom, such as 'Have a good time,' and the no-doubt innocently-intended 'Drink and Come'. Some students, more diligent or perhaps more accomplished than their fellows, are speaking English to one another. They'll go far. They already have.

## SCOTT POLAR INSTITUTE

The Scott Polar Institute is a reminder of the days, scarcely a century distant, when man seemed no threat to nature, but rather, when the odds seemed stacked the other way. The Institute, at the top of Lensfield Road, was built in 1934 as a result of the outpouring of public support following the death of the explorer Captain Robert Falcon Scott on his expedition to reach the South Pole in 1912. Inside, its light-filled galleries display the equipment, much of it touchingly primitive, which was used in the days when the Antarctic was a place no human could survive. Next to these are displays about contemporary climate change, which leave you wondering whether the Antarctic can now survive humans.

Back in 1912, Scott and his four companions reached their polar objective only to find their better-prepared Norwegian rival Roald Amundsen had beaten them by four weeks. On the return journey, all five perished. Their bodies were later discovered, together with Scott's moving diary of their last days, a document which more than made up in eloquence what his expedition had lacked in competence. Scott's words contributed to the legend which made this ill-fated venture perhaps the quintessential example of the British reverence of heroic failure.

It's long been customary to regard this admiration of defeat ironically, as though it were a pathetic grasping for positives in a general picture of decline. But England has hardly lacked historical successes, and this sympathy for the unsuccessful might actually be rooted in something more benign. Simple modesty for instance, and distaste for triumphalism. After all, it was this 1912 expedition which gave the world what must be one of the great understatements of all time, as frostbitten Captain Oates, fearing he was endangering his companions by slowing them down, stepped out into a white eternity with the quiet words: "I am just going outside and may be some time."

On several levels, the very appearance of the Institute epitomises the English spirit of adventure. There's that understatement again: from the outside, it looks not like an international scientific institution, but an unassuming country house. It was built that way, as though to give the impression that the single-minded pursuit of scientific endeavour in the most extreme environments on earth were a gentlemanly activity to pursue during one's spare time, and without appearing to try *too* hard. Then there's the very fact that the institute is named after Scott, who, while certainly the best-known polar explorer, was hardly the most successful. His contemporary, the great survivor Sir Ernest Shackleton, whose inspirational courage, initiative and sheer determination in the face of indescribable odds are the stuff of leadership training schemes to this day, is commemorated merely with a replica of his lifeboat tucked away at the side of the building.

Then there's the commemorative statue in front of the institute. It's of a naked young man, arms outstretched, face upturned to the grey, unforgiving sky. It was cast in 1922 by Scott's widow, Lady Kathleen. The model was A.W. Lawrence, younger brother of Lawrence of Arabia and later the Cambridge Professor of Classical Archaeology. It's a very fine piece, but surely only the English could commemorate polar exploration with a statue of a naked man.

Finally, there's the counterpart sculpture on the front of the institute. A dog. To be precise, one of the 1,204 huskies which took part in the British Antarctic Survey's expeditions from 1945 to 1993. Its plaque shows that dog teams were given collective names, from which, no doubt, individual names could be derived. The team names themselves give an insight into the minds of the dogs' human companions. Some display the cultural priorities of an earlier age – Admirals; Churchmen; Citizens; Counties; Darkie & Co; Debs; Gangsters; Huns; Number Ones and Wags. Some – Beatles, Troggs, Hobbits and Moomins – reveal origins in more recent times. Others show more timeless interests: Girls; Ladies and Players. Historic categories also seem to be popular: Amazons; Gaels; Giants; Picts; Spartans and Vikings. Finally, there are the seemingly unclassifiable: Hairybreeks; Komats; Lobsters; Terrors; and, with commendable unsentimentality, Orange Bastards.

# HILLS ROAD AND CHERRY HINTON ROAD

As I pass St Paul's Church in Hills Road I find myself, through long habit, reading those visual clues which might reveal its style of Anglican churchmanship: High, Low, Broad, or any of the many gradations in between. As so often in England, the definition is usually only hinted at, and rarely spelled out explicitly, as it might be in the unambiguous roadside signage of an American place of worship. In England, to find out anything for certain, you pretty much have to know it already. English society is a code with no key. That, of course, is the secret of this society's stability: define a boundary, whether around your property, your theology, your constitution or anything else, and you have something that can be disputed. Keep it unspoken, and conflicts can be tactfully evaded. You can't gainsay the unsaid.

In the case of St Paul's, there are few clues: no little spire above the crossing which would reliably – but not infallibly – denote an Anglo-Catholic church; no shouty orange posters which would be a pretty clear sign of an evangelical one. This is a pleasant redbrick Victorian structure in Perpendicular style, rather like a smaller and more modern version of Great St Mary's in the Market Square. You could pass it without a second glance unless you knew that, while it was still being built to bring religion to the rapidly expanding population of what was then known as New Town, it was the object of a celebrated architectural dispute when it fell foul of the self-appointed architectural taste arbiters of Victorian England, the Cambridge Camden Society.

This group, hugely influential in its day, were vestment-clad vigilantes: single-issue, highly-motivated, unafraid of confrontation and impossible to embarrass. They achieved their main aim within a couple of decades of pugnacious campaigning. Formed initially by Cambridge undergraduates, and soon counting hundreds of clerics and many bishops among its membership, The Camden Society had as its goal nothing less than the transformation of the architecture of the Church of England. It succeeded.

For these coped crusaders, the way forward was the way back. The C of E needed to be brought back to basics, which meant the aesthetic standards of the recently-formed ritualist movement within the Church, variously known as the Tractarians, the High Church, the Oxford Movement or the Anglo-Catholics. They sought to revive the worship and architecture of the pre-Reformation days. Copying the architecture of an earlier, more faithful, age would revive that very faith. Belief would follow building style. Piety could be summoned by planning. Doubt could be designed out.

Achieving those standards, whether by 'restoring' existing churches or influencing the design of new ones, involved keeping strictly to a checklist of the features of the revived Gothic medievalism which was the Society's house style. With the zeal of the committed, and unafraid of – indeed, positively relishing – the controversy attendant on precise definitions, they proceeded to define, delineate and to damn. And when they found any deviation, they went after it like avenging angels. As St Paul's found out.

When it took St Paul's to task, the Society's journal, *The Ecclesiologist*, was still in its infancy. But it was very much an *enfant terrible*. In its very first edition, in November 1841, in the first of what were to be a thousand reviews over its twenty-year lifespan, an article unsparingly castigated the design of St Paul's. The church's design was 'quite indefensible, even on the count of cheapness.' It listed St Paul's catalogue of architectural sins, which might not today be obvious to the uninitiated:

> ...the huge clock; the disproportionate octagonal Turrets; the great four-centered Belfry windows without cusping or mouldings; the figures 1841 in the spandrils of the clock; the square clerestory-windows; the enormous windows in the Aisles; the mullions made to stand on the same plane as the wall; the square

heads; the want of foliation; the jambs without mouldings; the graduated parapet of the Nave; the thin mullions and tracery of the east window, the difference between the supports of the western and the other galleries; the startling contrast of the red brick and the white quoins of dressed ashlar ; the trellis-work of black bricks; and many other things which time forbids us to notice.[4]

Obscure though they may seem to most modern eyes, these shortcomings drove the reviewer to a peak of righteous indignation. Where the church was decorated, it should have been plain; where it was plain, it should – of course – have been decorated; where its proportions were large, they should have been small, and every vice should seemingly have been versa. If this was what a return to the age of faith looked like, the builders of St Paul's might have regretted ever bothering. Stung, they protested, and the next edition of *The Ecclesiologist* published part of a 'Remonstrance' in which prominent citizens took issue with the reviewer. The journal, however, also published a much longer defence of the review which conceded no substantive points, though it did manage to express "regret that it was written in a bantering tone". Who knew that the defence 'it's just banter' had such an illustrious history?

Those disputes, when cusping could be controversial, now seem to belong to an age more distant from ours than the Victorians were distant from the Middle Ages. St Paul's – its main space now partly adapted as an all-purpose venue – now offers an extensive and blameless mix of activities: everything from silent prayer to salsa, and youth groups to yoga. Sportingly, its website recounts the Camden Society's 'searing' attack without rancour, noting mildly that: "The new church was a source of considerable embarrassment at the time." Ironically, the church's status as a onetime object of the opprobium of the Camden Society is given by Historic England as one of the reasons it is now Grade II listed. Give it long enough and hostilities become heritage.

Immediately behind the church is the former vicarage built in 1847 to a design by the great Victorian architect George Gilbert Scott. When this was being built during the height of the Gothic Revival, even the most farsighted could not have conceived the use to which it and its adjacent row of almshouses would be put just over a century and a half later, when they would house another committed, pioneering religious movement, albeit of a very different character. Since 2011, this has been the home of the

Cambridge Muslim College, founded by the Muslim Academic Trust[5] to promote the academic study of Islam in Britain. It runs diploma and B.A. courses approved by the Open University. It was the vision of Dr Timothy Winter, aka Abdul Hakim Murad, a longtime convert to Islam, and currently Director of Studies in Theology at Wolfson College, and the Shaykh Zayed Lecturer of Islamic Studies in the Faculty of Divinity at Cambridge University.

He's a regular contributor to BBC Radio Four's 'Thought for the Day', and it's part of his mission to ensure Islam in Britain isn't seen always through the lens of contemporary anxieties, but as part of a long and complex historical relationship. After all, Cambridge has a distinguished history in the world of Muslim scholarship: Abdullah Yusuf Ali[6], who graduated from John's in 1895, produced the best-known English translation of the Qur'an, while the most prominent Urdu poet of the Twentieth Century, Sir Muhammad Iqbal, graduated from Trinity in 1906.[7] Once, when Tim and I went out for a meal after I had given a lecture to the Muslim College and the Divinity Faculty[8], he kindly gave me a copy of one of his books which illustrate Britain's overlooked Islamic heritage; *Muslim Songs of the British Isles*, a compilation of Islamic songs, many dating to the early Twentieth Century and combining Muslim piety with English verse forms and traditional English and Celtic folk tunes.

More recently, his participation in a more contemporary musical project showed how even kindness can prove controversial when sensitivities are heightened. After the success of Pharrell Williams' catchy 2013 song 'Happy', whose viral video, viewed more than a billion times, showed people dancing around the streets of Los Angeles, some British Muslims decided to make their own tribute video to counteract the often dour portrayal of their religion in the U.K. Like the original, it showed smiling dancers miming to the lyrics, and it featured a celebrity cameo – in this case Abdul Hakim Murad, at whose unsmiling appearance the video screeches to a silent halt. After a long moment, he smilingly raises a cardboard sign with the words 'I'm Happy', and the music starts again. It was a nice riff on his reputation for seriousness, and the video was widely welcomed as a refreshing change from stereotypes. But not everyone was happy with Happy, or with dancing for that matter, or with what some of the dancers were wearing, or with the idea that Muslims had to prove anything to anyone. So Tim soon found himself having to explain the necessary compromises of cultural bridge-building to some of his more conservative co-religionists.

As with the Camden Society and its architectural antipathies, strong beliefs can cause sharp disagreements, even over apparent superficialities. But, for Christian and Muslim, whatever may be the storms on the surface, the real tide of faith has always moved according to its own deep motion. Christianity, and its controversies, may have ebbed, but Islam is flowing ever more strongly. In Mill Road, on the site of the old Robert Sayle warehouse, stands Tim's most recent achievement: the new £23m, thousand-seater Cambridge Mosque, its golden dome rising above the surrounding terraces.

Designed by the Jewish architect David Marks, and decorated by the expert in sacred geometry Keith Critchlow, the building, opening on to Mill Road, is glass-fronted – a deliberate attempt to let light in upon the mysteries of an often-misunderstood faith.

After a brief inquiry at the gatehouse – "Sure, mate - go on in" – the visitor can stroll into the courtyard, where a solar-powered fountain is the centrepiece of an Islamic garden whose four corners represent the four sections of Jannah – The Muslim Paradise. Inside, after the main lobby, footwear has to be removed before you enter the actual prayer hall itself, where the ceiling above the vast, empty, light-filled, carpeted space is held up by sixteen slender tree-like pillars which spring up and spread out like the fan vaulting in King's College Chapel. Ayesha, my helpful guide, in hijab and hi-viz, explains that twelve of the columns represent the Twelve Imams of Shia Islam, while the remainder represent the Four Rightly-Guided Caliphs of Sunni Islam. No sectarianism here: the only book allowed is the Qu'ran, so that no-one's later interpretations of the holy text can become a point of contention. Along one side of the hall is the section reserved for women, the division marked by a latticed screen of varying height, to cater for the different levels of modesty with which the worshippers are comfortable.

Ayesha needs to help another visitor. She says I can stay as long as I like, so I take a seat – there are a few chairs, presumably for visitors or those unable to kneel – and I watch as the mid-morning spring sun pours through the golden dome and fills the space with light. Intricacies of sacred geometry and Islamic design are a closed book to me, and so is the Qu'ran; I have read it in Yusuf Ali's excellent translation, but that has only made me realise how little I know. But light I can understand. And silence. Yes, I can understand that all right. After a while, I make my way out. Opening the sound-proofed main doors, the roar of the Mill Road traffic resumes, mixed with the play of the Islamic fountain. Above me, I hear birdsong, and looking up, I see that, in the arms of one of the fan-vaulted pillars, a bird has already built a nest. I let myself out through the metal gate and look back at the dome outlined against the clouded sky. The Camden Society might not have approved of the architecture, but they might well have recognised the faith which inspired it, and which would build, in honour of eternity, a beautiful offering to time.

A little further on, in Cherry Hinton Road, the Cash for Clothes warehouse has a simple message on its banner advert: 'Bring your things inside. Thank you.' On the door, a sign says: 'Dear Customers! Temporary we don't buy books. Sorry.' There are a lot of signs advertising jobs in this street. Evening laundry shifts; bar staff; sales staff. Cambridge is statistically the easiest place in the United Kingdom to get work, with more jobs per jobseeker than anywhere else. Simple. Or should be. But many of the vacant jobs are low-wage, and the cost of living here is so high that those who would be prepared to work for that kind of money can't afford to live in the city.

A few minutes away, in Hartingdon Grove is a tiny building 'St Athanasius Greek School (Est. 1969)'. As I stop to take its picture, a heavy-looking guy with a cocker spaniel on a lead comes barrelling down the pavement. His teeshirt carries the familiar crown-and-slogan of the Keep Calm poster and its variants. This one could hardly be better timed – it says: 'I am Turkish and I can NOT KEEP CALM!' Finding myself standing outside the Greek school, a distant awareness of centuries of ethno-religious conflict flickers for a moment. But he passes without a glance.

Just around the corner is The Rock pub, aptly named, as it is where Syd Barrett reputedly used to drink. Though take that with a pinch of salt. From 1971 until his death in 2006, he was, after all, a recluse. Local legend says the pub's name derives from the nickname for Alcatraz island, because its late-night lock-ins are impossible to escape from. Take that with a pinch of salt too. A hundred yards down the street, next to the Betfred bookies, is the turning to St Margaret's Square, where Barrett spent his final years painting, tinkering with endless DIY projects – he was touchingly hopeless at both – and avoiding the occasional determined fan who got through the protective cordon of polite evasion and deliberate misdirection[9] with which the residents guarded their strange and vulnerable neighbour.

Number six is well-chosen for a recluse: at the end of a cul-de-sac hidden away in a maze of identical-looking streets. After Barrett's death, the house and its contents were sold; the former attracting many more viewers than would be normal for a nondescript semi, and the latter going at auction for much more than would have been warranted by their artistic – or their DIY – quality. According to all reports, the house's eventual buyers knew nothing about Syd Barrett. I don't intend to bother them. But on closer inspection, I find that the house is, in fact, empty. There's a To Let sign. Taking the path trodden by many Floyd fans over the years, but this time knowing there will be no answer, I walk up the path, and look in through the curtainless window. Stripped floors. Empty shelves. Nothing to see here. Like its former owner, the shell is still there, but the life has gone.

## CAMBRIDGE FOLK FESTIVAL

As I arrive at the car park at Netherhall School, and wind down my window to speak to the steward, I realise my car radio is, as always, tuned to Classic FM. Not very folk-festival. I wonder if I should turn it off. But I decide to leave it on: I should be true to myself. Although folk music was part of the culture back home, and although I can I recall, as a child, going to sleep listening to Radio Two's *Folk Weave* on a tinny transistor radio, I'm not going to pretend I'm a lifelong folkie.

For the same reason, I've resisted any sense of obligation to dress for the occasion; instead of what I imagine must be the obligatory folk-festival waistcoat. I have a charity shop blazer, which seems just the thing for a day like today, sunny but with a bit of a breeze. In my bag, however, I do have an emergency waistcoat, like when you might put a tie in your pocket when visiting a posh restaurant, just in case.

When I get to the festival site, which surrounds Cherry Hinton Hall, it turns out there *is* a dress code, at least an unofficial one. But not waistcoats. Hats. Squashed felt ones; pointy ones like pixies'; black ones like witches'; peaked ones like sea captains'; pork pies; baker boys'; even the odd Panama. But for the serious folkie, the aspirational choice seems to be a top hat garlanded with flowers, or steampunk style, with goggles.

The Cambridge Folk Festival began in 1965, as the vision of a group of socialist activists and folk musicians seeking to put Cambridge on the sixties counter-cultural map. It's now a fixture in the festival calendar, hosting the likes of Paul Simon, Joan Baez, Christy Moore, Imelda May, K.T. Tunstall, Joan Armatrading, The Proclaimers, Sinead O'Connor, Ladysmith Black Mambazo, k.d. lang and Van Morrison, and attracting thousands to Cherry Hinton for a long weekend every July. This year, the line-up includes Jake Bugg, Loudon Wainwright III, Martin Simpson, Oysterband, Sharon Shannon, and the folk movement's grande dame, Shirley Collins.

I've come here to meet John Holder, a veteran of those earliest days. When the organisers of that first festival needed poster artwork, they turned to John, a talented bluegrass guitarist then making a name for himself as a freelance illustrator in Fleet Street. So from that first festival, and for the next thirty years, he gave the event its distinctive visual identity. And after more than half a century, he's still a regular, running drawing workshops there with fellow artist Jim Butler. I've called in to see them at work.

John picked up his love of bluegrass from the American servicemen stationed on US airbases in his native Suffolk, who would play songs from their homeland in the local pubs. And he learned his artist's craft at Cambridge Art School in the early sixties at the same time as the future members of Pink Floyd, and along with Paul Hogarth, who illustrated the covers of Graham Greene's Penguin books, and with his lifelong friends the caricaturists Roger Law and Peter Fluck, who later found fame with the satirical puppet series *Spitting Image*. As well as his work for Sunday supplements and for advertisers – he made enough money from the artwork for Phileas Fogg crisps to pay off his mortgage – he has illustrated several series of works for the Folio Society, as well as providing *Country Life* with the images familiar to many a manor house coffee table.

I find John's drawing workshop is already well underway. In the roped-off enclosure outside his tent, he has a full house of a dozen students of all ages. He and Jim are teaching them how to draw ... hats.

Jim sketches as he talks: "The thing with hats is ..." A fedora takes shape beneath his hands in a few charcoal strokes. "...I have learned that ... being worn by people ... they move ... they don't keep still." The hat is complete: shape, shadows, creases. Incredible. Could I do that? I am about to learn the secret of how to draw moving hats, when a band starts up in the nearby marquee, and the talk is drowned in jangling guitars and earnest, breathy male vocals. My grasp of the essentials of hatography is now a patchwork of snatches of advice audible between the music: "... patience ... it might be that he moves round again ... if you find he wanders off, it's not the end of the world ... the side of his head ... it took me an hour and a quarter to draw John's hat ... that patience is really really important." He's not joking: he's not shown a flicker of disturbance at being drowned by the neighbouring sound system. Now it's changed to breathy female vocals, intent and sincere, over a bed of wailing guitars.

There's live music on the Den stage now, real old finger-in-the-ear fol-de-rol stuff. The singer is closing his set by getting the audience to sing along with a chorus: "Say hey for the cheese of old England! In old Ing-er-land very hard cheeeeese". Or *trying* to get them to sing along. There's no response, and I don't blame them – it's as stale as last year's Wensleydale. "I hate this kind of music," mutters John.

He has a much better idea. Worry Dolls: a young band who were formed at Sir Paul McCartney's music school in Liverpool and are now big on the American circuit. John spotted them at a gig and suggested them to the festival organisers. They agreed. As it happens, I'd spotted their name in the line-up too, and it had intrigued me. Today, they're on the main stage and John wants to say hello. He has an access-all-areas pass, and thinks its magic might somehow get me in too, like an invisibility cloak. He suggests we try to blag our way backstage to meet them before they start their set. This is the most daring thing I have *ever* done. What is happening to me?

Actually, of course, it's all just about confidence. Not appearing suspicious. Not even feeling guilty. Looking like you have a right to be there.

As we head round behind the main stage, there are two girls on duty at the gate, young enough to be my daughters, or John's granddaughters. They're entirely immersed in their mobile phones and don't even look up as we breeze past.

We're in.

We're not.

One of them looks up briefly. "Pass?" she says. "He's with me," says John. "Yeah," she says. "He needs a pass," and looks back at her phone again. Busted.

I watch the gig from the main arena. Worry Dolls turn out to be two young women in floppy felt hats; they're backed by bearded guys in checked shirts playing double bass and keyboard. Briefly, between the hats, I glimpse a girl on drums. They're good: bluegrass-influenced Americana, with harmonica, guitar and banjo.

I notice the remote-controlled TV cameras swinging over the arena. The festival's being filmed for Sky and BBC Four. I'm sure I see the lenses swivel in my direction. It's this blasted blazer. A rookie mistake. I used to run camera crews for the BBC. I should have remembered: camera operators search for the anomalous. In a crowd of conventionally-dressed people, it will be the guy with a top hat with flowers round the brim. In a crowd of people in top hats with flowers round the brim, it will be the guy in a blazer. I'm a marked man.

I know the danger of being overdressed. Once, taking part in the 2002 Berlin *PoesieFestival*, and on my way to a reading in Potsdamer Platz by the Beat poet, Lawrence Ferlinghetti, I found myself walking through the Christopher Street Parade, the city's enormous all-day gay pride march. Later, I found that my plain black suit had stood out so much that CNN had featured a long lingering tracking shot of me on their TV coverage. My fellow poets, watching it in their hotel lobby while waiting for a taxi, thought I had come *out*.

So, while not wanting to claim a status to which I have no right, and while also trying not to appear homophobic, I then had to somehow get myself back *in*. So, no, I don't want to attract any cameras today. I find the biggest top-hatted guy nearby – there are plenty to choose from – and shuffle into his shadow. Now, cameras, do your worst. You'll have to settle for a shot of the man in a painted frock-coat. And how square would that be?

Sheltered by the big guy, I can relax and take a look around. There's a faint tang of beer in the air. A zing of cider. A faint whiff of what might be marijuana. One chap has a teeshirt with 'Trust Me I'm a Jedi' on the front. Another has 'I may be old, but at least I got to see all the good bands.' Two others, inexplicably, have matching teeshirts, one with '...Penelope Keith', the other with '...Felicity Kendall': some kind of in-joke for people old enough to remember *The Good Life*. Which is a large proportion of the crowd. That said, though, there are young people too. One of the teenagers in front of me is wearing one of those hoodies with the names of school leavers on the back. What kind of school, I wonder? I look at the names: Daisy; Olivia; Ralph; Caro; Cosmo; Ludo; Hugo; George; Alexander; Jasper; Chloe; Barnaby; Lola; Maia; Xavier. Ah. *That* kind of school.

Worry Dolls' set is over, and I make my way out, picking my way between the audience, who are reclining in deckchairs or on picnic rugs. All is courtesy and good cheer. There's zero litter. And no drunkenness that I can see, though there's plenty of beer. One guy is drinking hands-free, with a pitcher of ale secured round his neck on a cord. John tells me there's scarcely ever any trouble. Last year a security guard had to ask a guy to put out a joint. That was about it. It's impressive. As I pass the Friends of the Earth tent, I am seized with a visceral impulse. I will help save this planet, this green arcadia where children of nature walk barefoot on the good earth and wear its gift of flowers in their hair. And on their hats.

The impulse is short-lived. I'm old enough now to know that the cravings of the recovering idealist, like those of the recovering addict, will pass. They seize you, like the hand of the Ancient Mariner, but their grip has no endurance. Resist them, wait them out, and in ten minutes the grasp will slacken and you can shake yourself loose and go, sadder and wiser, uncommitted, untainted, and unsaved.

I have a couple of pints with Jim and John in the beer tent. Afterwards, I take a look round the merchandise stalls. A bearded guy is being fitted with an alpaca-wool poncho, the attendant smoothing it down, viewing it from different angles. How can you be *fitted* for a poncho? There's a musical instrument stall. I stop to browse, flicking through books of music I can't read. There's a stack of Irish bodhran hand-drums, placed one on top of the other in ever-smaller tiers, like a sonic wedding cake. After that second pint of Milton Nero Stout, an Irish bodhran drum is starting to look like a seriously sound investment. In a corner of the bar, a jamming session is in full swing with a kid aged about twelve giving it the whole riddly-diddly thing, and it's going down like a storm in Galway Bay. These bodhrans come with a DVD and instructional booklet too. How hard can it be? I picture myself in the warmth of my local on folk night, thrumming away in the background, with an air of deep concentration, fiddles swaying on one side, mandolin jangling on the other. The Milton Nero Stout has lowered my defences; I find myself feeling for my wallet.

Passion and parsimony are at war within me. Parsimony wins. As with the impulse to become an eco-warrior a few minutes ago, this craving too will pass. I force myself to step outside, where a young woman is fitting her baby with a red top hat. Starting him young. The fresh air has cleared my head, and already the bodhran is fading into a Celtic twilight of memory.

I decide to take a seat to do some people-watching. Better than that. I can do some people-*drawing*. Inspired by what I've learned from John and Jim, I take out my notebook, which has now become an artist's sketchbook. What to draw? After sitting in on the tutorial, I find myself wanting to stare at people's hats. Fearful of attracting suspicion, I take to stealing surreptitious glances at them. I fear I must look like a hat fetishist, if there is such a thing.[10] Jim was right, though, real people do move around a lot. I'm not going to have much joy trying to sketch their headgear. I need a more static subject. In the centre of the arena is a giant willow sculpture of an anthropomorphic badger. It must be twenty feet high. It's standing on its hind legs with its arm raised in greeting. Or is it in warning? Either way, at least it won't move. I sketch it. It doesn't look very realistic. I decide to sketch some of the festival-goers instead. They come out looking like badgers too. Though perhaps this is just my personal artistic vision, Like Dali's clocks, or Lowry's stick men. A signature style; a leitmotif. This is why I shouldn't go to festivals. I'm just too impressionable. But that's also what's great about the Cambridge Folk Festival, like all events of its kind: for a few days you can imagine how good things could be. For a few hours, the world is made right. Then you rejoin reality. I make my way back to the car, start up the ignition, and turn on Classic FM.

# ADDENBROOKES

Towards the end of Hills Road, terraces give way to detached homes, town houses yield to villas; gardens spread, the tree-cover expands, incomes and house prices rise. And that, in recent years, has become a problem. These expansive – and expensive – plots of Arts-and-Craft houses which seem to be an unchanging part of classic English suburbia are in fact a fragile, threatened environment. As always, it all comes down to money. In a city where house prices are rising faster than anywhere else in the country, those sprawling Edwardian homes with their red-tiled flared roofs and their graceful mullioned bay windows, those generous rambling gardens with their mature trees and plantings, are just so much wasted space. The answer? Buy the house, demolish it and whack a high-density apartment block on the site. Sell the units, bank the huge mark-up. Repeat.

The thing is, pleasing though those early twentieth-century buildings may be, and much as they form a unified streetscape here in Queen Edith's ward, much as they embody a century of the city's history, they're not actually listed buildings. If a developer wants to buy them and knock them down, there's pretty much nothing to stop them. But some people are willing to try. Outside York House, 292 Hills Road, one of the area's most beautiful buildings, built in 1924 to a design attributed to Edwin Landseer Lutyens, a protest

has gathered; its members wear suits and ties, and have flowers in their buttonholes. These residents, appalled by the destruction of Queen Edith's heritage, are fighting the demolitions case by case, house by house. Speeches are made through megaphones. Yellow ribbons are attached to the gate, along with a bitterly ironic sign saying RIP.

A few yards away, the bulky expanse of Addenbrooke's Hospital shows how aesthetics so often lose out to more powerful considerations: commercialism in the case of the threatened houses of Queen Edith's; utilitarianism in the case of the hospital. Addenbrookes Hospital was originally founded in 1766 near the Fitzwilliam Museum and named for Dr John Addenbrooke whose legacy funded its establishment. In 1976 it moved to Hills Road. But the new complex did not meet with universal approval. In his 1978 book, *A Portrait of Cambridge*, the historian and former Senior Proctor of the University, C.R. Benstead, remarked that when viewing the new buildings "one's glance may linger in pained astonishment."[11] Forty years later, however, familiarity has bred acceptance. And four decades of a world-leading reputation as a pioneering centre for life-saving transplant operations surely buys the right to have any aesthetic shortcomings overlooked. When it comes to doctoring, it's the cure that counts, not the costume.

On the perimeter of the site is a no-smoking sign which you cannot help but suspect is the latest in a series, which have moved from request to command with increasing exasperation. 'You cannot smoke anywhere.' So there. A staff member, unlit fag in hand, trudges past it to towards the site boundary, and legality. The whole site is a tangle of bike racks and vehicle ramps. Parking is at a premium. Bikes are shackled to every available post and rail. The main entrance is reached via a bright corporate lobby. On the wall are pictures of smiling commended employees and aspirational statements: mission, purpose, way, values, vision. A short distance along the corridor, the clinical quickly gives way to the commercial: gift shops, clothes shops, W.H. Smiths, Costa Coffee, M&S Food, and a full-scale food court with Starbucks and Burger King. It's half past five, and the court is filling up. So are many of the visitors, as they carry full bags of quarterpounders back to the wobbly plastic tables. I recall the comment of the Cambridge computer scientist, don and history blogger Chris Hadley:

> The saddest sight I have ever seen, which moved me to tears then and now in recollection, was a poor translucent little girl, desperately ill, staring at the "Happy Meal" her exhausted and broken parents had just bought her.

Since reading that, every time I hear the words Happy Meal, I feel sad. Sometimes happiness is the saddest thing of all.

The television is showing the quiz show *Impossible*. On one of the tables, a young woman in tartan pyjamas and fluffy slippers is sharing a coffee with what could be her sister. On another table, a grey-haired medic in scrubs, who looks like he's just come from a hard day in theatre, is talking with a keen young Asian doc. A few tables away, what looks very much like a doctor-nurse romance is reaching a critical stage: their hands, both holding mobiles, are almost, *almost* touching. There are no words. Then his pager goes. After he vanishes down the corridor, she continues looking in that direction, lost in thought; her hands on the fake woodgrain laminate haven't moved. On the wall is a sun-faded picture of King's College Chapel and an advert for a solicitors. On the nearby table an old guy in cream slacks and check shirt checks his watch for the twentieth time: late on in life, time is suddenly going very slow.

On the wall in the main concourse is a display board on which staff have stuck post-it notes with their personal pledges to celebrate the NHS' 70th birthday.

To give blood regularly.

Get my uke band to play for patients. Rocking Ukes of Ely.

To ensure as many of my departmental colleagues as possible know where to find relevant documents.

Spread joy in the Rosie.

I pledge to give blood soon.

I pledge to continue as a nurse until I am 70. I am 60.

I will try my best to be a better manager on a daily basis.

I pledge to uphold safe kind and excellent care as a scrub practitioner.

To give back as much as I've gained

Let's invest in what's really needed and allow all staff to do their jobs the best way they can each and every day. And eat cake.

To get my partner to give blood. (I will when I can again).

Try and give more blood.

## THE GOG MAGOG HILLS

The term East Anglian Heights is something of a misnomer. You scarcely need to change gear coming up the A1307 Babraham Road from London, and at three hundred feet at the summit, this low chalk down isn't exactly oxygen mask territory. But these things are relative, and despite their modest altitude, you'd have to travel thousands of miles to the Ural mountains, to find higher ground eastwards. As you reach the top of the Gog Magog Hills, you have a sweeping view down into Cambridge, with the bulk of Addenbrookes Hospital in the foreground, and the clusters of tower cranes showing how much this city on the plain is changing.

The Gog Magogs take their name from Geoffrey of Monmouth's often fanciful twelfth-century *History of the Kings of Britain*, where the giant Gogmagog is said to have been killed by Corineus, one of a party of survivors of the destruction of Troy, who, led by Brutus of Troy[12], had travelled around Europe before settling in Britain. Foundation myths were a big deal in the medieval period. Claims of ancient prestige helped justify contemporary power disputes; patriotism was boosted by patrimony. In the Twelfth Century, the entirely spurious idea that Britain had been founded by the hardy survivors of the greatest tale of antiquity, the *Iliad*, was potent propaganda for an expanding European power. As a spur to pride or action, a tale doesn't need to be true.

This ridge, whose best-known feature is the Iron Age hillfort on the summit of Wandlebury Hill, has attracted more than its fair share of fantasy. As early as 1212, the author Gervase of Tilbury in his *Otia Imperiala*, a 'Book of Marvels', referred to "a very ancient legend ... preserved in popular tradition" about the hillfort at 'Wandlebria', where, if a challenger entered the innermost ring at dead of night in moonlight and called out "Knight to Knight! Show yourself", a spectral knight would engage him in combat. Eventually, Sir Osbert Fitzhugh defeated the spectre, suffering, in the process, a wound that would open on the anniversary of the contest every year. He brought the knight's black horse to Cambridge Castle, though it escaped at cock-crow the next morning.[13] In 1932, the 'discoverer' of ley lines, Alfred Watkins[14], believed he had found two of his mysterious straight tracks running through its centre. In 1981, the hills, and the giant, featured briefly in the unforgettable – and unintelligible – three-hour BBC TV supernatural drama *Artemis 81.*[15] In 1991, a Dutch author, Iman Wilkens, even transported the entire history of the Siege of Troy to this site.[16] But it's probably the work of Thomas Charles 'T.C.' Lethbridge[17] that is the best-known piece of speculative history connected with this gentle tree-fringed ridge.

Lethbridge was one of those people cursed with private means and thereby freed from the constraints of common sense. Soon after coming up to Trinity from the family home in Somerset, he was taking part in Arctic expeditions. After college, veering into archaeology, he took up the honorary, but distinguished-sounding, post of Keeper of Anglo-Saxon Antiquities at the Cambridge University Museum of Archaeology and Ethnology. He also self-published his archaeological and historical ruminations, bypassing the harder, but ultimately surer, road of peer-review and institutional guidance. Instinct and belief were his guides; evidence was made to fit. During the Second World War, he decided he'd discovered a secret signalling system used by spies and composed of scraps of ephemera left in public places. His apparent academic respectability, and his evident sincerity, meant the authorities took his claims seriously. Guards on some of the military locations he identified were strengthened.

So when, by the 1950s he found scattered references to an ancient chalk figure having once been visible within the rings of Wandlebury Camp, a former earthwork of the Iceni tribe, he decided he would rediscover it. The few written sources were inconclusive, and the site had later largely been effaced in the Eighteenth Century by the building of Lord Godolphin's house and garden, of which only the stables now remain. But Tom Lethbridge wasn't going to let that stop him. Using the unorthodox and unreliable method of exploring with a sounding bar – a metal rod driven into the ground – he probed for areas of chalk softer than others, believing they were the now-filled-in trenches which had once formed the figure's outline. Gradually, round-eyed Celtic-looking figures emerged, with shield, sword and chariot. Lethbridge, triumphant, summoned the press, who were curious but sceptical. The archaeological establishment were dismissive, believing he had simply identified natural geological features, plough-marks and water-gullies; Lethbridge rejected their criticism as narrow-minded 'trade union' exclusivity towards an independent scholar. He resigned from the Museum in 1957, moving to Devon where he pursued ever more esoteric interests in ghosts, earth mysteries and extra-terrestrials. There, he could publish his speculations untroubled by academic scrutiny,[18] and he lived out his last decades ignored by the centre but acclaimed by the fringe.

This area has always attracted free spirits. In 1966, a group of students went to a secluded spot on the lower slopes of the ridge to experiment with magic mushrooms.[19] That wasn't in itself unusual then, or now for that matter.[20] What made this particular occasion notable was that one of the group was the twenty-year-old Syd Barrett, and another was a student film-maker from Cambridge, Nigel Lesmoir-Gordon, later a distinguished documentary-maker, but in 1966 just a kid with an 8mm cine camera and some time to kill. The five minutes of footage he shot became a legendary short film, 'Syd Barrett's First Trip', a disjointed sequence in which Syd, in pursuit of whatever hallucinatory scenario was unfolding behind his dark eyes, clambers determinedly over the rocks, stares with rapt attention at single leaves and at his hands and then strides across the ridge swinging his jacket defiantly. It has to be said, a trip like that is probably more entertaining for the experiencer than the observer, but hindsight means these shaky images, full of jump-cuts and camera flare, have a special poignancy, a past haunted by what we know the future was to bring.

I have come to Wandlebury Hill with Andrew Brown, who has photographed and blogged about the landscapes and the hidden pathways of Cambridge for years. He's the minister of the Cambridge Unitarian Church,[21] and finding offbeat paths has been something of a career for him. He was a professional jazz double bassist for years, and worked with Steve Harley of Cockney Rebel, until, tired of life on the road, he declined to play for an overseas tour and was sacked.

Jazz is still very much part of his life, though, and when I visited his church one Sunday morning, a pianist was playing pre-service improvisations. I've been to a few Unitarian churches, and to similar liberal congregations here and in the States, and jazz is pretty much the soundtrack of choice. Perhaps it's the freedom: the musicians unconstrained by the score, wandering in and out of the written directions as the feeling takes them; the minister free to dip in and out of the scriptures, riffing on what inspires him, skipping what doesn't. Andrew, presiding, retro-cool in tweed jacket and knitted waistcoat, moved seamlessly between pulpit and double bass. His sermon, or 'address' as they call it here, set out what he described as "a minimalist, religiously naturalistic way of being in the world ... an atheistic mysticism, free of mythical trappings ... but one still full of poetry and befitting reveries" Afterwards, he offered his microphone to the congregation for comment, rebuttal or question. A risky manoeuvre. I've seen this go badly wrong, and I braced myself for ramblings about UFOs, conspiracies, and misbehaving ex-husbands. But I needn't have worried. The questions were concise, thoughtful, insightful, and Andrew's answers honest and imaginative. There was so little belief in the supernatural that I could hardly say it strengthened my faith in God. But it certainly strengthened my belief in human beings.

Andrew may not be big on the supernatural, but as a philosopher and political activist, committed to peace and justice movements and refugee campaigns, he's surprisingly big on hauntings. He subscribes to the French philosopher Jacques Derrida's[22] theory of 'hauntology', which was developed in Britain by the theorist and music commentator Mark Fisher, also known as K-Punk, who, after a struggle against mental illness, took his own life in 2017 at the age of 48. It's the study of how the real (and imagined) past, and the real (and imagined) future affect our perceptions of the present, 'haunting' it with ghostly memories and unfulfilled futures. At a fairly superficial cultural level, this can mean something as simple as a preoccupation with reminiscence and retro aesthetics which distracts you from the present moment's responsibilities and opportunities; more deeply, it can be an aching sense of grief for futures that will never happen, most often the visions of utopian social justice which the apparent universal triumph of neo-liberal capitalism seems to have rendered permanently unviable.

At the top of the rise, we pause by a huge, bare-branched ash tree to take in the view. This place, says Andrew, is what inspired M.R. James to write a story like 'A View from a Hill,' in which an English antiquarian borrows some mysterious binoculars and finds himself able to see beyond the pastoral present to a disturbingly violent past, where a distant hill is crowned not with greenery, but with a gallows. It reminds Andrew of the travel writer Robert McFarlane's 2015 *Guardian* article, inspired by the 90th anniversary of that story, which claimed an insurrectionary subculture in the worlds of music, poetry and academia was using the gothic, the eerie and the occult to express the anti-pastoral anger of those who believe themselves marginalised by the kind of bucolic idyll marketed by capitalism.[23] Ghosts against greed. Wraiths against the machine.

At the cobwebbed base of the ash tree, there are the remains of tea lights, incense sticks, and carefully-arranged collections of snail-shells, twigs, leaves, stones and feathers. "Votive offerings," Andrew says. "Neo-pagans. There's a lot of kids taking it up now. Once I even came across an upside-down pentagram carved on a tree – which doesn't do it a lot of good." There's an understandable desperate desire to belong to something other than the shallow dominant culture, he says. Though, ironically, neo-pagan fashion has become just one more niche market for marketers to sell the kids things they don't need.

We make a circuit of the hillfort, at one point following the Roman road that cuts past the site. We're going counter-clockwise. The impulse to question, to subvert and disrupt is a sound one, but carries its own dangers, Andrew says. While capitalism's shortcomings are only too apparent, the Left can in its own way be as exclusionary as the Right, and, as a man of the Left, Andrew feels that modern left-wing thought, though long divorced from religious allegiance, has nonetheless inherited some of the less attractive aspects of the puritanism which is its ancestor: the emphasis on purity of belief; the proud signalling of personal virtue; the unhesitating, merciless condemnation of the transgressor; the intrusive assumption of jurisdiction over other people's thoughts; the preachy hectoring of the unconverted; the pursuing of ever smaller offences with ever greater zeal. It's particularly marked, he feels, in Cambridge, the cradle of the English Reformation, a city which, during the Civil War, was a stronghold of Parliament and the Puritans,[24] while Oxford, by contrast, was the Royalist capital. Undeviating liberal rectitude drives across the complexities of the intellectual landscape as starkly as any Roman road.

We have stopped at one of the memorial benches that seem to be the way people choose to commemorate their departed loved ones these days. The forest floor is a carpet of snowdrops. Above, in the clear January sky, two hawks are circling, like Yeats's falcon in its widening gyre. Things fall apart. The centre cannot hold.[25] A third hawk joins them. Andrew is concerned for the future of our modern, wealthy social democracies. As far as he's concerned, they cannot hold either. He's long been supportive of the work of The Dark Mountain Project, a network of writers, artists and thinkers "who have stopped believing the stories our civilisation tells itself." One story they have stopped believing is that environmentalism alone can avert ecological disaster. It can't, they say. There's going to be an age of ecological collapse, material contraction and social and political unravelling. Better to realise this than deny it. That way, you can prepare for, and contribute to, the future that will be, not the one you would like to have been. That dark future would be haunted by the ghost of the brighter future we had hoped for. "It's pessimistic to some extent," Andrew says. "But hopeful." Above, in the cloudless sky, the hawks now number five.

## GREAT SHELFORD, CAMBRIDGE SPIES

Cambridge has long had a connection with espionage. All those clever people. All those connections. All that idealism. The poet Thomas Wyatt[26] was an early example. Educated at St John's College, he was prominent in the court of Henry VIII, and was an overseas 'ambassador' during Henry's divorce and his break with Rome.[27] Francis Walsingham, Elizabeth I's spymaster, was another; he was at King's. Her magician John Dee, at John's, was another.

Then there was the playwright, poet and translator Christopher Marlowe.[28] It's believed that while he was still a student at Corpus Christi, he had already been recruited as a spy, as his college records show unexplained – and mysteriously unpunished – absences, together with a sudden increase in his spending power. Tellingly, when his qualification for his Masters degree was questioned because of his absences, the Privy Council itself intervened on his behalf due to the services he had rendered to Queen and country – hardly your average student truancy. The remaining years of his short life, as the most prominent dramatic tragedian of his age, were punctuated by mysterious gaps which later commentators have filled with a huge variety of theories. His untimely demise – stabbed to death in disreputable company in a house in Deptford – is attributed to everything from his being a secret Catholic, to his being a not-so-secret atheist, to gambling, a love triangle, or blackmail. You name it. Inevitably, there are also those who believe his death was faked and that he went on to join the repertory company of people who really wrote the plays of his contemporary William Shakespeare.

One thing that everyone agrees on, though, is that whatever spying Wyatt and Marlowe were engaged in, they were doing it for their own country. By contrast, the Cambridge Spies of the twentieth-century had very different ideas: they betrayed their own country to a hostile power. There was, however, a common factor between the Elizabethan spies and the 20th Century ones: a background of intense, existential ideological conflict. For the Cambridge Spies, Donald Maclean, Guy Burgess, 'Kim' Philby, John Cairncross and Anthony Blunt, it was Communism versus capitalism. For Marlowe, Walsingham and Wyatt, it was Protestantism versus Catholicism. As Ben Macintyre, in his 2014 book *A Spy Among Friends*, puts it:[29] "The violent ideological currents sweeping Cambridge in the 1930s had created a vortex which quickly swept up Philby and many other clever, angry, alienated young men." With Fascism growing in Europe it seemed that only Communism could oppose it. "Late at night, over copious drinks, in panelled rooms, students argued, debated, tried on one ideological outfit or another, and, in a small handful of cases, embraced violent revolution."

Outwardly, these young men were typical of their patrician class: highly educated, urbane, cultured, well-connected, confident, and as English as a cricket match. Inwardly, they had given themselves, heart and soul to the Soviet Union, and were dedicated to the defeat of the country of whose culture they seemed to be so reassuringly typical. It was the perfect disguise for the decades of deception that were to follow, as they reached ever higher positions in the British establishment: Burgess and Philby in MI6; Maclean in the Foreign Office; Blunt in MI5 and Cairncross in Bletchley Park. The Soviet intelligence agency could hardly believe its luck. Hundreds of agents and anti-communist activists died because of their actions, many after brutal torture. Only the paranoid suspicions of Joseph Stalin that the whole thing was an elaborate trap stopped its effect being even more devastating. English society had been subverted through what, in that age of deference, it had regarded as its especial strengths: restraint, honour, good manners, breeding. English gentlemen didn't doubt other English gentlemen. The Russians had weaponised snobbery.

In the final words of his introduction to his 1968 memoir, *My Secret War*, Philby remarks of his recruitment to Soviet intelligence; "One does not look twice at an offer of enrolment in an elite force." Doesn't one? Ben Macintyre comments on the attraction of elitism: "In some ways, Philby's story is that of a man in pursuit of ever more exclusive clubs." In a lecture in 1944, C.S. Lewis described the fatal British obsession with the 'inner ring', the belief that somewhere, just beyond reach, is an exclusive group holding real power and influence, which a certain sort of Englishman constantly aspires to find and join. Westminster School and Cambridge University are elite clubs; MI6 is an even more exclusive fellowship; working secretly for the NKVD within MI6 placed Philby in an elite club of one. "Of all the passions," wrote Lewis, "the passion for the Inner Ring is most skilful in making a man who is not yet a very bad man do very bad things."[30]

It certainly made Philby and his circle do very bad things. Though they were, of course, very good spies. The same, however, cannot be said for another espionage agent with a Cambridge connection – a spy whose career did not start in Cambridge, but which ended here.

With a name like Engelbertus Fukken, it's easy to understand the appeal of a change of identity. In 1940, when this young Dutchman, a dedicated Nazi,[31] joined the intelligence service of the German forces which had conquered his own country, he changed his name to Jan Willem Ter Braak, and in a matter of months was parachuted into England with a radio transmitter, a pistol, a supply of cash, fake papers and a fake backstory about being a refugee from the Nazis.

He was to prepare the way for the forthcoming invasion, and, for bonus points, to assassinate Churchill. He stayed in three successive addresses in Cambridge: 58, St Barnabas Road, just off Mill Road; then in 4 Green Street in the city centre, and finally 11, Montague Road, Chesterton. He remained at large for five months, longer than any other German agent in wartime Britain. But his false documents were his undoing: supplied by a British double agent, they contained deliberate mistakes sure to trigger official suspicion.

By late March 1941, short of cash, and under suspicion, he arranged to be picked up by plane. It never came, and, in despair, he took himself to an air raid shelter under Christ's Pieces and shot himself. His body was found a few days later, and his radio transmitter was recovered from the left luggage at Cambridge railway station. At the time, it was thought unwise to let the public know a Nazi spy had been at large for nearly half a year, so Fukken was buried in an unmarked grave at Great Shelford, a few miles south of Cambridge. Documents about the case were declassified in 1999, finally solving for the Dutchman's own family the mystery of his wartime disappearance– although perhaps not quite in the way they would have wished. Nonetheless, they asked the parish council to let them erect a memorial plaque, with simple details, and his real name: 'Engelbertus Fukken – 28 VIII 1914 The Hague, 30/31 III 1941 Cambridge'. The council agreed. Victors can afford to be generous.

However, even generosity has its limits. Nearly a year after the announcement that the grave was to be marked, I visited Great Shelford parish cemetery, which is reached via a narrow track past allotments on the outskirts of the village. By a process of elimination and cross-referencing with the rusty date-ordered cast-iron grave-markers, I found the right plot. It was exactly where it should be: at the very point where death's progress through the village's population in the 1940s would have reached at that time. The next departed villagers were laid down next to him in their turn; each taking their place in line in good, obedient English queueing style. But the spy's grave is just an unmarked patch of daisy-strewn grass.

I'm not surprised. The fact that the spy's family could even ask for the grave to be marked says much for their expectation of English politeness, generosity and magnanimity. But the English have plenty of pragmatic common sense too. This man was not an honourable adversary: a downed airman, for instance, killed above the fields of Cambridgeshire, in fair fight, even if in unfair cause. The Nazis had conquered this man's country and yet he joined

their secret service, and then volunteered to pose as a refugee so that he could bring the same tyrany to Britain. If the villagers of Great Shelford have had second thoughts about their initial generous response, I can't say I blame them.

I make my way out through the lych gate. As I do so, I feel the almost imperceptible tension of the spiders' webs which have attached themselves to me silently during my search, like those tiny compacts with corruption that no-one ever knows you have made, least of all yourself.

## FLEAM DYKE

The threat of invasion is a primal one. Hospitality abused; purity violated; the familiar estranged. Those ideas trigger the deepest aversions. To avoid them, people will move heaven and earth. In the case of Fleam Dyke, built in the Dark Ages, they moved the earth.

Exactly which danger this giant barrier was intended to exclude is uncertain. But for it to have needed such immense resources to contain it, it must have been an existential threat. Fleam Dyke is one of a number of similar structures which run like raised scar tissue across the landscape of east Anglia. Devil's Dyke lies to the east of it, Brent Ditch and Bran Ditch to the west, all of them cutting across the Icknield Way, the prehistoric ridgeway, later a Roman

Road, which runs northeastwards for 110 miles along the chalk heights from Dorset to Suffolk, and which can be claimed, with some justification, to be the oldest road in Britain. Today, the A11 dual carriageway follows the same ancient route.

At this distance, the different historical periods can be as difficult to identify to the untutored eye as rock strata to the non-geologist. First there were our prehistoric ancestors, who created the ridgeway thousands of years ago. Then, by about 500 or 700 years B.C., the people, culture and language had become what we would now call Celtic, with the Catuvellauni as the dominant local tribe. Next came the Romans, whose conquest, beginning in 43 AD, imposed a Latin superstructure on the native population for some four and a half centuries. Then, as Rome's grip weakened, finally ending in 410 AD, the Romano-Celtic society found itself facing new invaders: the Angles and the Saxons. It is from this period that Fleam Dyke is believed to date, as a barrier between the expanding Anglo-Saxon territories to the east, and those still under native Celtic control to the west. It would have not just been a military border, but a linguistic one, with the population to the east speaking the Germanic ancestor of English, and those to the west a close relative of modern Welsh; it would have been a religious border too, with the Celts adhering to the Christianity they had adopted during Roman times, and the Anglo-Saxons not yet converted to the faith which

Augustine of Canterbury would bring to them in the late Sixth Century.

Gradually, over decades and centuries, village by village, valley by valley, the Saxons, as they now were, moved westwards, building more dykes to consolidate the territory they had gained, like land reclaimed from the fens. The Celts, or Britons as they thought of themselves, retreated before them, their island being taken from them acre by acre. However, there is evidence that some stayed behind in the conquered territories as the lowest kind of serfs, and that they remained a distinct linguistic group until at least the Eleventh Century. In around 1050, the Gild of the Thanes at 'Grantabrycge', the modern Cambridge, laid down in its regulations the kind of support this mutual aid society could be expected to provide to a fellow guildsman who found himself having to pay 'wergild' or compensation to the relatives of any man he had killed. It was all based on the victim's status. There was a sliding scale:

> If any of the gild slay a man, and he be an avenger by compulsion (*neadwraca*) and compensate for his violence, and the slain man be a *twelfhynde* man, let each of the gild give half a mark for his aid: if the slain man be a *ceorl*, two oras: if he be Welsh (*Wylisc*) one ora.[32]

The exchange rate for a Welshman to a thane (a *twelfhynde* man) was, therefore, four to one. Which, while far from ideal, was a better than the going rate in more recently-conquered Saxon-controlled lands further west, where Welsh serfs were more numerous, and where the rate could be as low as twelve to one. The one-ora serf in Grantabrycge could console himself with the thought that, the laws of supply and demand being what they are, he at least had some scarcity value.

The dyke runs roughly north-south for about four miles between the villages of Fulbourn and Balsham. Excavations show it consists of three layers dating from the Fifth, Sixth and Seventh Centuries; it may have been topped with a palisade. It's now a Site of Special Scientific Interest and a Scheduled Ancient Monument. Over the last forty years or so, the decline in sheep grazing had allowed scrub to take over, turning the dyke into just one more apparently unremarkable dark stroke across the landscape like a hedge or railway line. Now, a conservation project is gradually clearing away the vegetation, and the stark outline stands out across the fields again, an isolated man-made contour line.

For Andrew Brown, who is walking the dyke with me, this has long been a favourite haunt. He used to walk this exposed, elevated pathway between fen and sky for hours as he worked out his own response to his unexpected calling from the music world to the ministry, while trying to integrate both. It's not an easy path, especially when his faith is characterised by seeking, not by certainty, by reason, not by revelation. Does he even believe in God? "The short answer is no," he says: he is as opposed to simplistic theistic assumptions as any materialist. But life is not as simple as belief or unbelief: "The long answer is yes."

Holding such opposites in a lifelong creative tension, it's small wonder he's drawn to this ancient liminal frontier outside the city limits, and entirely unknown to most of its inhabitants. He would stop here to read the works of Lucretius[33], the Roman Epicurian philosopher writing some half-century before the start of the Christian era, who believed in no transcendent world, and sought none, who accepted that life was, as he put it in his sole work, *De rerum natura*,[34] just "one long struggle in the dark," who dismissed religion and who cultivated equanimity as he contemplated the ultimate dissolution of all things. While reading, Andrew would listen on his headphones to the music of George Butterworth, the English composer killed on the Somme in 1916 at the age of 31, and revered for his intensely English pastoral settings of the melancholy *Shropshire Lad* poems of A.E. Housman, whose own stoical atheism was rooted in his deep Latin scholarship.[35] Like Lucretius, Andrew taught himself to be content for his atoms to be dispersed on the wind. With such unconsoling consolations was his freethinking faith refined.

The dyke crosses the old dismantled railway, now filled with juniper trees; this is one of the areas the conservation work has left overgrown as it's the habitat of the rare green hairstreak butterfly. A short distance away, just before the A11 itself cuts across the dyke, is Mutlow Hill, an earth tumulus created possibly two thousand years ago, at a time when the names of Celt and Saxon would have meant nothing. The current name is Saxon, though: 'moot' being the word for meeting place. It was a meeting place in the Bronze Age, when the people created it from chalk rubble to hold the cremated remains of their loved ones; it was a meeting place when the Romans built a temple here[36]; and when the Saxons used it for their gatherings. Now, it's a place to stand between the railway and the road; between the chalk soil and the changing sky.

On a beech tree by the tump someone has sprayed a Celtic spiral. In the bark, a carved name: 'Grace'. We leave our signs. We mark our territory. We pass. Travellers, tribes, tongues, temples and totems come and go. Atoms cohere and dissolve. Across the A11, in the fields towards the east, stands an isolated farmhouse. Already secluded, it's almost entirely hidden behind a tall clipped privet hedge as high as the roofline. Above it, on a flagpole tall enough to be seen above the leafy ramparts, flies a giant Union Flag.

## Notes

1. 'An embarrassment to the city': what went wrong with the £725m gateway to Cambridge?'https://www.theguardian.com/artanddesign/architecture-design-blog/2017/jun/13/an-embarrassment-to-the-city-what-went-wrong-with-the-725m-gateway-to-cambridge June, 2017.
2. Site of Cambridge cattle market from the 1890s, when it moved from Castle Hill, until 1976.
3. Corpus Christi hall has a framed blue silk flag with the college arms, taken to the Pole by alumnus Dr 'Bill' Wilson, one of Scott's doomed party, and found with him along with the Bible and a copy of Tennyson's *In Memoriam*.
4. *The Ecclesiologist,* November, 1841, 9-12.
5. Whose three trustees include Yusuf Islam, the former singer Cat Stevens,
6. 1872-1953.
7. 1873-1938. Tame *op. cit.,* 177.
8. On the research of my book about Wales and Islam, *The Dragon and the Crescent* (Seren, 2011).

9. They used to feign ignorance and tell callers Syd Barrett lived a few streets away.
10. There is. They're called capellophiles.
11. *Op. cit.,* 163.
12. Not Julius Caesar's Brutus.
13. Gervase of Tilbury, *Otia Imperiala,* (c. 212) ed. F. Liebrecht, (Hanover, 1856). For a more readable version: Kevin Crossley-Holland, 'The Spectre of Wandlebury', *The Old Stories,* (Cambridge, 1997), 101-106.
14. 1855-1935. *Archaic Tracks Round Cambridge* (Hereford, 1932), 14.
15. Starring Hywel Bennett, with Sting in his first TV role and Daniel Day Lewis in a walk-on.
16. *Where Troy Once Stood,* (London, 1991).
17. 1901-1971.
18. Paul Newman, *The Lost Gods of Albion,* (Stroud, 1999), 114-125.
19. The location is always given, even by participants, as 'The Gog Magog Hills'. In fact, it was Cherry Hinton Chalk Pits, now a nature reserve, and part of the same chalk ridge, though half an hour's walk from the hilltop.
20. The hills were often a place of questionable diversion. In 1620, bear-baiting was advertised there as 'The Olympic Games'.
21. In Emmanuel Road, near Christ's Pieces, built in 1927 to a design by Beatrix Potter's cousin, Ronald Potter Jones (1876-1965), with a fine wooden neoclassical interior.
22. 1930-2004.
23. "The eeriness of the English countryside", April, 2015 https://www.theguardian.com/books/2015/apr/10/eeriness-english-countryside-robert-macfarlane
24. Such as one of its MPs, Oliver Cromwell, a Cambridgeshire man and alumnus of Sidney Sussex, where in 1960, a mummified head, reputedly his, was buried in a secret location by college authorities. It had been retrieved in the late Seventeenth Century from Westminster Hall, where it had been displayed since Cromwell's posthumous hanging. Experts differ as to its authenticity.
25. W.B. Yeats: 'The Second Coming'.
26. 1503-1542.
27. Reputedly lover of Anne Boleyn. Nicola Shulman: *Graven with Diamonds: The Many Lives of Thomas Wyatt, Courtier, Poet, Assassin, Spy,* (London 2011). See also Charles Nicholl: 'The Many Lives of Thomas Wyatt by Nicola Shulman' – review, *The Guardian,* April, 2011.
28. 1564-1593.
29. London 2014, 36.
30. *Ibid.,* p41.
31. A photograph shows him with a Hitler moustache.
32. Arthur Gray, 'On the Late Survival of a Celtic Population in East Anglia', *Proceedings of the Cambridge Antiquarian Society,* 15(1), 42–52 and 53–62 (1911).
33. Titus Lucretius Carus, who died in the late 50s BC.
34. "Of the nature of things".
35. Houseman, author of the poem, 'Loveliest of trees the cherry now', is commemorated by an avenue of cherry trees along the Backs. Tame, 80.
36. Antiquarian R.C. Neville excavated in 1852, finding Bronze Age cremation urns and the remains of the later Roman temple.

# WEST

# MUSEUM OF CAMBRIDGE, AND KETTLE'S YARD

"She's out the back. Plotting the revolution."

The steward at the wood-panelled entrance of The Museum of Cambridge points to where I can find the artist and community activist Hilary Cox Condron.

When she's not using artwork to give voices to the voiceless and expression to the excluded, Hilary can often be found at the Museum, which stands at the junction of Northampton Street, Magdalene Street and Castle Street.

In the workshop across the courtyard, the insurgents, a group of mostly mature women, are hard at work. The table is covered with posters of clenched fists in a variety of colours. But mostly red. I hesitate at the threshold, wary of interrupting, conscious how finely balanced the scales of history can be. But Hilary spots me and invites me in. "Are you teaching?" I ask, looking around at the circle of intent activity. "We're working together," she corrects me. The group is producing materials to commemorate the centenary of women's suffrage. I make what I hope are approving noises, conscious that nothing an inheritor of millennia of patriarchy can possibly say can be adequate. "That was good timing," one of the women says to me suddenly; a sardonic comment, I assume, on my tardy appearance at this late stage in the long struggle of human emancipation. I'm searching for a suitably conciliatory response, when she produces a tray of cakes and offers them to me. "Freshly made", she says.

Leaving the workers absorbed in their tasks, I go back into the museum, whose interior, all low ceilings, artisan implements and creaking floors, is scarcely altered since its days as the seventeenth-century White Horse Inn. It opened as the Cambridge and County Folk Museum in 1936, with the defiant mission of showing that Cambridge has always been more than just the University, and that people here have lives beyond the degrees and discussions of academia – lives worth remembering.

There's the city's industrial history, for instance. On display downstairs is a venerable Pye radio, its speaker contained in a wooden art deco sunburst-patterned screen, and a Pye television, bought in 1953 for its owners to watch the Coronation. Both were made in Cambridge in factories belonging to the company created in 1896 by William Pye[1], as a spinoff from his scientific work at the Cavendish Laboratory. It was a leading name in electronics until the firm finally folded in 1988.

Prior to television, of course, people had to make their own entertainment, and the poster for 'A Cambridge Coronation Festival. June, 1838' shows just how they did it:

Rustic sports on Midsummer Green
Newmarket Baulk[2]
Jumping in Sacks
Biscuit Bolting (one pennyworth to be eaten)
A jingling match[3]
Wheelbarrow race
Bobbing for oranges in wash trough
Royal Pig Races to win an elegant, piebald, short-legged, curley-tailed PIG
Grinning match
Ram race
Rooting extraordinary.[4]
Dipping for Eels
A whistling match.

Thank God for television, that's all I can say. I mean, look at what people used to get up to without it. Competitive pedestrianism, for instance. On a mantelpiece in one of the rooms is displayed the magnificent prize belt of Chesterton man Charlie Rowell[5], the undisputed 'King of the Peds', the champion of champions in the late Nineteenth Century when the pedestrianism craze gripped the United Kingdom, United States, Australia and New Zealand, attracting huge crowds, massive betting, and making its greatest exponents household names. Known as 'The Cambridge Wonder', Rowell could cover 150 miles a day and in 1879 won the equivalent of a million dollars in today's money for two races.[6]

Upstairs, there are paintings by Mary Charlotte Green[7], aunt of the novelist Graham Greene, and the person who taught the illustrator Gwen Raverat how to draw. They show the backstreets of Cambridge – inn yards, livery stables, blacksmiths' forges – which she was careful to record before development swept them away.

   In one room, among time-worn toys and spooky dolls' houses (which I can never see without thinking of M.R. James' 'Haunted Doll's House'), is 'The Bard's Chair.' Now I've seen a few bards' chairs in my time. They're the centrepiece of the eisteddfodic culture in which I was raised, where life holds no greater honour than to be ceremonially enthroned in the chair crafted by ancient tradition especially for each eisteddfod, and incised with words and images unique to each year's different location. As befits a symbol not just of success, but of survival, these chairs are mighty oak cathedra that would make the Iron Throne on *Game of Thrones* look like a piece of picnic furniture.

This is not like that. It seems to be a dining room chair with a bit of gold ribbon and some plastic oak leaves glued on. It is, apparently, the seat of the 'Cambridge Bard', an ancient tradition dating from 2016 and open, the website says, to "any word weaver (poet, storyteller, comedian, dramatist, singer/songwriter) with a voice and the power to use it."

In another room are the top hat and gigantic boot of the 'Histon Giant', Moses Canter[8], a onetime Stourbridge fair boxer who stood seven feet tall and weighed 23 stone. He grew vegetables on Histon Moor, pulling the harrow himself like a horse.[9] Nearby are the relics of Elizabeth Woodcock of Impington, who survived eight days in a cave of snow after falling from her horse in a blizzard in February 1799 while drunk. The story of her amazing survival – she attracted the attention of her rescuers by making a flag from her red petticoat and pushing it out through the snow on a stick – made her a national celebrity, and gifts flooded in from wellwishers. Unfortunately, many of the gifts were in liquid form: it being thought that spirits would aid her recovery. It had the opposite effect: she died from drink five months later, aged 43.[10]

You have to pay to get into the Museum of Cambridge; this memorial to the working people still has to work hard for a living. But leave the folksy memorabilia behind and take a few steps up Castle Street to the Kettle's Yard gallery, and – thanks to generous funding and a substantial endowment – you can stroll like a patrician free of charge into an internationally-renowned art space based on a sensibility so achingly rarefied that even the most refined galleries seem gauche by comparison.

It was in 1956 that the art collector and former assistant curator at the Tate, Jim Ede[11], and his wife Helen bought four derelict cottages near the road junction. They began turning them into a gallery to display artworks in a domestic setting. Over the next ten years Ede kept an open house for art lovers and students, who could enjoy his exquisite collection, including works by Great War artists like David Jones, and Henri Gaudier-Brzeska, the prodigiously talented French modernist sculptor and painter killed in the trenches in 1915 aged just 23. Ede's 1931 book about him, *Savage Messiah*, was made into a film by Ken Russell in 1972, and his collection of the artist's work is one of Kettle's Yard's treasures. Ede had a shrewd eye for overlooked artists, befriending and buying from them, and amassing a priceless collection of contemporary art, which he displayed around the cottage-galleries with perfectionist precision.

Of course, such exquisiteness had its downsides. Helen had to lock her room to keep it from being perfected. And, once, a female guest taking tea with the couple in the living room recalled seeing Ede getting more and more visibly uncomfortable until he could restrain himself no longer and leaned forward to say: "Margaret, Margaret dear: do you think your handbag might look better on the *other* side of the chair?"

Though intensely personal in its character, the house/gallery was also resolutely public in its purpose. Ede loaned artworks to students to display during the term, and in 1966, he gifted the buildings and the entire collection to the University, which, after he retired to Edinburgh in 1973, retained the entire complex as a work of art in itself. It was all left untouched in 2015, when a major new extension was added, with the revamped complex later reopening, with modern facilities added on.[12]

To get into the old part of the house you have to tug a bell pull. Visitors enter one small group at a time. Once inside, you find yourself facing one of David Jones' ethereal pencil-and-watercolour pictures where animals scarcely distinguishable from their habitat glide through cathedral-like forests, dense with pencilled undergrowth. You can sit in the chairs, and take in the subtly different view obtained from each. In fact, you *should* sit in the chairs. Once you realise that every seemingly random position you adopt is an artistic perspective, you'll never see any interior the same way again. Each view is a different angle on creation; each a different facet of reality. The world looks different from each corner. Each is worthy of respect; each equally valid; each has its vistas and its blind spots. As the French philosopher Gaston Bachelard says in his *Poetics of Space*: "...every corner of a house, every angle in a room, every inch of secluded space in which we like to hide, or withdraw into ourselves, is a symbol of solitude for the imagination; that is to say, it is the germ of a room, or of a house."[13]

A side table holds a spiral pattern of near-spherical stones, and an arrangement of shells and driftwood. The sound of the traffic outside seems to have disappeared, Nothing is labelled; bells summon you from room to room. For the first time in my life I find myself moved by abstract art. On the bedside in Helen's bedroom is *Farewell, Happy Fields*, the autobiography of the poet Kathleen Raine,[14] who studied at Girton, a few minutes' bike ride up the road.[15] The cover shows a picture of the young author, with her shy, shadowed, unflinching eyes. What a great poet she was. Her incantatory 'Northumbrian Sequence IV' has haunted me since my youth: 'Let in the wind. Let in the rain. Let in the moors tonight...'.

The exit takes you into the new extension: all honey-coloured brick walls, white plaster interiors and recessed lighting. The new coffee shop is packed to capacity. There's the faint scent of toasted ciabatta. In the foyer is a Kindersley studio plaque listing the donors to the project. From inside the gallery comes the whoosh, growl and bleep of a video installation about migration; a loop of film shot in Caribbean and African coastal locations, in which, to a soundtrack of booming ocean waves, impassive locals gesture and stride in slow motion through an otherwise deserted landscape, or sit, motionless, at picnic tables at the rim of a derelict tropical swimming pool. Throughout, the camera lovingly examines the detritus and trash underfoot: overturned furniture, broken picture frames, shattered mirrors: room after chaotic room of debris. I'm not sure it would have been Jim Ede's idea of an aesthetically-pleasing interior. But he could have had no end of fun tidying it up.

## NEWNHAM

On the river meadows at Sheep's Green, a student is reading peacefully, his back propped against a recumbent, ruminating cow. Man and nature in harmony. It's the kind of scene that might have appealed to the quirky vision of the artist Gwen Raverat, grand-daughter of Charles Darwin, who grew up in the late Victorian age in Newnham Grange on Silver Street, overlooking the meadows.[16] The Darwin family, which intermarried with the almost equally illustrious Wedgwood pottery dynasty, is a distinguished one, producing generations of artists, scientists, and leaders in every field. The Cambridge branch, founded by Charles' second son George, later *Sir* George, Darwin, was no exception. He was the Plumian Professor of Astronomy and Experimental Philosophy at the University, and his family came to occupy many of the commanding heights of city society, with the apparently effortless ease of those who seem destined to succeed by some social principle of natural selection, almost as ineluctable as the biological process discovered by their most famous member.

*Period Piece* is a classic evocation of a late Victorian and Edwardian upbringing in an unusually cultured and immensely well-connected upper-class household, with more than its fair share of eccentricities. Although Raverat was writing towards the end of her life, *Period Piece* captures, disarmingly, the often inverted values of her childhood self, where trivial affairs are described in terms of violent passion – desperation, murder, fury, despair – while all real matters of life and death are passed over with serene understatement. There's that beguiling, ruthlessly efficient social survival skill doing its invisible work again: hide your hurts; conceal your commitments; display only what you don't really value. Generation after successful generation of English patricians can't be wrong. Social Darwinism in action.

That effortless expectation of achievement is a powerful indicator of success; it transmits itself from generation to generation like a dominant gene. Newnham, an enclave of affluence even in prosperous Cambridge – the ward has three of the city's ten richest streets, and the lowest crime rate – is an ideal environment for it to thrive.[17] While house-hunting in my first year as a student, I was shown around some potential lodgings in Newnham – all muesli and music stands – by an eight-year-old girl: "and we're hoping to put a screed down here, but it's *so* difficult to get the workmen ..." I ended up staying in Owlstone Croft, then a nurses' hostel for Addenbrooke's hospital nearby, where my college rented a couple of floors. My first time away from home. First lots of things. This utilitarian accommodation complex, now part of Queens' College, is tucked away between the village and the River Cam next to a wooded area, now a nature reserve, and long known as 'Paradise'.

This paradise, though, once concealed a serpent. For more than six months from October 1974, an assailant known as the Cambridge Rapist terrorised the city, striking six times, with ever greater violence, breaking into his victims' houses with seeming impunity. A team of sixty officers took part in the biggest manhunt in the county's history. It was at Owlstone Croft that he was finally stopped. The attacker had broken in, but was disturbed, pursued, cornered and caught, while trying to flee disguised as a woman. Unmasked, he turned out to be Peter Samuel Cook, then 46, a delivery man whose longtime sideline as a burglar had taken a terrifying turn. He died in prison in 2004. John Burnside's 2001 novel, *The Locust Room*, is set against the background of fear and suspicion caused by Cook's still-notorious crimes. Today this secluded corner of the village overlooking Grantchester Meadows is again a peaceful backwater, that intrusion of evil long past. For most people, any echoes recalled by this area are more likely to relate to the early Pink Floyd song 'Grantchester Meadows', by Roger

Waters, which, to the accompaniment of birdsong, evokes a pristine rural eden: "Icy wind of night, be gone / This is not your domain."[18]

That song is, of course, a postlapsarian desire for a lost innocence. When it was being written, Pink Floyd's first frontman, Syd Barrett, had already been ousted painfully from the band he helped form, due to his drug-fuelled unpredictability. Two years earlier, Barrett had chosen the title of the first and only full album he was to record with the band, *The Piper at the Gates of Dawn*, taking the phrase from his favourite children's book. It retrospect, there is a particular poignancy in the way of Kenneth Grahame's elegaic Edwardian idyll, which we now know was soon to be swept away by the tide of war, with the idealism of sixties pop culture, which we now know was combined to sweep away the likes of Syd Barrett on a tide of acid. Some pipes should not be listened to. Some gates should not be gone through. Some dawns can be too dazzling.

That same fatal embrace of art and ecstasy seemed to be at work in the relationship of two of Newnham's other famous one-time residents, Ted Hughes and Sylvia Plath. A Fulbright scholar, Plath studied at Newnham College itself, that idyllic, turreted, bay-windowed, all-female, High Victorian haven founded in 1871.[19] Hughes and Plath married in 1956, four months after they met. They moved to the modest terraced house at 55 Eltisley Avenue, Newnham, where, while Hughes was teaching at Coleridge

Community College,[20] they rented a ground floor room between autumn 1956 and the summer of 1957. In the February of that year, Grantchester Meadows witnessed a strange ritual, as Hughes and Plath carried out into the fields a sculpted clay head of Plath made by a fellow student. Plath didn't want to keep it but had a superstitious fear of destroying her own image. She and Hughes eventually left it in the branches of an old willow tree, expecting it to quickly decay. But it didn't, as Plath tells in her poem 'The Lady and the Earthenware Head':[21]

> Yet, shrined on her shelf, the grisly visage endured,
> Despite her wrung hands, her tears, her praying: Vanish!
> Steadfast and evil-starred,
> It ogled through rock-fault, wind-flaw and fisted wave—
> An antique hag-head, too tough for knife to finish,
> Refusing to diminish
> By one jot its basilisk-look of love.

A short distance away, down a well-worn footpath is a wooden door. Behind it, for those who dare, is Paradise: the long-established clothes-optional swimming club. "There's a wonderful mix of demographics" one of the regulars tells me: "Businessmen come wearing their suits, hang them on trees, go swimming and then go to work." On a sunny day, she says, it's mainly older men with perfect full-body tans. Plus the odd student. She goes there late at night after dancing. "It's wonderfully transgressive," she says.

Which is great. But, as a non-swimmer, this would be no paradise for me. My school operated a strange policy – inexplicable though unchallenged – whereby they only gave swimming lessons to those who could already swim. It was almost Darwinian in equipping those most likely to survive. That, combined with my chronic physical inhibition, became a lifelong incapacity, not to say aversion. Not that I feel the lack of the ability. Rather the contrary. I'm actually at much less risk from drowning than if I *could* swim. I was a journalist for many years, and countless times I saw, or wrote, headlines containing the words 'swimmer' and 'drowned'. Rip tides, exhaustion, concussion while diving, cramp, cold, booze, the bends. It's counter-intuitive, I know. But with rare exceptions it's true – it's swimmers who drown. Admittedly, if I ever find myself on a sinking ocean liner, I'll be on my way to Davy Jones faster than you can say Leonardo di Caprio. But, as I assiduously avoid going anywhere near water if I can possibly help it, for most practical purposes, I'm as safe as houses. Take that, Darwin.

# GRANTCHESTER

Two miles drive south of Cambridge city centre – or a two-mile punt from the Mill Lane station if your triceps are up to it – lies Grantchester. It's an ancient village, referred to in the Eighth Century by Bede, by Nennius in the ninth,[22] by the Domesday Book in the Eleventh, by Chaucer in the Fourteenth, and, as mentioned, by Pink Floyd in the Twentieth. More recently, it became the setting for an eponymous ITV detective drama set in the 1950s, based on the stories of James Runcie, son of the former Archbishop of Canterbury Robert Runcie. But despite Fifties whodunits and Sixties music, there is really only one artistic connection that matters here: for most visitors, Grantchester's cultural clock stopped in 1912 – at precisely ten to three.

Near the centre of the village is the Rupert Brooke pub, named after the poet, who, perhaps more than any other, epitomises the tragic collision of Edwardian idealism with the horrors of the First World War. A playful, wistful poem he wrote about the village ends with the line; "Stands the church clock at ten to three? / And is there honey still for tea?"

Born in 1887 in Rugby, where his father was a schoolmaster, Brooke came to King's to study classics, where his good looks, athleticism, charisma and his exceptional promise as scholar and poet, quickly made him one of the most prominent men of his generation. He was a member of the elite secret debating society The Apostles, and the leader of the socialist Fabian Society, while also being on intimate terms with the family of the Prime Minister Herbert Asquith. He came to live in Grantchester in 1909, first in Orchard House, and then, from 1910 until 1912, at the Old Vicarage, where he was the centre of a kind of Bloomsbury Group on tour, which included the economist John Maynard Keynes, the philosophers Ludwig Wittgenstein and Bertrand Russell, the painter Augustus John and the novelists E.M.Forster and Virginia Woolf. Here, Brooke attempted to get back to nature by means of long walks, longer talks, and minimal clothing, in what Woolf – who went skinny-dipping with him in the Cam in 1911 – called his 'neo pagan' life. While still only in his early twenties, he was already a celebrity: "the handsomest man in

England," according to W.B.Yeats. Contemporaries regarded him with awe, if not worship. He loved, and was loved by, women and men.[23] It was as though pre-war England, sensing somehow that its own end was near, had loaded him with all its riches.

It was a lot to live up to. A failed love affair, coupled with confusion about his sexuality, triggered a breakdown, and he took himself abroad: Germany, America, and the South Seas. To his huge circle of friends, he sent back travel articles and a stream of letters and poems, including, in 1912, his whimsical, nostalgic 'The Old Vicarage Grantchester', written in homesickness at a café table in Berlin, in which he praises Grantchester as a kind of English paradise while comically dismissing neighbouring parishes for all kinds of fanciful failings. It's not a great poem perhaps, but has been well described as being "surely as good as a minor poem can be,"[24] and it earns its place in the collective memory because, concealed beneath the jokes, the mock-heroicisms and the knowing ironies with which Englishmen then and now must hide their deepest feelings, it is one of the greatest expressions of the patriotism of place, of how England can be loved for what it is, not what it does.

It is customary to think sentimentally of Brooke as the last representative of an old world, altogether too innocent to survive the brutal modern age. Read his best-known poems, where diaphanous abstractions swirl around statuesque personifications, and that's certainly the impression you get. But read *all* his poems,

and letters and you get a different picture: he was far from innocent, and far from outdated. In his relentlessly performative, exhaustingly ironic letter-writing,[25] he is reminiscent of a contemporary gap-year 'traveller', a postgrad digital nomad, vlogging his way around the world with his camera pointing at himself. There is actually something reassuringly familiar in finding that youthful self-obsession is not merely a modern phenomenon, any more than idealism is something belonging only to a vanished past. After all, we borrowed the word narcissism from the ancient Greeks' story of the first and most famous selfie.

Brooke returned from his travels shortly before war broke out, and quickly enlisted, finding, finally, a purpose for – and possibly also an escape from – his life. Winston Churchill, then First Lord of the Admiralty, offered him a commission in the Royal Naval Division. He went to war willingly. A sonnet he wrote at this time, entitled 'The Soldier', was read out by Dean Inge at St Paul's Cathedral on Easter Day 1915. It began:

> If I should die, think only this of me:
> That there's some corner of a foreign field
> That is forever England...

Less than three weeks later, on St George's Day, its author was dead, killed by blood poisoning while on a troopship en route to Gallipoli, and laid to rest on the Greek island of Skyros. His death was a national tragedy. Churchill himself wrote his obituary.

> Joyous, fearless, versatile, deeply instructed, with classic symmetry of mind and body, ruled by high undoubting purpose, he was all that one would wish England's noblest sons to be ...

Classical references had frequently been invoked to describe Brooke. In 1910, his friend the poet Frances Cornford, depicted:

> A young Apollo, golden-haired,
> Stands dreaming on the verge of strife,
> Magnificently unprepared
> For the long littleness of life.

That life was not long, of course, and in the end, Death needed only its smallest emissaries to bring this young god to the grave.

In death as in life, Brooke was always well connected. His statue stands today in the garden of the house he once rented, the Old Vicarage in Grantchester. It was unveiled by Lady Thatcher in 2006, at the invitation of the house's owners for more than thirty years, Lord Jeffrey Archer, the Conservative politician and author, and Dame Mary Archer, the scientist and – fittingly for one living in the former home of the 'golden-haired Apollo' – expert on solar energy.

Brooke's statue, in military uniform, stands in the centre of a little lawn just inside the wide gates of the Old Vicarage's circular gravel drive, where I park up. A thunderstorm is just about to break, and the housekeeper kindly brings a spare umbrella as she comes to show me inside. I am taken through to the drawing room where Dame Mary will join me shortly.

Writing to his cousin Erica Cotterill, Brooke had described this house as: " ... a deserted, lonely, dank, ruined, overgrown, gloomy, lovely house: with a garden to match. It is all five hundred years old, and fusty with the ghosts of generations of mouldering clergymen. It is a fit place to write my kind of poetry in ..."[26]

It is anything but ruined now. What had been Brooke's ramshackle, book-strewn study, lit by a low-slung oil-lamp, is now colour-supplement perfect. Over tea and Duchy Originals biscuits, Dame Mary explains how the house came into her family's possession. Brooke himself had considered buying it, a hope his mother fulfilled after the war, when she gave it to Brooke's close friend from college days, Dudley Ward, as a memorial to her son.[27] It remained in Ward's family until 1979, which is when the Archers came in.

"It was because Jeffrey had one of his periodic reverses and we had to leave London," Mary Archer says. A rising star in the Tory party, Jeffrey had resigned his seat as an MP when facing bankruptcy after losing a fortune as a victim of a fraudulent investment scheme. Cambridge, where Mary was already lecturing at Newnham and Trinity, and where she was only the second woman at the High Table, offered more affordable accommodation. "Jeffrey would have nothing but this, obviously," Mary says. By this time he had reinvented himself as a popular novelist, and he bought the house with the money from his 1979 bestseller *Kane and Abel*. "I did not love it at first sight," Mary Archer says of the house, "But I have come to love it."

As we're talking, Lord Archer, wearing his characteristic cricket sweater, joins us, en route to his writing room. This is not actually our first meeting. Thirty years ago, during the 1987 General Election, in my first job as a newspaper reporter in the south Wales Valleys, I covered a speech he was giving in support of the Conservative candidate in Merthyr Tydfil. This was – and still is – a constituency where the Labour majority is the size of a bestselling novelist's sales figures, and it's fair to say that, even during that Tory heyday, it was going to be an uphill struggle. Not that this was apparent from the confidence Jeffrey Archer projected in our

interview, or to his full house Con Club audience. I stood at the back of the room, leaning my notebook on the bar, facing the speaker across sea of blue-rinsed heads. He seized the theatrical opportunity: "I see there's a gentleman of the press here!" he said, pointing at me like his toxophilic namesake, and then directed his entire speech at me and, through me, to the waiting world. Or at least, to that part of it who read the *Merthyr Express*.

It was a bravura performance, and there were, of course to be many more over the following years, as the 'periodic reverses' – and recoveries – of Jeffrey Archer's career, were played out in Parliament, papers, prison and publishing, becoming themselves the stuff of legend. He was something of a legend in our house too when I was growing up: the story of how he lost a fortune and regained it by writing a book – a book about losing and regaining a fortune – appealed strongly to my father, whose own building company had gone to the wall in 1976, and who himself then had to reinvent his career.[28] Archer novels arrived from the book club at regular intervals; hardback heralds of a world where setbacks and successes, virtues and vices are secondary to the stories which they serve, and where drama itself is a kind of destiny, where the tale is what's important, not the truth.

Jeffrey heads out to his writing retreat, which can just be glimpsed in the garden: a castellated former folly, decorated with relief sculptures by Eric Gill, an artist whose work, Jeffrey tells me, he is happy to collect despite the misgivings that are often now expressed about the sculptor's private life. Jeffrey writes according to a disciplined schedule: two-hour blocks and timed with an hourglass. This is the afternoon shift. A century apart, the Old Vicarage's two authors seem to embody opposite poles of a writer's life: the one brief, gilded, fragile, and producing only a handful of pieces; the other long, tarnished, indestructible and producing titles by the dozen and sales in the hundreds of millions.[29] Abel and Kane. Good stories need both.

Brooke's memory is well-preserved at the Old Vicarage. Mary Archer has researched and published two books about the house and the association with Brooke, having, she says, "fallen in love" with him, and she has worked closely with the Rupert Brooke Society.[30] I mention how strange it seems that Brooke, whose life seemed always to be so charmed, was always looking back at some vanished arcadia: his schooldays, his youth, the village he had left to go travelling.

"Brooke was filled with nostalgia for a lost age, but was a much more complex man than is often thought," she said. "It was *a fin de siecle* feeling. Was it that he no longer felt himself to be the golden-haired Apollo that Frances Cornford made him out to be? Was it the loss of an innocence that he never really had? But it gives him a yearning quality which is poignant and attractive, and rather sad at heart."

On a little table by the window overlooking the courtyard, she shows me a display of memorabilia, including some of Brooke's medals and his silver cigarette case, all of them kept, like his memory, bright.

## MADINGLEY AMERICAN CEMETERY

In Madingley American Cemetery, it is England, for once, that is the foreign field. The cemetery, just outside the city, started to receive burials in 1943, mainly from the U.S. aircrew stationed in England who had died here. In 1956 it was opened as the United Kingdom's only permanent United States military cemetery. Given in perpetuity by Cambridge University, it's maintained by the U.S. equivalent of the Commonwealth War Graves Commission, the American Battle Monuments Commission, whose on-site staff make sure the 3,782 crosses and 25 Stars of David are washed by hand, three times a week.

I have come with two American visitors, Richard, my son-in-law Zach's grandfather, and Hunter, Zach's young cousin. Richard wears a baseball cap with his unit insignia. He served in Vietnam, operating a .50 calibre Browning machine gun from a chattering Bell Huey Cobra chopper above the jungles. He spends a long while with the displays which depict a war which took place three decades before his own, but still closer to his own war than Vietnam is now to the present day. The exhibition shows the gigantic scale of the American wartime presence in the United Kingdom, and the stupendous resources that nation expended in order to bring the conflict to an end.

My father was only slightly too young to serve in the war, but he completed two years' National Service with the Royal Engineers, and, like many of his generation, he retained a fascination with the miltary. A lifelong admirer of America, he would have loved to have seen this place.[31] He used to say the Americans carried out daytime bombing missions, while the British carried out the nighttime ones. This was, so the British said, because night-flying was too difficult for the Yanks. They, in turn, retorted that the British only flew at night because it was safer.

Day or night, theirs was a deadly dangerous business. A total of 3812 service personnel are buried here, and a further 5127 whose bodies were never found are commemorated on the memorial wall. Among the latter is a recipient of the United States' highest award for gallantry, the Medal of Honor, Leon Robert 'Bob' Vance. In the nearby museum, a picture shows him as a smiling twenty-something, looking every inch the hero. He has a chin you could land aircraft on. He's in good company at Madingley: the wall also commemorates Joseph P. Kennedy Jr, eldest of the children of Joseph P. Kennedy Sr, and brother of J.F.K. He died in 1944 when the experimental explosive-packed plane he was test-piloting blew up prematurely; further along is the bandleader Glenn Miller, whose plane vanished over the Atlantic later in the same year.

The door of the chapel is teak and bronze, decorated with sculptures of a DUKW amphibious vehicle, a Sherman tank, a half-track and a motorboat. It's a military modeller's heaven, an Airfix Valhalla. On the wall is a map of Europe with the North Atlantic criss-crossed by the flightpaths of little metal aeroplanes. At one end, a mosaic of nearly a million pieces shows ghostly aircraft and the spirits of aviators making their way to their celestial landing ground. Back outside, the sun is shining on the ranks of gravestones ranged down the hill, and in the slight westerly wind the Stars and Stripes are flying above a corner of Cambridgeshire which will be forever America.

# HUNTINGDON ROAD

The *Via Devana*, aka the A14, runs as straight as the Romans could make it, northwest from Castle Hill out towards Huntingdon. On the left, it passes a tiny park where the Old Three Tuns used to stand, a favourite tavern of Dick Turpin the highwayman, but demolished in 1936. A short distance further on, it passes Murray Edwards college, formerly known as New Hall, a women's college on a 1964 campus by Chamberlin, Powell and Bon, the architects of the Barbican. The complex, characterised by white domes, sunken gardens and colonnades, was described, memorably, by P.D. James as looking like "a harem ... owned by a sultan with liberal views and an odd predilection for clever girls."[32] A little further on, the road passes Girton college, built in the 1870s and 1880s in turreted redbrick Gothic style by Alfred Waterhouse. C.S. Lewis called it 'The Castle of Otranto'.[33] Originally women-only, it became co-educational in 1976. Its location, some two miles from the city centre, was designed to minimise risk to reputations on both sides of the stark Victorian gender divide.

Past the city boundary, the road becomes a dual carriageway, although the route is currently sclerotic with roadworks as the network expands its capacity to cope with the city's growth. As a result, Herbie's Diner can only be reached through a maze of barriers so complicated it looks like one of those roadblocks that appear at the end of movie car chases – all chevrons and flashing lights. The sign 'Herbie's Diner Still Open for Business' defies the obstacles. Opened in early 2016, some ten miles outside Cambridge, Herbie's[34], with its retro 50s/60s decor, and its red-and-white striped vinyl dining booths, looks like it would be at home next to some dusty highway in the American South West, rather than next to the Swavesey Travelodge and the hand car wash.

It's a sunny day, and the only sunglasses I've been able to find in the car are a round pair that make me look like Woody Harrelson's Mickey in *Natural Born Killers*. Except with more hair. And fewer guns. My Texan son-in-law Zach has seen a diner or two in his time, and apparently this one passes the authenticity test. Probably with Woody Harrelson still somewhere in the back of my mind, I find myself ordering a bottle of 'Baby Faced Assassin', an IPA which, at 6.1 ABV, is close to being the .44 Magnum of the beer world. The label says it goes well with spicy food and strong cheese.

There's no shortage of either. Among the usual dogs and fries, some of the more ambitious menu items carry names which are simultaneously challenge and threat: the Tower of Terror (triple chillis) and The Joker. The latter, at £29.95, is a teetering skewered skyscraper comprising: one beef pattie; one grilled chicken breast; one southern fried chicken; one pork pattie; one spicy bean burger; some BBQ pulled pork in between layers of bread topped with cheese and finished with chilli cheese, fries and six onion rings. Finish it in under twenty minutes and you get it for free and your face goes on the Wall of Fame. Posthumous fame, probably. I opt for the Route 66 burger. Almost all the names here trigger memories of the America we think we know from music and movies. Listening to the tunes of the Fifties and Sixties playing on the jukebox brings a pang of nostalgia for a time I never actually knew. It shouldn't hurt, but it does, like pain in a phantom limb.

For years I used to go on a literary tour in the States every autumn, and stopping at a diner – preferably one of those streamlined, railcar-style stainless-steel ones – was always a highlight of any road trip. I've never actually travelled down Route 66, but, as we leave Herbie's, I make a mental note to make that journey one day. Outside though, there's another route to follow, and this one too is legendary.

The Greenwich Meridian was established in 1851 and was accepted internationally by 1884 as a means of defining longitude, essential for maritime navigation. From its starting point at the Royal Observatory at Greenwich it lasers across the country invisibly, dividing east from west. Heading north, it bisects Cambridgeshire, entering the county just west of Melbourn, where it's marked with a stone monument like a large milestone. At numerous points along the route its intangible presence is made real by such markers: in Meldreth, a fine granite sundial, unveiled by the Astronomer Royal, Sir Martin Rees; at Orwell, a series of little green discs on the trees, and then another monument,[35] looking like a large white cricket ball, seamed by the dark meridian. Between Little and Great Eversden, it's marked with a bright blue bollard; in Toft, another fine sundial in Cumbrian slate. And so it goes on: Meridian Close; Meridian Drive; the Meridian Golf Club, and plaques and trees and woods and markers tracing this unseen mathematical motorway across the countryside.

At Swavesey, a mile or so just north of Herbie's, the meridian has five markers: four plaques on posts and a sundial at the primary school. Nearby is Swavesey Village College, one of a dozen such establishments in Cambridgeshire set up by Henry Morris,[36] the county's visionary Director of Education for more than thirty years from 1922. He took up his post at a time when Cambridgeshire was the second-poorest county in England, the destitution of its rural hinterland contrasting shamefully with the wealth of the city. Morris' answer was all-age, cradle-to-grave village schools, educating children during the day, and adults in the evening, in buildings which would themselves be inspiring masterpieces of contemporary design – in the 1930's he even enlisted the great modernist architects Walter Gropius and Maxwell Fry to design Impington Village College, now Grade I-listed. Egalitarian in his aims, patrician in his manner – in fact, an out-and-out snob – he was charming, arrogant and imperious by turns as he pursued his grand scheme in the face of his councillors' caution. Faced with objections about cost, he supplemented the council's budget with donations from wealthy patrons at home and internationally. He founded five Village Colleges during his tenure: Sawston, (1930), Bottisham (1937), Linton (1937), Impington (1939) and Bassingbourn (1954), while others, such as Swavesey in 1958, opened after his retirement. Others followed, most recently, at Cambourne, which opened in 2013, while the model was also taken up by other counties, notably Leicestershire. The schools' approach has modified over the years, of course; society is no longer as cohesive, or as poor, as when Morris' scheme was conceived. But the village colleges continue the aim of serving not just pupils, but the entire community.[37]

The *Via Devana*, which ran from Colchester to Chester, forms the boundary to the parish of Swavesey. Roman pottery has been found in the village, and a female Roman skull was discovered in the next-door town of Over, which stands on a slightly higher gravel hill to the north. The Saxon name Swavesey denotes the landing place, or island, of Swaef, indicating that this low Jurassic Clay ridge on the River Ouse was once a major inland port. By 1261 it was important enough to have an eight-day fair which thrived for five hundred years, declining only from the 1740s. The docks, now grassed over, form the village green[38], and the floodgates on the watercourse beneath Station Road are a reminder of the ever-present danger of inundation, a fact even more apparent a short distance up the road at Over, where the spring rains have turned field after field of the adjacent farmland to lakes. The interior of St Mary's Church carries markings showing where floods reached in previous years, while the gables of some of the older houses show the influence of the Dutch engineers who worked here draining the fens in the Seventeenth Century, with a system of dykes, still in existence.[39]

The meres and river meadows on and around the Great Ouse are home, temporary or permanent, to Canada geese. swans, coots, bitterns and herons. Even seals have been spotted here, some fifty miles from the sea. The banks are fringed with osiers, once used for making baskets, and teasels, once used for separating wool – reminders of the once self-sufficient fen economy whose independence was guarded so fiercely by the inhabitants that they were known as Fen Tigers. Such economic autonomy is a distant memory now, as with all the communities around Cambridge which are now commuter villages, gradually expanding, a dozen houses here, a hundred or so there. Standing on the banks of the Ouse in this parish which is half water and all fen, it's hard to believe that urban Cambridge is only a few miles distant. But it's roads, not rivers, which shape the countryside now, and the only tides now are the traffic, flowing daily back and forth down the A14.

## LITTLE GIDDING

As pilgrimages go, this has been a bit of a cheat. On my part at least. The other pilgrims have done it the hard way, starting at Leighton Bromswold Church and schlepping across the countryside the five miles to Little Gidding, stopping en route for prayer, reflection, worship, and, at Hamerton, a toilet break. I have simply driven straight up the A14, followed the sat nav down narrow country lanes where grass pushes a green mohican strip through the middle of the tarmac, through villages where everything seems to be 'The Old' something or other – the Old Forge, Old Vicarage, Old School, Old Post Office – pulled up in the little car park, and walked the few yards to the Church of St John the Evangelist, where, through the door which stands open to the late afternoon sunshine, I can hear the opening prayers as evensong just gets underway.

It's standing room only. The fifty or so pilgrims have filled the church, a heavily-restored medieval barrel-vaulted building, laid out, college-chapel-style, with pews facing one another across a central aisle. A huge Alsatian is lying in the doorway licking his paws; his owner, in combat fatigues, is absorbed in his service sheet. Outside, sheep are bleating and blossom is drifting down from the fruit tree by the entrance. In the candlelit semi-darkness inside, pilgrims with backpacks and anoraks are seated on the chancel step, where the priest conducts proceedings with a service sheet in one hand, while in the other she holds a lead with a terrier dog on the end of it. Other dogs roam around the sanctuary. Evensong. In a country church. With dogs. It can't get more English than this.

Oh, actually, it can. The congregation rises to sing 'He Who Would Valiant Be'. It's a favourite of mine. Who could not relish singing a verse beginning "Ho-obgoblin, no-or foul fiend / Can daunt his spirit..."? Sadly, however, we're not using John Bunyan's gutsy 1684 original lyrics straight from *The Pilgrim's Progress*, but Percy Dearmer's toned-down 1906 version; "Since, Lord, thou dost defend / Us with thy spirit." Nonetheless, we still get to sing the line which my old BBC boss used to say should make this the official hymn for all news editors: "Whoso beset him round / With dismal stories..." At this service, I might be standing at the doorway; I might be a latecomer, but I'm right at home.

That homeliness was really always the idea with Little Gidding, ever since Nicholas Ferrar[40], a pious High Anglican, together with his extended family and friends, made it the centre of an experiment in Christian living combining work and worship, family and faith. The Puritans of that time immediately before the Civil War hated and suspected its atmosphere of ritualism, even though its members had no formal rule except the *Book of Common Prayer*. But Charles I loved the place and visited three times, finally, and most poignantly, in 1645 while seeking refuge after his disastrous defeat at the Battle

of Naseby. The community did not long survive the death of the
family members, and by the late 1650s had disbanded. But it left the
legacy of an ideal that, in the Twentieth Century, would inspire
T.S.Eliot, an American convert to Englishness, to the High Church
and to Royalism, who saw in Nicholas Ferrar's humble enterprise an
ideal to inspire his own troubled times, as his adopted country faced
the existential crisis of the Second World War.

In his 1942 poem 'Little Gidding', published as the last part of his
great late work, *Four Quartets*, Eliot invoked the power of sacred place
as a spiritual principle strong enough to stand against any danger:

> the communication
> Of the dead is tongued with fire beyond the language of the living.
> Here, the intersection of the timeless moment
> Is England and nowhere. Never and always.

Even though he affected the manner of the Old World English
gentleman, Eliot was at heart a New World pioneer; his outward
conformity disguising his inward intrepidity:

> We shall not cease from exploration
> And the end of all our exploring
> Will be to arrive where we started
> And know the place for the first time.

He found what he believed English people had lost, and what
twentieth-century people in general lacked – belonging, belief:

> A people without history
> Is not redeemed from time, for history is a pattern
> Of timeless moments. So, while the light fails
> On a winter's afternoon, in a secluded chapel
> History is now and England.

Which is why they come back, year after year; those who believe;
and those who wish they could. That's one of the great things about
the old C of E: even at the times when you don't believe anything,
you can still belong.

I mentioned the homeliness: "Let us stand to pray ...", the priest
says. "No, it's me now," says another clerical voice: the Bishop of
Ely, the Rt. Rev. Stephen Conway. He's leading the pilgrimage, and

it's time for his sermon. He takes his place at the chancel step among the terriers. Eliot gets a mention, of course. And Nicholas Ferrar, whose flower-garlanded tomb stands like an altar table just outside the door. But the Bishop ends by quoting Ferrar's great friend, the seventeenth-century poet-priest George Herbert,[41] who, largely from his own resources, had restored the church at Leighton Bromswold, where today's pilgrimage began. On his deathbed, Herbert entrusted his poetry to Ferrar, to publish or to burn as he saw fit. He published, to the gratitude of posterity.

Evensong is over. Lord now lettest thou thy servant depart in peace. The pilgrims collect their belongings and make their way out. I'm already in the doorway, so I step out ahead of them. The last shall be first. For the tea and cakes anyway. I pay my contribution and join the pilgrims as they leave their walking shoes and staffs in the nearby community house and queue up for their tea and Victoria sponge. This building, Ferrar House, used to be the home for Little Gidding's second experiment in communal living, the Community of Christ the Sower, which was formed out of the Friends of Little Gidding in 1970, and which carried out its mission of stewardship and hospitality until 1998, when it dispersed, having lasted just a generation, much the same as Nicholas Ferrar's original community. But then, the worth of an enterprise, or a life, isn't measured merely by its duration. The guy with the combats and the Alsatian – who is, I learn, called Valentine – had been a member here. The connection is still strong. Others have come to Little Gidding more recently, summoned by the same longing that drew Eliot:

Through the unknown, remembered gate
When the last of earth left to discover
Is that which was the beginning;

The walkers are arranging transport back to their cars, which have been left at Leighton Bromswold. I give three of them a lift: a retired Scottish engineer, an ex-journalist now a country priest, and a university administrator who's also a poet. We pass the church with the inscription on its façade, 'This is none other but the House of God and the gate of heaven'. Well, on a rainy Saturday afternoon, there are worse places to be than that. As we make our way to the car park, one of the pilgrims is still humming, absent-mindedly, 'He Who Would Valiant Be.'

## GRANGE ROAD

Tree-lined Grange Road runs roughly parallel with the Cam along its west bank through overspill faculty centres, sports grounds and college buildings, all overshadowed by the giant brick-built secular cathedral of Giles Gilbert Scott's University Library, completed in 1934. Just off Grange Road, down a private drive belonging to Corpus Christi College, is Leckhampton House, a late Victorian mansion, now postgraduate accommodation, originally built in the 1880s for Frederic W.H. Myers[42], the classicist, and founder of the Society for Psychical Research. In *Period Piece*, Gwen Raverat describes her father and uncle taking part, more out of good manners than belief, in a séance conducted by Fred Myers, one of the founding fathers of spiritualism in Britain.

His picture is the focal point above the sanctuary of Cambridge Spiritualist Church, a former Methodist chapel on Newmarket Road, just opposite McDonalds. It shows Myers, solemn, black-bearded and black-hatted, gazing upwards at an unexplained light source. It is pointed out to me with great pride by Tom, the charming and entirely sincere man who greets me when I venture inside one Sunday evening for my first ever visit to a spiritualist church. It is not, however, my first encounter with spiritualism: my sister-in-law, Lesley, is a professional psychic medium, from a family of psychics. I've never had a formal sitting with her, but I did once catch the second half of one of her public demonstrations of what spiritualists call 'platform work'. It was a fundraiser for a local hospice, held in a town hall. The amount of detail she gave the audience defied even resolute scepticism. And in many passing conversations with me over the years, she has told me things she could not possibly have known. There are, no doubt, plenty of fraudulent mediums. But Lesley isn't one of them.

I tell Tom why I'm there, that it's my first time, that I'm not a spiritualist, but that I do have a family connection and that I'm open-minded. Cards on the table. After all, there's little purpose in trying to conceal anything from people who deal in supernatural knowledge. He invites me to sit near the front. I choose the back row. He joins me. There are just over twenty people there. Mainly older, but a few younger than me. I'll pass over the prayers, the unaccompanied hymns and the sermon by the visiting medium, Mark Williams, a tall, middle-aged, black-suited man with a gentle south Wales Valleys accent. The last half hour of the service was the real business of the evening: the mediumship. We are warned: "Don't feed the medium." That is, don't offer information unbidden, as it detracts from the evidential quality of his message. "Is there anyone here for the first time," Mark asks. There's no point in hiding. I put my hand up. I don't actually feel uncomfortable. Years of evangelical Christianity, hundreds of books, many an hour watching TV psychics, and many a conversation with Lesley have made me conversant with these conventions, just as they have made me alert to self-deception, cold-reading, and fraud.

"I have the sense of a father figure," says Mark, extending his hand in my direction. Seconds into the reading, and I'm the focus of the session. "A tall man, carries himself very well. Can you take that?" "I'm sorry," I say. "I can't". Both my father and father-in-law had died from lung cancer within a few months of each other eight years earlier, but neither were tall. Anyway, a father figure could be *any* older male. "I can take that," says Tom, next to me, gamely. "But not tall." "Perhaps it's not tall, then," says Mark. "But straight, upright. Carries himself well." OK, I can go along with that too. It could be my father-in-law. "I can take that too," I say. "But not tall."

Mark is now indicating his chest. "Was there a heart problem?"
"Yes."
"Difficulty breathing at the end?"

Well, I think to myself, isn't there *always* difficulty breathing at the end? But, I say, "Yes."

"Did he work a lot with papers?"

"Possibly," I say. He was an engineer; it would have involved paperwork, but it's not the most obvious connection.

"You have an older brother."

"Yes."

"He works with contracts."

"Yes." He's a lawyer.

"He helped with paperwork when your father passed."

"Possibly. I'm not sure. Father-in-law."

"Sorry, father-in-*law*. I got that wrong. He liked sport. Tennis. I can see him watching cricket. Did he play cricket?"

He did like sport. But I don't know about tennis or cricket. "Probably," I say.

"He's showing me a watch. A pocket watch. Do you have his pocket watch?"

"Not a pocket watch."

"Not a pocket watch, then. I'm sorry, that was wrong. But a wrist watch."

"Yes, a wrist watch."

"It's gold".

"Yes." It is. Solid gold. It was given to me on his death: an expensive piece which I wear in his memory. Though just this week it's in the shop being repaired, and tonight my wrist, for once, is bare.

"There's an inscription on the back".

"I'm afraid not."[43]

"You've been looking at a picture of him this week."

"Yes". Now, there's a good chance an audience member at a spiritualist gathering will regularly look at the picture of someone they have lost. But in all honesty I don't look at pictures of my late father-in-law that often. Though for the past two weeks, I have, unusually, been kept company by a picture of him. Sally had been sorting out papers and left a big picture of him propped up on the settee in my study.

There's a bit more about him being a man who was respected, who was no-nonsense, someone people listened to when he spoke. All true enough, but fairly generic. Then…

"He's giving me the name Ian."

"That was his middle name." Now this was impressive. My

father-in-law's name was Ian. His wife called him Colin Ian. If the medium had said Colin, I would have been a convert on the spot. But all the same, that was still pretty close.

Mark closes by leaving the message that I need to trust my first instincts in a big decision that is coming up. I thank him – and, I suppose, my father-in-law too – but, privately, I'm not aware of any impending big decisions. I do have a big potential change coming up in the next few months, but it isn't anything I can make a decision about. Still, as someone naturally cautious, who distrusts spontaneity, it would never hurt to trust instinct for once.

Mark moves on to two other people. Neither goes as well as my reading. Every time the sitter is unable to endorse the proffered information, Mark just says, with disarming humility. "Oh, I'm sorry. I got that wrong." He gives one other name, though, Anne. It is the name of the sister-in-law of the lady to whom he's delivering the message. Not a wide miss, but not a bullseye either.

The demonstration is over. The medium departs quickly to catch his train. I stay for a quick chat with Tom, a regular here for twenty years and a participant in the church's healing groups. "I'm glad you had a good reading," he says. "There's nothing worse than when people come for the first time and the medium's rubbish." That certainly wasn't my experience. But if only he had given the *first* name, not the middle. If only it had been a *wrist* watch straight off, not a pocket watch. As I make my way out into the night, the congregation are taking part in a fundraising raffle, their psychic powers, presumably, suspended, just for now.

## ASCENSION PARISH BURIAL GROUND

There could hardly be a more apt name for the house where the Viennese philosopher Ludwig Wittgenstein spent his last days. Storey's End is a 1913, three-floor, neo-Georgian building on tree-lined Storey's Way, which lies between two of Cambridge's more modern colleges, Churchill and Murray Edwards. Here, Wittgenstein lived for his last months until his death from cancer in 1951 aged 62. "Tell them I've had a wonderful life," were his last words.

He wasn't wrong. Born into one of Europe's richest families, he was the kind of genius even other geniuses deferred to; the kind of polymath who makes a Renaissance man look one-dimensional: scientist, musician, warrior, philanthropist, inventor, architect, designer, teacher, and, of course, philosopher – the discipline by which he earned his place in the history of thought. He first came to Cambridge before the Great War, to study with Bertrand Russell, who persuaded him to join The Apostles. On the outbreak of war, he returned to fight with the Austrian forces, distinguishing himself repeatedly for reckless bravery and an unshakeable sense of justice, social responsibility and duty. After a time as a prisoner of war, then as a rural schoolteacher and as an architect, he returned to Cambridge in 1929 to a fellowship at Trinity College and later a chair in philosophy,[44] remaining there until 1947, and, after some further peregrinations, returning there a few years later to die. He is buried only a few minutes' walk from Storey's End, in the Ascension Parish Burial Ground, where his is the most illustrious of the scores of famous burials.

At the entrance to the burial ground, a sign on the noticeboard says 'Please be aware that you enter at your own risk'. Risk of what? Of feeling inadequate, perhaps. The historian Dr Mark Goldie, author of *A Cambridge Necropolis*, has suggested that there is probably more IQ lying in this acre than in any other in the country: three Nobel Prize winners, seven members of the Order of Merit, eight College Masters, 39 people in the Dictionary of National Biography and 15 Knights of the Realm.

One of them, Sir Frederick Gowland Hopkins, managed a hat trick; Nobel Prize winner (Chemistry 1929), member of the Order of Merit (1935), and Knight of the Realm (1925). He is buried with his wife Jessie Ann, whose epitaph reads, with scientific precision: 'For 49 years she kept the cares of the world away from him.' A.C. Benson, author of the words of 'Land of Hope and Glory', is here too, as is the poet Frances Cornford,[45] grand-daughter of Charles Darwin and mother of John Cornford, the Communist poet killed aged 21 in the Spanish Civil War. Her memorial with its fine lettering, reputedly by Eric Gill, is on the very edge of Cambridge, fixed to the cemetery wall. Look over, and there's just a field of long grass and thistles, a row of trees and the sky. The epitaph, from one of Cornford's own poems, was a favourite of Philip Larkin's:

> My love came back to me
> Under the November tree
> Shelterless and dim.
> He put his hand upon my shoulder,
> He did not think me strange or older,
> Nor I him.

Wittgenstein's grave is recumbent rather than vertical; the stark lettering – just his name and dates – oriented not to the passing visitor but to the sky. The grave is maintained by the British Wittgenstein Society. Devotees, moved more perhaps by emotion than by the logic which was the master passion of this rigorous, piercing-eyed, minimalist ascetic, have left gifts of flowers on the stone. Coins have been pushed into the earth next to him; their denomination, their country of origin, indistinguishable; taken out of legal tender by their decay. Someone, Jewish-style, has left a stone on the grave, a hard flint. Someone else has left a feather.

This man who did not suffer fools gladly, but who in wartime chose to suffer with the common soldiers rather than take advantage of his privilege, lies among the most ordinary people of his adopted country. The names on the graves around his resting place seem chosen for their unpretentiousness: Albert, Annie, Nellie, Harriet, Gladys, Stanley, Edna, Nancy, Kitty, Elsie and Archibald.

However, it is not primarily to visit Wittgenstein that I have come here. The person I have come to see has no flowers on her grave. Fredegond Shove,[46] a minor poet connected with the Bloomsbury Group, was born in 1889. She was Virginia Woolf's cousin but never attained the stature of her famous relative, and, being a retiring sort, never tried. I would never have heard of her had not her uncle, the composer Ralph Vaughan Williams, set some of her work to music. It was at a concert in St George's in Hanover Square, London, that I first heard Shove's 'The New Ghost', which begins:

> And he cast it down, down, on the green grass,
> Over the young crocuses, where the dew was.
> He cast the garment of his flesh that was full of death,
> And like a sword his spirit showed out of the cold sheath.

This was not word-play. This was experience. At the time, I didn't even know if Fredegond was a man's name or a woman's. But I knew I had to find out more about this author, which is why, months later, I found myself in this wooded mid-Victorian cemetery. It took me a long while to find the grave where she lies with her husband, the economist Gerald Shove.[47] And when I did, I found that ivy had long hidden the name, and the year, 1949, when she herself went to meet the Maker who, if her poem was an accurate guide:

> ...kissed the unsheathed ghost that was gone free
> As a hot sun, on a March day, kisses the cold ground.

It is so overgrown that there is clearly no Society, no devotee keeping her memory from obscurity. Of course, if Fredegond – a mystic and convert to Catholicism – was right and her ghost has indeed gone serenely to eternity "like a naked cloud holding the sun's hand", then it doesn't matter if her grave is tended or not. For very different reasons, I doubt whether Wittgenstein, lying a short distance away, would have cared much whether his own resting place was tended or not either. After all, this is the man who said:

> Death is not an event in life: we do not live to experience death. If we take eternity to mean not infinite temporal duration but timelessness, then eternal life belongs to those who live in the present.

As I am neither mystic nor philosopher, I scrape the ivy and lichen away so that Fredegond's name can be read again – at least for a while.

# EDDINGTON, NORTH WEST CAMBRIDGE

The west wall of the Ascension Parish burial ground has long marked the very point where the city becomes the country. But if you look westwards across those open fields, you can make out a dust cloud, and within it, the outline of tower cranes, and you can hear the faint rumble of the earthmoving machines which are pushing the city limits, as A.C. Benson might have said, "wider still and wider."

North West Cambridge is the city's new frontier. Those wide-open prairies just sitting there, waiting for the hardy pioneers, the sodbusters, the speculators, to come and turn them into civilisation. To the overheated city, with its overpriced bedsits, its unaffordable studio flats, North West Cambridge seems to say: give me your tired, your huddled masses, yearning to breathe free, yearning for an executive apartment with a Juliet balcony and a hardstanding for the Mini.

It's certainly a bold enterprise: a billion-pound spend; a 150-hectare site on the former University farms; 1500 new homes – half of them affordable – for university staff and key workers. There'll also be accommodation for two thousand post-grads, a substantial but previously- overlooked group, vital to the city's future reputation for innovation. In a triangle formed by Huntingdon Road, Madingley Road and the M11, an army of builders are constructing an entire new town, complete with school, superstore, community centre, doctor's surgery, nature reserve, shops, hotel, power plant, and, with a view to the future, 'senior living home', all of it to high environmental standards, with green roofs, triple glazing, locally-generated underfloor heating, and swales to harvest rainwater. The core of the development has been named after Arthur Eddington[48] the astronomer, physicist and mathematician who helped explain Einstein's theory of relativity. He is buried in the Ascension parish burial ground, within sight of the emerging new community which will bear his name.

Construction will take fifteen years. So it's not surprising, when I visit with the art historian Duncan Robinson CBE, that it's still a work in progress. Duncan is the only person to have been both Director of the Fitzwilliam Museum, and Master of Magdalene College, where he was succeeded by Archbishop Rowan Williams. We have come to give this new development an early architectural appraisal.

Although the site has been designed to be friendly to bicycles, to public transport and to pedestrians, there are still a few on-street parking spaces, and, for convenience, and because there's little traffic this summer Saturday afternoon, we decide to use one. It's not a success. The meters are out of order. I use the car park beneath the Sainsbury store at the heart of the site. A trolley escalator takes me back to street level, where I find Duncan inspecting the array of refuse chutes; they look like ordinary rubbish bins, but they actually channel waste to giant underground containers, which are then removed bodily. It's ingenious, eliminating wheelie bins, but Duncan points out, it's having some technological teething problems too: the bins are sealed and marked

as not in use. We decide to get a coffee in the store café in Sainsbury's. Inside there's no sign of a café, so I ask a cashier to point me in the right direction. "You can get one there," he says, indicating at a small coffee stand, without seating, near the entrance. Better than nothing. Actually not. It's unstaffed, and a sign says sorry, the coffee machine is out of order.

We take a walk around the site, which doesn't yet quite have that lived-in look. But give it time: plenty of young trees have been planted, and the designers have made an effort with the building surfaces, which are in variegated buff-coloured brick recalling the city's domestic architecture, and with occasional details in what looks like terracotta. It's a bit blocky and institutional, though, with all those flat roofs; a bit like what a village would look like if designed by someone who'd spent their whole life on educational campuses. And, outside term-time, it's very quiet, with only the distant roar of traffic on the A14. In a few years it will be easier to get a feel for how its shaping up as a community: once those blocks are fully occupied; once that award-winning primary school, its closed gate decorated with a giant metal map of the world, has a playground full of shouting kids.

Next to the school is a tall industrial-looking rectangular building. From a distance, we're trying to work out what it might be when we spot a young man with long hair taking photographs of it, moving urgently as he snaps it from various angles. Clearly an architecture buff. I wonder what he's making of Eddington? We walk over to have a word, just as he darts out of sight behind the building. We find him sitting on a high wall, legs crossed – he's wearing shorts and white ankle socks – while posing for photographs for his companion, a man in a jaunty matelot-striped teeshirt. Close up, we see the long-haired guy is not actually that young: he's well into his thirties, and his companion well into his forties. The younger man jumps down and I take the opportunity to ask him if he's studying architecture. Yes, he says. In fact he's an architect himself. I turn to his companion, who's looking on appreciatively. An architect too? No, he says benignly: an *admirer* of architects. Both of them seem hyper, overflowing with nervous energy. They both look keen to be away, though they are polite, if brief, in responding to my questions.

The rectangle we're looking at is, they tell me, the MUMA[49] building, a community and art centre nominated for the Stirling Prize. The younger man looks up at it with reverence. So what does he make of Eddington as a whole? He thinks hard. Finally he says: "The streets are too wide." He's right, I realise. They *are* too wide. That explains that slightly spaced-out feeling you get walking through them. Though that's not the only thing round here that's spaced out. "Got to go," says the younger man. "Our parents are waiting for us." Parents? But they're gone, bounding away like puppies in the direction of the nearby children's playground, which is empty apart from two small Asian children playing silently on a see-saw under the supervision of their texting dad. The two guys reach the fence, stop a moment, then veer away. "Too big for the slide!" one of them shouts at us happily and, jumping like hurdlers over a low wall, they disappear around the corner. We watch them go. Whatever *joie de vivre* Eddington seems to lack, those two were certainly making up for it.

## Notes

1. 1869-1949.
2. Climbing a greasy pole.
3. Blind man's buff.
4. A bran tub.
5. 1852-1909.
6. http://www.kingofthepeds.com/
7. 1860-1951.
8. 1810-1860.
9. Moses Carter's Stone, carried there for a bet, stands outside the Boot pub in Histon. Ian

MacEachern, *Curiosities of Cambridge. A County Guide to the Unusual*, (Market Drayton, 1991), 19.

10. A memorial stands in a field near Impington where her ordeal took place.

11. 1895-1990.

12. Next to the gallery is St Peter's Church, now an exhibition space. The Roman *tegulae* (roof tiles) in its outer walls are the only remaining visible evidence of Cambridge's Roman past. (Mee 13).

13. 1884-1962, *La poétique de l'éspace*, 1957.

14. 1908-2003.

15. Raine went to Girton to read Natural Sciences in 1926, got a 3rd in Psychology and returned in 1954 as a research fellow for five years.

16. A blue plaque on Boots the Chemist in Sidney Street commemorates Charles Darwin's lodgings when a student at Christ's.

17. 'The 10 most expensive streets in Cambridge – you'll need at least £1.8 million to move in' *Cambridge Live*, 29.09.16 https://www.cambridge-news.co.uk/news/property/revealed -10-most-expensive-streets-11957936

18. For the band's 1969 album, *Ummagumma*. Fellow band member David Gilmour had moved at the age of ten to Grantchester Meadows.

19. Cambridge's first college for women. Girton, was founded two years earlier.

20. Martin Garrett, *op. cit.*, 152.

21. *Ibid.*, 154.

22. Who called it by its Welsh name Cair Grauth, 'Fort Granta', the name Welsh speakers still use today for the whole of Cambridge: Caergrawnt.

23. Danuta Kean, 'Battle of the heart: Was war poet Rupert Brooke a closet heterosexual?' The Independent, 25.01.09.

24. By Mary Archer, *Rupert Brooke and the Old Vicarage Grantchester*, (Cambridge, 1989), 34.

25. Mary Archer says rightly: "Brooke was ... a hyperbolical letter writer", 31.

26. Mary Archer, *op. cit.*, 13. The house in fact was late seventeenth-century and had not been a vicarage since 1850.

27. According to Ward's daughter Elisabeth, he "never in later life spoke of his friendship with Brooke, perhaps from grief or embarrassment," Mary Archer, 37.

28. He became a college lecturer, though not a millionaire.

29. At the time of writing, 33 titles and sales of over 270,000,000.

30. She notes, sportingly: "Jeffrey is linked to the house in another unusual way, by *The Guardian*'s master crossword setter Araucaria, whose clue: 'Poetic scene has, surprisingly, chaste Lord Archer vegetating (3, 3, 8, 12)', has as its anagram solution THE OLD VICARAGE GRANTCHESTER." *Op. cit.*, 64

31. He died in 2010, days after I received my honorary D.Litt. from Anglia Ruskin. I showed him the framed certificate on his deathbed, and the flowers given as part of the presentation accompanied his coffin.

32. In her 1972 murder mystery, *An Unsuitable Job for a Woman*.

33. A 1764 novel by Horace Walpole set in an ancient castle; it spawned the Gothic novel genre.

34. The name of the sentient VW Beetle which starred in a series of Disney movies starting in 1968 with *The Love Bug*.

35. Again, unveiled by Sir Martin Rees, in 2000.

36. 1889-1961.

37. David Rooney, Henry Morris, *The Cambridgeshire Village Colleges and Community Education*, (Cambridge, 2013).

38. Nearby are the buildings replacing some of the 28 thatched properties lost in the 'Great Fire' of 1913. One of the more elegant replacements is an early work of Clough Williams Ellis, later famous for Portmeirion, his Italianate fantasy village in north Wales.

39. Pumping is now electric-powered. Over's last windmill closed in the 1890s.

40. 1593-1637.
41. 1593-1633.
42. 1843-1901.
43. Unless you count the word 'Accurist'.
44. On October 1946, at a meeting of the Moral Sciences Club in Room H3 at King's College, he was involved in a legendary altercation with fellow exiled Viennese philosopher Karl Popper, in which he brandished a poker threateningly, or used it to point an emphasis (depending on whom you believe). See David Edmonds and John Eidinow, *Wittgenstein's Poker*, (New York, 2001). The bar at the University Arms hotel offers a cocktail called 'Wittgenstein's Poker.'
45. 1886-1960.
46. Rhymes with 'stove'.
47. A Newnham alumna, she and her husband lived in Cambridge in later life.
48. 1882-1944.
49. McInnes Usher McKnight Architects.

# OUTSIDE

# THE SOURCE OF THE CAM

It isn't every day you find a new goddess. But for Alan Meek, scanning his way with his metal detector through a field some seventeen miles south west of Cambridge in September 2002, his divining turned up a bona fide divinity. He unearthed a hoard of 27 gold and silver objects which later investigation showed were a Romano-Celtic deposit of votive offerings to the goddess Senuna, the deity of the river which springs from the rocks a mile or so distant, and which, further down its course, is known as the Cam.

The hoard, now safely behind glass in Room 49 at the British Museum, includes a silver figurine and twenty gold and silver votive plaques, a portion of those many costly sacrifices which the ancient Britons and their Roman overlords thought were worth paying, whether in propitiation or gratitude, to holy rivers and wells the length and breadth of Britannia. Half the plaques in the cache were inscribed in Latin to the goddess Senuna, previously unknown to history except in one possible reference in the seventh-century *Ravenna Cosmography*, which mentioned a river in southern Britain called the Senua. Twelve of the plaques depicted an image of a female figure with a spear, shield and owl – a symbol of wisdom. These are the traditional attributes of the Roman goddess Minerva, but seem here to have been applied to her native Celtic sister in an example of what theologians call syncretism, but which we might now call multi-culturalism.[1]

It appears the discovery site may have been a wellhead for the river which bore the goddess' name, and that the hoard had been deliberately hidden sometime in the Third or Fourth Century, perhaps by a devotee at a time of conflict between Christianity and the older religions. Put aside for a season, to await better days. It was a long wait. But, some seventeen hundred years later, thanks to electromagnetic technology, Senuna was back in business. A group of neo-pagans, the Temple of Brigantia, in Maine, New England, crafted a ritual to honour her: an eclectic mix of archaisms ('forth', 'mighty') and contemporary therapeutic vocabulary ('community', 'support', 'interconnected'). They reported that it went down well with the divine being, who was clearly prepared to move with the times: "all of us who partook of that work believe that Senua[2] exists as a deity, that she heard and received our prayers, and that she was pleased to receive our attention after being so long neglected."[3]

The exact location where Alan Meek found the cache is officially 'undisclosed', in order to discourage less responsible detectorists from plundering the area in search of further treasures. The fact that the wellhead has long silted up makes it all the more undiscoverable. But there's no such official coyness about the present source of the river, a mile or so distant in the picture-postcard North Hertfordshire village of Ashwell Springs, where, immediately off the main street, in a natural ash-tree-fringed rock amphitheatre, the water gushes from the bare rock as though Moses himself had just struck it with his staff.[4]

On the Sunday afternoon that I visit, the annual festival is in full swing. There's a cricket game taking place on the village green, and a full-scale funfair on the field next door. A steward with a hi-vis vest and a broad Scots accent is guiding traffic, while the day's activities are being announced by a red-robed town crier in a tricorn hat and wearing a chain around his neck. Any house with a claim to historical interest of office has been tagged with a laminated sign telling its history. A morris man with flowers round his hat makes for the door of the pub. Outside a shop sit three old geezers with beards and waistcoats strumming guitars, and singing a tuneless self-penned song about sitting outside a shop on a Sunday afternoon strumming guitars.

At Ashwell Springs, the river is known as the Rhee, an old Saxon word for a water course. Further on, it develops a dual identity, as its name becomes interchangeable with the Cam. Then, a mile south of Grantchester, it joins its fellow tributary, the Granta, which arises some 25 miles away in Essex, and for a brief stretch, the river is known as the Granta until it reaches Silver Street bridge in the centre of the city when it becomes the Cam again.[5] Although the river might no longer bear her name, Senuna, recently awakened from nearly two millennia of slumber, might well be pleased to see the thriving city of learning that has arisen on her banks. After all, she was – or, according to the Temple of Brigantia, *is* – the goddess of wisdom

## ELY PLACE AND ST ETHELDREDA'S

Her name might not exactly trip off the tongue, and she might not be an A-lister these days as saints go, but back in the Seventh Century St Etheldreda was box office. This daughter of an East Anglian king was a woman who did things on her own terms. She wanted to be a nun, but accepted a dynastic marriage on condition she could retain her virginity. When her husband tried to renege on the deal, she left him and entered the religious life at Ely, rebuilding that city's war-damaged church in some splendour, freeing her bondsmen and becoming one of the most powerful women of her age. When she died, she was proclaimed a saint, and when her tomb was relocated seventeen years after her death, her body was said to be have been found to be uncorrupted. The same claim was made when it was moved again, in 1106, four hundred and fifty years after her death. So when the Bishop of Ely, traditionally one of the most influential English dioceses, needed a London palace as a *pied à terre*, it was natural that its chapel should be dedicated to this remarkable local heroine. St Etheldreda's opened in 1290, and became one of only two buildings in London to survive from the time of Edward I. It also became the site of a legend as apparently indestructible as the body of St Etheldreda itself – the belief that Ely Place, now a little cul-de sac of mainly Georgian houses in the Holborn area of London, is not really part of the capital at all, but is really part of Cambridgeshire.

It is an appealing tale, and you can find many a website and wishful thinker who will tell you that, to this very day, Ely Place is administratively part of Cambridgeshire and that its own tavern, Ye Olde Mitre Inn, has its licences granted by the Cambridge magistrates. More ambitious versions of the tale will even claim that villains fleeing the law could take refuge in the pub, safe in the knowledge that, in this 'exclave' of Cambridgeshire, only officers from that constabulary could arrest them. It's sadly not true, of course, and was already being debunked as groundless as early as 1876, but until the late Eighteenth Century it did have some basis in fact. The Bishop of Ely, who until 1836 had extensive powers, including the ability to appoint magistrates and to arrange assize courts *in Cambridgeshire*, exercised that power from Ely Place when he was in residence. The Bishop's Palace was the property of Ely diocese until 1772, when it was sold to developers who demolished everything except the church and who rebuilt the area as the quiet and orderly Georgian street that it is today. It does retain this peculiarity, however, that it is the only private street in London, with its own commissioners regulating its affairs, and a barrier denoting its boundary with the outside world, where a black-clad beadle with dark glasses keeps watch from a neat little guardhouse, equipped with a clipboard, radio and kettle.

During its time as the Bishop's Palace, Ely Place certainly played its role in history. John of Gaunt lived there, and in Shakespeare's *Richard II*, it is at this palace that the playwright has John of Gaunt deliver one of the most famous speeches in the English language, when he eulogises "this sceptre'd isle ... this England." Then in *Richard III*, Shakespeare has the Duke of Gloucester distract the inconvenient and soon-to-be-imprisoned bishop by calling his attention to the strawberries for which the palace's gardens were famous:

> When I was last in Holborn,
> I saw good strawberries in your garden there
> I do beseech you send for some of them.

The commissioners still arrange the street's annual Strawberry Fayre celebrations in memory of the long-vanished garden which exists only now between the pages of Shakespeare's works.

Later, King Henry VIII and his first wife, Catherine of Aragon, stayed at the Palace for five days as guests of the Bishop in 1531 at a time when the cracks in the marriage were starting to show – they dined in separate rooms. Later still, once Henry had split with Rome over his divorce, the first Protestant Bishop of Ely built The Mitre Tavern close to the palace for the benefit of his retinue. In the centuries that followed, St Etheldreda's survived the Reformation, the brief restoration of Catholicism under Mary Tudor, the re-establishment of Protestantism, the Great Fire of London in 1666 (the wind turned just as the flames were reaching the church), the demolition of the palace in 1775, and a German bomb in 1941. In 1714 it was the scene of a sensational trial when the Fellows of Trinity attempted to depose their tyrannical and rapacious Master, Richard Bentley, by appealing to the Bishop of Ely. The Bishop ruled against Bentley – who fainted from shock – but was then himself taken ill and died before he could put his judgment into effect. Bentley's reign of terror eventually lasted 42 years. In 1878, St Etheldreda's became a Catholic church again, and for many years retained the distinction of being the oldest in England – all the others being post-Reformation.[6]

Today, St Etheldreda's is one of London's most atmospheric places of worship. I visit it on a December day between Christmas and the New Year. The poster outside advertises "one of the most magical wedding venues in London". Inside, I have the place to myself – stone-flagged floors, recessed lighting, alcoved statues, Our Lady, St Francis; the Stations of the Cross. From outside comes the faint hum of a generator and the chink of hammers from renovation work on the mews house opposite. The weak winter sunlight light struggles in through the dense, abstract stained glass in the nave. It is still some days before Epiphany, so the sculpted figures of the Magi are only half-way on their journey along the stone sill of the glorious West window to complete the cast-list at the crib. They do things properly at St Etheldreda's: the Magi must inch along, a little further each day, until they reach the fulfilment of their hopes. Wisdom cannot be rushed.

Outside again, a little side alley leads to Ye Olde Mitre pub, so named because of the episcopal connection. Upturned barrels outside act as planters-cum-ashtrays. Behind the quarry-glass are a couple of fake skulls. The pub itself is small and packed. In the corner of the bar behind a glass case, is the stump of a cherry tree, said to have formed the boundary between the Bishop's Palace and the palatial home of Elizabeth I's favourite Sir Christopher Hatton. When he took a fancy to the site, the queen forced the Bishop to hand it over to him on pain of being defrocked. The area became known as Hatton Gardens, and is now the City's jewellery quarter. In many ways, The Mitre is a typical City boozer, filling up at the end of the working day with suited office workers spilling out onto the pavement, ties off, fags out, volume up, for an hour or so of cathartic clamour before they scatter for the tube.

I have come here with Mick Gowar, poet, folklorist, lecturer, guitarist, and a man who has forgotten more about Cambridge than I will ever know, though for once, we have found a bit of Cambridge which is new to him.

The couple on the next table are from Cambridge too, it turns out. In no time, they are swapping stories of local characters:

"Do you remember the lady who used to ride around on a bike, with a bucket on her head?"

"Yes, and the guy who used to dress as Sinbad?"

"There's a statue of him..."

"They say if you live in Cambridge you never grow up."

They have to go. "We're attending an event in Ely diocese." They're going to a dinner held in the crypt of St Etheldreda's. They didn't need telling about the Cambridge connection. Ely Place may not really be part of Cambridge administratively – if it ever was – but it remains, inalienably, part of Cambridge mythology.

We have to take our leave too. Outside, in Hatton Gardens, the street is a mass of cables, trucks, and lighting rigs; a film crew are wrapping after a day's work on a movie about the 2015 Hatton Gardens raid – the biggest burglary in British legal history, when a gang of veteran jewel thieves tunnelled into the vault of a safety deposit company and got away with an estimated £14 million. They were eventually arrested – or more correctly, nicked, as it was The Sweeney[7] who collared them – and are now doing time. The heist was a pretty retro affair – the oldest villain was 77, the youngest 59 and the average age of the six who were jailed was 66 – but there's no evidence they were old-school enough to consider taking refuge from justice in the Mitre. Nonetheless, in this corner of the city that has more than its fair share of stories, they have certainly added one more layer of legend.


# PINK FLOYD

There's a flying pig above the Victoria and Albert Museum. Not, perhaps, a sight that would have been foreseen by the founders of this institution in 1852, when it was conceived as a Museum of Manufactures, a permanent legacy of the Great Exhibition of 1851. But perhaps not so incongruous after all, as the inflatable porker is here to advertise the work of a group of artists who certainly know how to put on a show.

The retrospective exhibition, *Pink Floyd: Their Mortal Remains*, has proved especially attractive to a particular demographic: guys over sixty. Free spirits with free bus passes. Many appear to be attending on their own, their nostalgia trip a solo tour. But they're out in force. Dark teeshirts with once-edgy slogans are worn outside trousers, partly a defiant style statement, partly a necessity as raunch gives way to paunch. The young museum attendant who is managing the queue, has drawn a rope across the entrance to control the numbers. While waiting, the grey-haired guy at the front is trying to engage her in banter. It isn't going well.

"Don't worry, I'm not a gatecrasher," he joshes her.

"You are not ... what?" she says, dubiously.

"A gatecrasher."

"Gate? Crasher?" This is not a term she's familiar with. The guy decides it's time for an English lesson.

"Yes. It's an expression. When you want to come in without paying, you crash the gate."

She's distinctly uneasy now: She looks anxiously across at the security guard.

Mercifully, her walkie talkie squawks, authorising her to lift the rope, and Grey Haired Guy is in. Legitimately. No gates crashed. She watches him warily.

We're given our wifi-enabled headphones, and, to the private soundtrack of wailing guitars, are off down a psychedelic black-and-white spiral-patterned tunnel to the Nineteen Sixties. A return journey for many of these guys, I guess, but a first-time trip for me.

It's not just older geezers, to be fair. There are plenty of ordinary tourists, and some, but not many, young hipsters. There is, however, a generally intent and reverential air to the whole thing. In a room papered with trippy, acid-induced posters, where a black-and-white film of a sequence from Alice in Wonderland plays on a loop on a video wall, and a classic red phonebox serves as a mini display cabinet for magazines, record sleeves, and gig tickets,[8] four men are absorbed in study of a family tree of the band's antecedents: the line of succession of rock royalty; I suspect they'll know these branching, proliferating lineages as well as any religious scholar could follow a genealogy back to Genesis. Better, probably.

As far as I can see in the subdued light, it all seems to start with Geoff Mott and the Mottoes, followed by Those Without, the Ramblers, Bullitt, Jokers Wild, The Newcomers, The Ramblers (again), The Tailboard Two, Sigma 6, The Abdabs (screaming, presumably? Yes, the very small print says 'aka The Screaming

Abdabs'); Leonard's Lodgers and, penultimately, The Tea Set. Who
begat Pink Floyd.

The display material deals gently with Syd Barrett's departure
from the line-up. Alongside a picture of that knowing, vulnerable
face, the caption says, with careful understatement: "By late 1967,
lead guitarist and composer Syd Barrett found popular success an
increasing strain." It is probably imagination that makes you see, in
those early images, and Nigel Lesmoir-Gordon's flickering
cine-film footage, a foreshadowing of what is to come, and to find
in those hooded eyes, which already seem to have seen too much, a
family resemblance to Jim Morrison, Kurt Cobain, Richey
Edwards. Retrospect makes patterns and purpose out of random
realities.

But, in the display case devoted to the band's Cambridge roots,
hindsight is accurate enough in finding poignancy in the pictures of
the young Barrett in the 7th Cambridge County School Scout
group, along with images of Gilmour and Waters in school
photographs and rugby teams. There are tickets for gigs in
now-vanished venues, and a strikingly accomplished technical
drawing of Cambridge Railway Station and a street scene from
1962, done while Waters was a student of architecture, a reminder
of the technical mastery, not just of musicianship but also of visuals
and stage set design, which kept the band at the cutting edge of
cultural innovation for decade after decade.

Pink Floyd, one of the best-selling bands of all time, and the creators of some of the most influential artworks of the last fifty years, were formed in London in 1965, but were rooted in Cambridge. In fact, the exhibition shows that the Cambridge connection is even stronger than I supposed. As well as the fact that Barrett, Waters and Gilmour had all grown up in Cambridge, their circle of friends and associates during their early years in London was made up substantially of a Cambridge town diaspora. Storm Thorgerson[9] and Aubrey Powell, the graphic designers who devised some of the band's most iconic album covers with their Hipgnosis company[10], were from Cambridge, and even their road manager, former Mill Pond puntmaster Alan Styles, was a native of the city.

Entire rooms are devoted to examples of the band's equipment – pedals, woofers, moogs, minimoogs, cables, drumkits, mixing desks, animation suites, and, of course, guitars. Lots of guitars. Floyd's influence on visual culture is explored, including the work of Hipgnosis whose covers range from the rainbow prism on the cover of *Dark Side of the Moon* (still selling seven thousand copies a week) to the burning business executive on *Wish You Were Here*, to the flying inflatable pig above Battersea Power Station on *Animals*. The achievement is all the more impressive for having been realised in an analogue rather than a digital world. Finally, after you make it past the giant Gerald Scarfe-designed tyrannical teachers and goose-stepping fascistic hammers of *The Wall*, you find yourself in a large room where a wraparound video screen – headphones off now – delivers some of Floyd's most powerful performances in earthshaking surroundsound.

"Did it take you back?" asks the lady at the exit as I return my headset. I'm just one more old guy revisiting his past. She remembers it well, she tells me. She was born in 1960; four years earlier than me. She grew up with all this. I have to tell her that, in all honesty, Pink Floyd hadn't actually been part of my youth; not because I was too young, but because my interests had lain elsewhere. But, knowing what I know now, since I entered that swirling psychedelic Alice-in-Wonderland rabbit-hole a couple of hours ago, I feel nostalgia for a place I've never been, I feel the loss of a youth I never had, and I envy those paunchy blokes with their merchandise and their memories. Wish You Were Here? I just wish I had been.

# THE OXFORD AND CAMBRIDGE CLUB

The district of St James's in central London takes its name from the convent of St James the Lesser, which stood here for centuries, providing a home for people with leprosy, and those who ministered to them. That came to an end in the 1530s when Henry VIII took advantage of his Dissolution of the Monasteries to evict the inmates and build a palace for himself and Anne Boleyn.[11] This has been a place of power ever since: home to generations of royalty; the senior royal court of the United Kingdom; the Court of St James to which foreign ambassadors are accredited, and the place where the Accession council meets to proclaim the new sovereign. The Chapel Royal, whose windows look out on to St James's Street, has been the scene for centuries of dynastic drama: this is where Elizabeth I prayed for deliverance from the Spanish Armada, and where her half-sister 'Bloody' Mary's heart is buried in a silver casket under the chancel step. More recently, Queen Victoria married here; so did George V, and it has also witnessed the baptism of Prince George.

In the days when political power and patronage flowed from the royal court, it made sense for the well-connected – and the ambitious – to base themselves nearby, so the adjacent streets of Pall Mall and St James's Street quickly became filled with the kind of private clubs that provided a home-from-home for gentlemen who wanted to be as close as possible to the levers of power. While the drama of politics may now mainly be played out in front of the television cameras on the stage of Westminster, it's still here in Clubland that much of the script is devised. Power has converged and concentrated here, like in Alfred Watkins' system of ley lines. And almost as invisibly. Walk down St James's Street, and, in between the cigar shops, wine merchants and purveyors of tweed, you'll pass White's Club, the oldest and most exclusive of them all. Then Brooks's, then Boodle's. Then the Carlton, for Conservatives, which admitted women only in 2008. Even Margaret Thatcher was only an Honorary Member until then. Next, close to the junction with Pall Mall is Mark Masons' Hall, the headquarters of a branch of Freemasonry even more esoteric than most. Many evenings, usually at seven or nine, its black-clad members can be seen arriving or leaving by taxi, all carrying the distinctive layflat cases, somewhere between the size of a briefcase and an artist's portfolio, in which they transport their regalia. But you could pass all of those places without knowing it, as none of them advertise their presence; not one carries so much as a nameplate. If you know, you just know. If you don't, you just walk on by, none the wiser.

Just opposite, close to the corner of Pall Mall and Marlborough Road, next to the headquarters of the Commonwealth, is the Oxford and Cambridge Club. Again, there's no sign to publicise the fact, but this is the apex of Britain's Golden Triangle: the notional three-cornered figure formed by Oxford in the west, Cambridge in the east, and London in the south, and which contains within it the greatest concentration of academic expertise and institutional wealth in the country, focused as though by a prism, and represented in its quintessence here, where Oxford, Cambridge and London all converge.

The club is a fine neoclassical mansion, purpose-built in 1838 for the then Oxford and Cambridge University Club by Sir Robert Smirke, who also redesigned the interior of the Chapel Royal a few hundred yards away. Like all such clubs, you have to be elected to membership, and to qualify here, you need to have a degree or an honorary degree from either Cambridge or Oxford, or have full membership of either university's halls, colleges, or governing bodies. I don't qualify on any account. But Duncan Robinson, with whom I'm dining here today, as former Master of Magdalene and Director of the Fitzwilliam, is almost over-qualified.

Dinner is preceded by drinks in the bar, where a picture of the first Duke of Wellington (an Honorary Member) gazes down. The club has an enviable art collection. A little later, in the Coffee Room, as the main dining room is known here, I remark on a large portrait of George IV, and a dim memory stirs of having seen it in the collection of Thomas Lawrence's[12] portraits of Regency and Napoleonic War luminaries in the Waterloo Chamber at Windsor Castle. "Is that a Lawrence?" I ask. "*After* Lawrence," says Duncan, gently. He has just been to the Charles I exhibition at the Royal Academy, where that ill-fated monarch's collection, dispersed by Cromwell, has been re-assembled. The first Charles had been a shrewd art collector, and so had George IV, as Prince of Wales, as Prince Regent and then as King. The portrait here depicts him in the Coronation robes he designed himself, complete with collars of the Orders of the Golden Fleece, Guelphic, Bath and Garter. His Imperial Crown and his right hand rest on the 'Table des Grands

Capitaines', which depicts the great commanders of antiquity, and which was a prized possession of his defeated enemy, Napoleon.

George IV was famous, among other things, for the lavishness of his catering arrangements. The three hundred guests at his coronation banquet in Westminster Hall, the last held in England, were treated to: soups; venison; veal; mutton; beef; braised ham; savoury pies; geese; braised capon; lobster; crayfish; cold roast fowl and cold lamb; jellies, creams and sauces, as well as thousands of side dishes. By the end of the supper, the new King had almost collapsed from his gastronomic exertions.

Our supper today is, by comparison, much more restrained, though still very fine. I have the red mullet, followed by the beef rosette with oxtail hash and neeps (it's shortly after Burns night, and neeps are still enjoying their brief annual outing to the big city). For pudding, salted caramel ice cream (caramel and salt – strangers for so long, but now inseparable); the ice cream comes with a wafer printed with the crest and title of the Oxford and Cambridge Club. For a moment, I think of taking a souvenir photograph, but I remember that phones are forbidden here, along with briefcases, folders and anything that looks like it might be used for business.

Looking around the Coffee Room, there's visible diversity in age, gender and ethnicity. Barriers were lowered here earlier than in many comparable places, with women members admitted in 1996, which may not have been exactly the cutting edge of female emancipation, but which was, in the environs of Clubland, almost dangerously egalitarian. Duncan and I find ourselves talking about the subtle barriers which, intentionally or not, can exclude the uninitiated access to university and for instance, there's that well-intentioned politeness that would not dream of insulting you by assuming that you do not know the social rules – and which therefore never explains them to you. As the former Master of Magdalene, he's particularly aware of how these unwritten standards can sometimes take a linguistic form, with counter-intuitive pronunciations acting as a code – with pronunciation diverging more from spelling the further up the social scale you go. The cognoscenti are exempt from the dull literalism of the hoi polloi. He recalls once, as a young man, being in conversation with an English grandee of the artworld who asked him if he had ever been to *Mill*un. When he looked nonplussed, the grandee simply repeated the name, with some impatience, if not actual exasperation: *Mill*un, dear boy, *Mill*un! It took a moment to work out that the questioner meant Mil*an*, and had been expecting him to pick up seamlessly on his use of the archaic Shakespearean pronunciation. Not the best way to indicate the geographical place, to be sure; but certainly an effective way of reinforcing a *social* place. Which was, of course, the whole idea. Still, old barriers can eventually be overcome. After all, this Club is formed from an amicable marriage of Oxford *and* Cambridge, and if that isn't progress, what is?

## Notes

1. It was a surprisingly diverse world: One of the Latin inscriptions on the votive offerings said 'Servandus Hispani ('from Spain') willingly fulfilled his vow to the goddess.'
2. The inscriptions on the votive offerings are variously Senuna, Sena, and Senua.
3. http://www.janeraeburn.com/senua/
4. Numbers 20:11.
5. The settlement was originally called 'Grantabridge', a name whose pronunciation softened over the years to 'Cambridge'. In an unusual case of reverse etymology, the river was then renamed to conform to the changed pronunciation. The entire river was called the Grant or the Granta until Shakespeare's day.
6. It held this title until 1971 when the Church of England, in a spirit of letting bygones be bygones, gifted the Catholic Church an even older building at Malton in North Yorkshire.
7. Cockney rhyming slang for The Flying Squad ('Sweeney Todd'), the Metropolitan Police unit responsible for dangerous, specialist and armed operations. The term was popularised by a 1970s TV series of the same name.
8. The phonebox was designed by Sir Giles Gilbert Scott, who also designed Battersea Power Station, which appeared on the cover of the Pink Floyd album *Animals*, hence its use s a recurring motif in the exhibition.
9. 1944-2013.
10. The name, which appeared as a graffito on the door of the practice's London premises, was probably a coinage of Syd Barrett's.
11. In the Tapestry Room at the palace you can still see the 'H&A' monogram at one end of the magnificent carved Tudor fireplace. At the other end, it is just an 'H', because by the time the carver had reached that end of the piece, Henry and Anne's marriage, and Anne's life, had come to an end.
12. 1769-1830, the greatest English portrait artist of his day.

# WORKS CONSULTED

Anonymous, *A Roof-Climber's Guide to Trinity*, Cambridge, 2010

Archer, Mary, *Rupert Brooke and the Old Vicarage Grantchester*, Cambridge, 1989

Bachelard, Gaston, *La poétique de l'éspace*, Paris 1957

Barrowclough, David, *Bloody British History; Cambridge*, Stroud, 2015

Bell, John, *Cambridgeshire Crimes*, Cambridge, 1994

Benstead, C.R., *Portrait of Cambridge*, London 1968

Bottema, Els, and Kindersley, Lida, *The Shingle Street Shell Line*, Cambridge, 2018

Boyd, Fiona, Cardozo Kindersley, Lida Lopes and Sherwood, Tom, *David Kindersley*, Cambridge, 2015

Boyd, Fiona, Cardozo Kindersley, Lida Lopes and Sherwood, Tom, *David Kindersley, Volume 2, The Man*, Cambridge, 2016

Brigham, Allan, Clark, Gordon, and Filby, Peter *Mill Road Windmill, Cambridge*, Cambridge, 2013

Brooke, Rupert, *The Collected Poems*, London, 1983

Bruce, Alison, *Cambridge Blue*, London, 2008

Burnside, John, *The Locust Room*, London 2001

Cardozo Kindersley, Lida Lopes, *The Cardozo Kindersley Workshop, A guide to commissioning work*, Cambridge, 2013

The Community of Christ the Sower, *The Little Gidding Prayer Book*, London, 1986

Crossley-Holland, Kevin, *The Old Stories*, Cambridge, 1997

Curry, David, *The Men That Never Clocked Off, Ghost stories from Cambridge airport*, Cambridge, 2004

Durrant, John, *Cambridge, The Changing Face of the City and its People*, Stroud, 2000

Edmonds, David and Eidinow, John, *Wittgenstein's Poker*, New York, 2001

Garrett, Martin, *Cambridge. A cultural and literary history*, Massachusetts, 2004

Gibson, Arthur, *God and the Universe*, London, 2000

Gray, Ronald, and Stubbings, Derek, *Cambridge Street-Names. Their Origins and Associations* Cambridge, 2000

Gray, Terence, *Why Lazarus Laughed: The Essential Doctrine Zen-Advaita-Tantra*, London, 1960

Hawking, Stephen, *My Brief History*, Random House, 2013

Hawking, Stephen, *Black Holes and Baby Universes*, London, 1993

Hayman, Ronald, (ed) *My Cambridge*, London, 1977

Heaton, John and Groves, Judy, *Wittgenstein for Beginners*, Cambridge, 1994

Hughes, Ted, *Poetry in the Making*, London, 1967

Keynes, F.A., *By-ways of Cambridge History* Cambridge, 1947

Lister, Raymond, *With My Own Wings, the Memoirs of Raymond Lister*, Cambridge, 1994

MacEachern, Ian, *Curiosities of Cambridge. A County Guide to the Unusual*, Market Drayton, 1991

Macintyre, Ben, *A Spy Among Friends*, London, 2014

Mee, Arthur, *Cambridgeshire*, London, 1939

Newman, Paul, *The Lost Gods of Albion*, Stroud, 1999

Pagnamenta, Peter, (ed) *The University of Cambridge: an 800th Anniversary Portrait*, London, 2008

Raphael, Frederic, *The Glittering Prizes*, London, 1976

Raverat, Gwen, *Period Piece, A Cambridge Childhood*, London, 1963

Rawle, Tim, *Cambridge Architecture*, London, 1993

Rooney, David, Henry Morris, *The Cambridgeshire Village Colleges and Community Education*, Cambridge, 2013

Scammel, William, (ed) *Winter Pollen: Occasional Prose*, London, 1994

Sharpe, Tom, *Wilt*, London 1976

Shulman, Nicola, *Graven with Diamonds: The Many Lives of Thomas Wyatt, Courtier, Poet, Assassin, Spy*, London 2011

Tames, Richard, *An Armchair Traveller's Guide to Cambridge*, London, 2013

Taplin, Phoebe, *Country Walks Around Cambridge*, Stroud, 2015

Watkins, Alfred, *Archaic Tracks Round Cambridge* Hereford, 1932

Watkinson, Mike and Anderson, Pete, *Crazy Diamond: Syd Barrett and the Dawn of Pink Floyd*, London, 1991

Wickham, Glynne; Berry, Herbert and Ingram, William, (eds), *English Professional Theatre, 1530-1660*, Cambridge, 2000

Wilkens, Iman, *Where Troy Once Stood*, London, 1991

# THE PHOTOGRAPHS

Reality Checkpoint, on Parker's Piece 18

Malcolm Guite 19

Bicycles in Trumpington Street 22

Mark Wormold with the stained glass memorial to Ted
Hughes 30

Lord and Lady Eatwell's garden party, at Queen's College 32

The World War Two messages on the ceiling of the Eagle pub 36

Simon Satori Hendley and the bomb damage on the walls of
Trinity College 42

Falun Gong demonstration in King's Parade 44

Prayer station in Market Square 49

The houses tragetted by Latin grafitti 56

Cambridge Guided Busway 61

The Gospel Hall, Arbury 63

Mural on Arbury Court 64

James Murray-White and the memorial to James Cromwell 65

Memorial to Tony, the dog of Prince Chula of Siam 66

Lida Cardozo Kindersley in her North Chesterton studio 69

Lida Cardozo Kindersley working on William Blake's gravestone 70

David Kindersley's grave in North Chesterton 71

Crafts workers at the Cardozo Kindersley Studio 72

Cambridge North Station 76

Cambridge Science Park 77

Pillbox on Cambridge Science Park 78

Ian Rawlinson and the anthrax burial site, Arbury 78

The Polish Centre, Chesterton 80

Home cooking at the Polish Centre, Chesterton 81

St Andrew's Church, Chesterton 83

Jim Butler in the Urban Larder Café, Mill Road 92

Sign in the Empress pub, off Mill Road 94

Shrine Room in the Cambridge Buddhist Centre,
Newmarket Road 97

The Cambridge Museum of Computing History 106

Match day at Cambridge United's Abbey Stadium 112

Today's Stourbridge Fair, a tribute to a one-time economic
powerhouse 115

A street sign recalling produce at the Stourbridge Fair 117

Johnny Dee performs at Stoke cum Quy Steam Fair 119

Spectators at Stoke cum Quy Steam Fair 120

Pro Remain protesters at Cambridge railway station 128

Hoarding at CB1 development 130

Clothes collection business 138

John Holder and his workshop participants at the
Cambridge Folk Festival 141

Hats at the Cambridge Folk Festival 143

Starting young at the Cambridge Folk Festival 145

The threatened Lutyens house, Queen Edith's 146

Addenbrooke's Hospital 147

Cherry Hinton chalk pits, scene of Syd Barrett's first trip 152

Andrew Brown on Wandlebury Hill 154

Engelbertus Fukken's unmarked grave, Great Shelford 159

Fleam Dyke 160

Mutlow Hill, Fleam Dyke                                          163

Pye television at The Museum of Cambridge                        167

Charlie Rowell, the 'Cambridge Wonder' at The Museum of
Cambridge                                                       168

Kettle's Yard Gallery                                           170

St Peter's Church, outside Kettle's Yard Gallery               171

Ted Hughes and Sylvia Plath's former home in Eltisley Avenue,
Newnham                                                         174

The Old Vicarage, Grantchester, today                          177

Statue of Rupert Brooke at The Old Vicarage, Grantchester      179

Dame Mary Archer in the garden of The Old Vicarage,
Grantchester                                                   180

Rupert Brooke memorabilia in The Old Vicarage, Grantchester    182
Madingley American Cemetery                                     183

Madingley American Cemetery                                     183

Herbie's Diner, A14                                             185

Meridian marker, Swavesey                                       187

Floods at Over                                                  188

Great Ouse river at Over                                        189

The Chapel at Little Gidding                                    190

Pilgrims' evensong at Liddle Gidding                            191

The pilgrims' centre at Little Gidding                          193

Storey's End, where Ludwig Wittgenstein died                   198

Eddington – bin not working                                     202

Sainsbury, Eddington                                            202

MUMA Building, Eddington                                        203

Source of the Cam, Ashwell Springs                             208

## THE PHOTOGRAPHS 227

Ely Place, London                                                    211

Mitre pub, Ely Place                                                 213

Pink Floyd exhibition at Victoria and Albert Museum,
London                                                               216

# ACKNOWLEDGEMENTS

Firstly, heartfelt thanks to Peter Finch, the *Real Series* editor, for his vision in devising the series and his wise, patient and insightful guidance throughout the writing process. Thanks to Mick Felton and all at Seren for their customary excellent production work. I am indebted to the many kind people who gave me their time, hospitality and expertise as I researched *Real Cambridge*. I am especially grateful to those who are named (in alphabetical order) below: Lord and Lady Archer; Deborah Alun-Jones; Katy Bailey; Will and Lucy Beharrell; Allan Brigham; Andrew Brown; Jim Butler; Lida Lopes Cardozo Kindersley; Hilary Cox Condron; Taradasa Dharmachari; Lord and Lady Eatwell (Suzi Digby); Nigel Ferrier and Linda Symonds; Arthur Gibson and Niamh O'Mahony; Mick and Ann Gowar; Malcolm Guite; Jennie Hogan; John Holder; Michael Hrebeniak; Bill Jenks and the Camboaters; James Murray-White; Robert Lloyd Parry; Carolyn Redmayne; Selwyn Richardson; James Riley; Ian Rawlinson; John and Hilary Roadley; Duncan Robinson; Simon Satori Hendley; Lily Tomson; Mark Wormald. Thanks also to the staff of the English Department at Cambridgeshire College of Arts and Technology, now Anglia Ruskin University, who, in the 1980s offered me a place on the course which changed the direction of my life. My special thanks, and love, go to my family: to my eldest daughter, Cambridge City Councillor Haf Davies, and my son-in-law, Zach Lewis, who kindly opened their home to me during my researches, and to my wife Sally and youngest daughter Alaw, for their patience and support as I went in search of *Real Cambridge*.

# THE AUTHOR

Grahame Davies is a Welsh poet, author and lyricist, who has won numerous prizes, including the Wales Book of the Year Award.

He is the author of seventeen books in Welsh and English, including: *The Chosen People*, a study of the relationship of the Welsh and Jewish peoples; *The Dragon and the Crescent*, a study of Wales and Islam; a novel, *Everything Must Change*, about the French philosopher Simone Weil, and the popular work of psychogeography, *Real Wrexham*.

A native of Coedpoeth near Wrexham, now based in Brecon and London, he has a degree in English from Anglia Ruskin University, Cambridge, and a PhD from Cardiff University, where he was an honorary fellow in the department of religious studies. He was awarded an honorary D.Litt from Anglia Ruskin University, and is a Fellow and Governor of Goodenough College, London. He travels internationally as a reader and lecturer, carries out numerous high-profile poetry commissions, and is a much sought-after lyricist for classical composers.

His poetry has been translated into many languages and has appeared in publications such as: *The Times*, *The Times Literary Supplement*, *The Guardian*, *Poetry London*, the *Literary Review* in America, *Orbis* (#136 Spring 2006), *Yearbook of Welsh Writing in English*, *Absinthe* (Michigan, USA, 2007), *Kalliope* (Germany, 2009), *Poetry Review*, and Everyman's Library Pocket Poets series *Villanelles* (2012). His work is widely anthologised and is on the education syllabus in Wales.

# INDEX

Abdul Hakim Murad 136-37
Abdullah Yusuf Ali 136, 137
Abrahams, Harold 47
Addenbrooke, Dr John 147
Addenbrooke's Hospital 146-49, 173
Akinfenwa, Adebayo 113
Amundsen, Roald 131
Archer, Dame Mary 179-81
Archer, Lord Jeffrey 179-81; *Kane and Abel* 180
Ashwell Springs 209

Bachelard, Gaston: *Poetics of Space* 171
Baedecker Raids 42
Balsham 161
Barrett, Rosemary 91
Barrett, Syd 90-91, 139, 151-52, 174, 216-17
Barton 70
Bassingbourn Village College 188
Battle of Naseby 191-92
Beharrell, Lucy 121
Beharrell, Will 121
Benstead, C.R.: *A Portrait of Cambridge* 147
Bentley, Richard 212
Bishop's Palace 211, 213
Blake Societye 68-70
Blake, William 68-70
Bletchley Park 157
Bloomsbury Group 176, 200
Blunt, Anthony 156-157
Bodley, George Frederick 34
Boleyn, Anne 218
Bottema, Els
Bottisham 121-22
Bottisham Village College 188
Brancusi, Constantin 10
Brigham, Allan 93-94
British Library 30, 70, 194
British Museum, The 208
British Wittgenstein Society 199
Brown, Andrew 152-55, 162-63
Bunhill Fields Cemetery 68
Bunn, Ivan 75
Bunyan, John 116, 117; *The Pilgrim's*

*Progress* 68, 115, 191
Burgess, Guy 156-57
Burghley, David Lord 47
Burnside, John: *The Locust Room* 173
Butler, Jim 92-93, 140, 141, 144-45,
Butterworth, George 162

Cairncross, John 156-157
Cambourne Village College 188
Carroll, Lewis 25
Cambridge Rapist 173
Cambridge spies 155-59
Catherine of Aragon 212
Chakrabongse, Prince Chula 65-66
Chan Ny 61, 65
*Chariots of Fire* 47
Chesterton, G.K. 54-58, 69, 82-83, 104, 114, 117, 158, 168
Church of St John the Evangelist, Little Gidding 190-93
Churchill, Winston 158, 178,
Clarkson, Thomas 84
Clayton, Nicky 33-34, 218
Coe, Sebastian 47
Coleridge, Samuel Taylor 14, 19
Conan Doyle, Arthur 104, 123
Conway, Rt. Rev. Stephen 192-93
Cook, Peter Samuel 173
Cornford, Frances 178, 182, 199
Covent Garden 92
Cox Condron, Hilary 166
Cram, Steve 47
Crick, Francis 14, 34-35, 36, 47
Critchlow, Keith 137
Cromwell, Oliver 11, 14, 219
Cross, Ben 47
Crowley, Aleister 41
Cullen, Susannah 84

Dale, Mrs. Celia B. 75
Dark Mountain Project 155
Darwin Green 58
Darwin, Charles 14, 129, 172, 176, 199
Darwin, Sir George 172

Davies, Grahame: *Real Wrexham* 11

Dee, John 155
Dee, Johnny 118-19
Defoe, Daniel 68, 115
Degas, Edgar 11
Digby, Suzi 31-34
Domesday Book, The 11, 107, 176
Domesday Project, The 107
Donne, John 14, 19
Dutch box bikes 9

Eatwell, Lady Susan 31-34
Eatwell, Lord John 33
Ebere, Eze 113
*The Ecclesiologist* 134-35
Ede, Helen 10, 169
Ede, Jim 10, 169, 172, *Savage Messiah* 170
Eddington, Arthur 201
Edward I 8, 210
Edward IV 33
Edward VI 48
Edwards, Peter 27
Einstein, Albert 123, 201
El Seed 63
Eliot, T.S. 14, 192-93; *Four Quartets* 192, 'Little Gidding' 192
Elizabeth I 83, 155, 213, 218
Ely 210
Emery, Nathan 33-34 *Bird Brain* 34
Equiano, Olaudah (Gustavus Vassa) 84

Fabian Society 176
Ferrar House 193
Ferrar, Nicholas 191-93
Fisher, Mark 153
Fluck, Peter 140
Football Association 20
Forrest Thomson, Veronica 63
Franklin, Rosalind 35
Fry, Maxwell 187
Fukken, Engelbertus 157-59
Fulbourn 161

*Game of Thrones* 76, 169
Gaudier-Brzeska, Henri 10, 169
Geoffrey of Monmouth: *History of the Kings of Britain* 150
George, Mick 112, 113
George IV 219, 220

George V 218
Gibson, Arthur 121-25; *God and the Universe* 124-25
Gilbert Scott, George 135
Gilbert Scott, Giles 194
Gill, Eric 10, 70, 71, 181, 199
Gilmour, Dave 90, 216-21
Glasgow Sun Foundry 18
Godmanchester 8
Gog and Magog (giants) 10
Gogmagog (giant) 150
Goldie, Dr. Mark: *A Cambridge Necropolis* 198
*Good Will Hunting* 121-22
Gowar, Ann 39
Gowar, Mick 39, 213-14
Grahame, Kenneth 174; *The Wind in the Willows* 85, 104-05
Grantchester 70, 176-82, 209
Gray, Roland 74
Gray, Terence 98
Great Chesterford 8
Great Eversden 187
Great Shelford 155-59
Green Dragon Inn 57, 117
Greene, Grahame 168
Greene, Mary Charlotte 168
Greenwich Meridian 186-87
Greenwich Royal Observatory 186
Gropius, Walter 187
Guite, Malcolm 18, 19, 40

Hadley, Chris 148
Hamerton 190
Hatton, Sir Christopher 213
Hatton Gardens 213, 214
Hawking, Stephen 41, 47, 49, 85
Henry III 21, 82
Henry VI 33, 44
Henry VIII 44, 48, 155, 212, 218
Hepworth, Barbara 10
Herbert, George 19, 193
Hipgnosis 217
Hobbs, Sir John Berry 'Jack' 20
Holder, John 140-145
Housman, A.E.: *A Shropshire Lad* 162
Hrebeniak, Michael 110-114, 116-118; *Stirbitch: An Imaginary* 116
Hughes, Carol 29

Hughes, Ted 14, 26-34, 174-75, 'The Thought Fox' 30
Huntingdon 184, 201

Icknield Way, The 159-60
Impington 169
Impington Village College 187-88

James, Clive 14, 26, 28
James, M.R., 41, 102-03, 153; *Nightfrights* 102; 'The Haunted Dolls House' 102, 168; 'Canon Alberic's Scrap-Book' 103; 'Casting the Runes' 103; 'A View from a Hill', 153
Jenks, Bill 57-58
King John 82, 115
John of Gaunt 211
Johnson, Samuel 27
Jones, David 10, 169, 179

Keyes, Dr. John 46-47
Keynes, Florence 116
Keynes, John Maynard 116, 176
Kindersley, David 70-71, 172
Kindersley, Lida Lopes Cardozo 69, 71-73
Kindersley Workshop 67, 70-73
King's College London 35
King's Cross Station 129

Lady Jane Grey 48
Larkin, Philip 199
Latimer, Hugh 40
Law, Roger 140
Lawrence, A.W. 132
Leighton Bromswold 190, 193, 194
Lesmoir-Gordon, Nigel 151-52, 216
Lewis, C.S. 19, 25, 157, 185
Linton Village College 188
Lister, Raymond: *With My Own Wings* 95
Little Eversden 187
Little Gidding 190-94
Lloyd Parry, Robert 103-05
Lutyens, Edwin Landseer 146

Macintyre, Ben 156-57; *A Spy Among Friends* 156
MacLean, Donald 156-57
Madingley American Cemetery 70,

182-84
Malone, Gareth: *The Naked Choir* 32, 34
Margaret of Anjou 33
Marie de Saint Pol 26
Marks, David 137
Marlowe, Christopher 14, 41, 46, 156
McFarlane, Robert 153
Mee, Arthur 43
Meek, Alan 208-09
Melbourn 186
Meldreth 186
Milton 74
Moran, Caitlin 39
Morris, Henry 187-88
Muhammad Iqbal, Sir 136
Murray-White, James 58-67
Muslim Academic Trust 136
Mutlow Hill 162
Myers, Frederic W.H. 194

Naylor, John 41
Newton, Sir Isaac 11, 14, 47, 49
Nicholson, Ben 10
Nobel Prize, The 35, 198, 199
Norwich Players 98

O'Mahony, Niamh 121-25
Oates, Captain Lawrence 132
Old Vicarage, Grantchester 176-82
ORA Singers 32-33
Orchard House 176
Orwell 186
River Ouse 188-89
Over 188-89
Oxford 8, 9, 21, 25, 43, 107, 155, 219, 221
Oxford and Cambridge Act 22
Oxford and Cambridge Club 218-21

Parker, Matthew 46
Parliament 21, 22, 155, 181
Parr, David 93
Peasant's Revolt 21, 115
Philby, Kim 156-157; *My Secret War* 157
Pink Floyd 11, 15, 90, 91, 140, 173, 176, 214-17, *Their Mortal Remains* (exhibition) 214; *Animals* 214; *Dark Side of the Moon* 214; *The Piper at the Gates of Dawn* 174; *Ummagumma* 11; *The Wall*

214; *Wish You Were Here*, 214
Planer, Nigel: *The Young Ones* 101
Plath, Sylvia 29-30, 74, 174-75; 'The Lady and the Earthenware Head' 175
Powell, Aubrey 217
Pye, William 166-67

Raine, Kathleen: 'Northumbrian Sequence IV' 171; *Farewell Happy Fields* 171
Raphael, Frederic 37; *The Glittering Prizes* 23
Ravenna Cosmography 208
Raverat, Gwen 168; *Period Piece* 172-73, 194
Rawlinson, Ian 75-81
Read, Piers Paul 23-24
Rees, Sir Martin 186
Ridley, Nicholas 26, 40
Riley, James 23-25

Robinson CBE, Duncan 201-204, 219-21
Rogers, Sir Richard 129
Rowell, Charlie 168
Runcie, Robert 176
Runicc, James 176
Rupert Brooke 47, 176-82; 'The Soldier' 178
Ruskin, John 91
Russell, Bertrand 47, 122, 176, 198
Russell, Ken 170
Rosa, Salvator: 'L'Umana Fragilita' 104

St Etheldreda 210
St Mary's Church, Over 189
Satori Hendley, Simon 40-43; *Apathy: A cause not worth fighting for* 41
Sawston Village College 188
Scarfe, Gerald 217
Scott, Captain Robert Falcon 131-33
Scott, Lady Kathleen 132
Senuna 208-10
Shackleton, Sir Ernest 132
Shakespeare, William 47, 156; *The Merry Wives of Windsor* 47; *Richard II* 211; *Richard III* 211-12
Sharpe, Tom 26; *Wilt* 91
Shove, Fredegond 200
Shove, Gerald 200

Simpson, John 20
Smirke, Sir Robert 219
Spencer, Stanley 11
*Spitting Image* 140
Stalin, Joseph 157
Sterr, Margaret 21
Stow cum Quy 118-21
Stubbings, Derek 74
Styles, Alan 217
Swavesey 185, 187-88
Swavesey Village College 187-88

Taradasa Dharmachari 96-99
Tate Gallery 10
Temple of Brigantia 209-10
Ter Braak, Jan Willem 157
Thatcher, Margaret 107, 179, 218
Thomas Charles 'TC' Lethbridge 10, 150, 151
Thorgerson, Storm 217
Titian 11
Toft 187
Trumpington 61
Tudor, Mary 40, 48, 212, 218
Turner, J.M.W. 11
Tyler, John 90
Tyler, Wat 21

Varoufakis, Yanis 122
*Varsity Handbook* 19
Vassa, Anna Maria 84
Vaughan Williams, Ralph 200
*Via Devana* 184, 188
Queen Victoria 218
Von Stockhausen, Hans 31

Wainwright, Oliver 129
Walsingham, Francis 155-56
Wandlebury Camp 151
Wandlebury Fort 9
Wandlebury Hill 150, 152
Ward, Dudley 180
Waterhouse, Alfred 26, 185
Waters, Roger 11, 90, 173-74, 216-17
Watkins, Alfred 150, 218
Watson, James 14, 35, 36, 47
Wilberforce, William 84
Wilkins, Maurice 35
William the Conqueror 11
Williams, Archbishop Rowan 201

Williams, Mark 195-97
Williams, Pharrell: 'Happy' 136
Williams, Raymond 23
Winter, Dr. Timothy 136-37 *Muslim Songs of the British Isles* 136
Wittgenstein, Ludwig 14, 47, 49, 122, 176, 197-200
Wood, Christopher 10
Woodville, Elizabeth 33
Woolf, Virginia 176, 200
Woolsthorpe Manor 11
World Cup 10, 110
Wormald, Mark 26-34
Wormwood Hill 9
Worry Dolls 141-42, 144
Wren, Christopher 26
Wyatt, Thomas 155, 156
Wycombe Wanderers 111, 113-14

Xu Zhimo, 'Farewell to Cambridge' 45

Yeats, W.B. 98, 155, 177

CAMBRIDGE AND ENVIRONS

Arts & Culture
Archaeological Museum 74; Cambridge and County Folk Museum 166; Cambridge Bard 169; Cambridge Folk Festival 15, 44, 93, 139-45; Cambridge Museum of Computing History 105-09; Festival Theatre 95-98; Fitzwilliam Museum 11, 102, 103, 147, 201, 219; Kettle's Yard 10, 166, 169-72; Mathematical Bridge 11; MUMA 204; Museum of Archaeology and Ethnology 150; Museum of Cambridge 166-69; Museum of Technology 102-05; Scott Polar Institute 131-33; Sedgwick Museum of Earth Sciences 11; Town not Gown Tours 93; Whipple Museum of the History of Science 104; Zoology Museum 10
Colleges
Cambridge Muslim College 136; Christ's College 61; Churchill College 22, 197; Clare College 9, 22, 35; Corpus Christi College 9, 11, 25, 35, 41, 46, 156, 194; Darwin College 22; Downing College 25;

Girton College 18, 22, 23, 171, 185; Gonville and Caius College 9, 14, 23, 46-47; Homerton College 90; Jesus College 24; King's College 9, 37, 41, 44, 45, 46, 102, 155, 176; Lady Margaret Hall 86; Magdalene College 14, 22, 23, 110, 201, 219, 220; Murray Edwards College 185, 197; New Hall College 185; Newnham College 29, 30, 35, 172-176, 180; Pembroke College 9, 19, 25-30, 31, 33; Peterhouse College 9, 25, 26; Queens' College 31-34, 173; Robinson College 25; Sidney Sussex College 9, 11, 25; St John's College 35, 84, 155; Trinity College 11, 41, 47, 56, 70, 76, 136, 150, 180, 198, 212; Wolfson College 110, 136
Commerce & Retail
Arbury Court 63; Daily Bread Wholefood Shop 62; Grafton Centre 99; Grand Arcade 24; Heffers Bookshop 47; Lion Yard 24; Market Square 46, 48-49, 128, 133
Higher Education (Non-University)
Anglia Ruskin University 11, 19, 39, 90-91, 100, 225; Cambridge School of Art 91; Cambridgeshire College of Arts and Technology (C.C.A.T.) 13, 14, 19, 57, 75, 90-91
Industry
Cambridge Science Park 76; Moonshine Brewery 130; Moulton Park Industrial Estate 62
Places of Religion
St Andrew the Great (St. Sepulchre's) 9; St Andrew the Less Church 100; St Andrew's Church 82-84; St Bene't's Church 9; St Botolph's Church 9, 30; Buddhist Centre 11, 95-99; Cambridge Mosque 137-138; Cambridge Spiritualist Church 194-197; Cambridge Unitarian Church 152; City of Zion Church 105; St Edward, King and Martyr Church 9, 39-41; St Etheldreda's Church 210; St Giles with St Peter Church 10; Great St Mary's Church 9, 133; King's College Chapel 13, 22, 44, 64, 137, 148; Leper Chapel 11, 60, 104; Little St Mary's Church 9; St Luke's Church 71; St. Michael's Church 9; North Arbury

Chapel 62; St Paul's Church 133-136; Round Church, The 9, 38; Unite Christian Church 71
Pubs, Clubs & Hotels
Anchor 30; Carlton Arms 65; Castle 43; Eagle 34-37; Fort St George 57; Jenny Wren 78; Mill 30; Old Three Tuns 184; Ship 62; Snowcat 78; University Arms Hotel 20; Waterman Arms 66; White Horse Inn 166; Mitre 210-211, 213, 214; Plough 84; Rock 139
Recreation
Abbey Stadium 11, 109-14, 115; Botanic Gardens 11; Cambridge Snooker and Pool Centre 105, 107; Cambridge United 109-14; Fenners 20; Paradise Nature Reserve 173; Paradise Swimming Club 175; Satyam Yoga Wellbeing Centre 65
Restaurants
Edge Café 75; Herbie's Diner 185-86; Hobbs' Pavilion 20; Klub Polonia 80-82; Relevant Café 93-95; Stir Café 65; Urban Larder Café 92
Schools
St Athanasius Greek School 138; Netherhall School 139
Streets
Arbury Road 65, 74, 75; Babraham Road 149; Beche Road 100; Bene't Street 34; Bradmore Street 90; Bridge Street 43; Broad Street 100; Campkin Road 63; Carisbrooke Road 58; Castle Street 10, 166, 169; Chapel Street 70, 82; Cherry Hinton Road 138-139; Chesterton Hall Road 80; Chesterton Lane 10; Chesterton Road 65, 80; Coldhams Lane 105; Downhams Lane 78; Downing Street 74; East Road 90, 99-102; Elizabeth Way 99, 100; Eltisley Avenue 174; Ely Place 210-214; Falcon's Yard 29; Free School Lane 35; Garlic Row 116; Glisson Road 90; Gonville Place 20; Grange Road 194; Grantchester Meadows 11, 173, 175; Green Street 158; Gwydir Street 93; Hartingdon Grove 138; Hawkins Road 78; Hawthorn Way 65; Hills Road 90, 133-135, 146-147; Huntingdon Road 184-190, 201; Jesus Lane 41; King's Hedges Road 79; King's Parade 44; Lensfield Road 131; Madingley Road 13, 201; Magdalene Street 10, 43, 166; Mercer's Row 116; Mill Lane 176; Mill Road 14, 18, 24, 75, 91-95, 99, 137, 158; Mitcham's Corner 65; Montague Road 158; Newmarket Road 11, 95, 96, 99, 100, 104, 110, 114, 116, 118, 194; Northampton Street 166; Northfields Avenue 62; Nun's Way 62, 79; Oyster Row 116; Parkside 99; Petty Cury 24; Queen's Road 13; Ramsden Square 79; Regent Street 20, 21; Rock Road 91; St Barnabas Road 158; St John's Street 8, 117; St Margaret's Square 91, 139; Sidney Street 41; Silver Street 172, 210; Storey's Way 197; Trinity Street 8, 46; Trumpington Street 26; Victoria Road 69-70; Water Street 55
University
Cambridge University 14, 21, 90, 136, 157, 182; Cambridge University Physics Laboratory 35; Faculty of Divinity 136; University Library, 29, 71, 194; Women's Union 29